# Antifascism

# Antifascism

*The Course of a Crusade*

Paul Gottfried

Northern Illinois University Press
an imprint of Cornell University Press
Ithaca and London

First published 2021 by Cornell University Press

Printed in the United States of America

Library of Congress Cataloging-in-Publication Data

Names: Gottfried, Paul, 1941– author.
Title: Antifascism: the course of a crusade / Paul Gottfried.
Description: Ithaca [New York]: Northern Illinois University Press, an imprint of Cornell University Press, 2021. | Includes bibliographical references and index.
Identifiers: LCCN 2021005662 (print) | LCCN 2021005663 (ebook) | ISBN 9781501759352 (hardcover) | ISBN 9781501759376 (pdf) | ISBN 9781501759369 (epub)
Subjects: LCSH: Fascism—History. | Anti-fascist movements—History.
Classification: LCC JC481.G5849 2021 (print) | LCC JC481 (ebook) | DDC 320.53/3—dc23
LC record available at https://lccn.loc.gov/2021005662
LC ebook record available at https://lccn.loc.gov/2021005663

# Contents

# ACKNOWLEDGMENTS

I would like to thank those who aided me in preparing this book while I labored on other chores, such as editing a venerable monthly magazine on "American culture and opinion" and collaborating with a cohost on a weekly podcast program. Working on this book became something that I was forced to pursue among other tasks. Fortunately, I was able to inflict my proliferating chapters on certain patient readers, particularly Joseph Cotto, who is my podcast collaborator; Robert Paquette of the Alexander Hamilton Institute; Alex Riley, professor of Social Thought at Bucknell University, and Ed Welsch, executive editor of *Chronicles*. Without their timely comments, I would still be organizing my thoughts for a book that would still be in outline form. I am also grateful to Stanley G. Payne, who is the dean of American and possibly world fascist scholars. Professor Payne praised my book on fascism most of all because of its discussions of antifascism. This convinced me that if I went back to my earlier research, I would focus on the antifascists from the 1920s to the present.

Acknowledgment is also due to my two perceptive readers, Professors Grant Havers and Paul Robinson, who, after reading my manuscript, exchanged notes with me about how to improve my text. I benefited enormously from both these exchanges. I should also acknowledge the assistance provided by *Chronicles* publisher, Devin Foley, who persuaded me to present my views on antifascism on several of his "Backchannel" podcasts. These talks and the chance to answers questions about my research helped clarify for me, perhaps even more than for listeners, topics I was then addressing. I should also mention in gratitude my wife Mary and computer expert Pamela Evans, both of whom repeatedly rescued me from my technical klutziness in retrieving lost texts.

Most of all I am grateful to Cornell University Press editor and longtime friend Amy Farranto, who helped me shake off my senescent lethargy to finish this work. Each time I sent some material to Amy with a hopeful message appended that this was the end, she came back with a note to write more. She also went over my completed chapters and removed superfluous passages (often drenched with sarcasm). Without Amy's editorial advice and steady words of encouragement, this project would not have come as far as it has.

# Antifascism

# INTRODUCTION

The following study of antifascism as a pervasive ideological force may be read as a sequel to my 2016 book *Fascism: Career of a Concept*.[1] The present work also revisits themes from my monograph on the post-Marxist Left, which originally appeared in 2005.[2] In both those studies, I gave considerable attention to the rising alarm throughout the Western world about the resurgence of fascism, together with the changing definitions assigned to that term. This study will explore in greater depth the shifting meaning of fascism and try to put it in historical perspective. A preoccupation with fascism has resulted, not least of all, from its emotive value for those who are already in positions of political, journalistic, and educational power. However else it may operate, arousing a fear of fascism serves the interests of the powerful. It also involves associating fascism almost exclusively for rhetorical purposes with Hitler and the destruction of European Jewry.[3]

Among our elites there is a growing unwillingness to treat fascism as a movement that belonged to a specific time and place. The term "fascism" functions as a resource that the speaker, whether a journalist, actor, comedian, educator, politician, or member of the clergy, can lay hold of to demonize an opponent. In the interwar period antifascist critics were usually coherent and criticized a movement that had taken power in a Western country. But critical discussions of fascism, particularly since World War II, have become both diffuse and imprecatory. Today the f-word is wielded mostly to bully and isolate political opponents or impose on the unwilling an unrequested therapeutic reconstruction.

Most alarmingly for many observers, antifascist activism has led to violence, a trend that escalated in the United States with the election of Donald Trump but has been going on for decades. From 1968 onward the Rote Armee Fraktion in Germany went on a rampage against supposed Nazis in the German government and business community. Before it came to an effective end in 1978, this German antifascist underground managed to murder thirty people while unleashing other forms of physical destruction. At the same time antifascist terrorism was launched by Red Brigades in Italy, which resulted in, among other casualties, the death of Premier Aldo Moro in 1978. In England since 1985 acts of terror against an alleged fascist threat have been perpetrated by, among others, Anti-Fascist Action (AFA). More recently, since the election of Donald Trump in 2016, Antifa activists have swung into action in large cities across the United States. In this country, however, such turbulent activism on the Left is nothing new. In the 1960s antiwar protests often turned violent, and in the late 1980s, Anti-Racist Action (ARA) was organized by leftist punk fans to fight the Right. According to Peter Beinart, this last group took its name because Americans were more familiar with fighting racism than they were with combating fascism.[4] This conflation of fascism and racism (along with other "isms") is something I address in this book.

After observing the eruptions of violence from bands of militants who claim to be protecting society against a violent Right that is often nowhere to be seen, I was motivated to examine the political culture fueling this trend. The crusade of violent antifascism is often no more than the final stage of a process of indoctrination that political, educational, and cultural elites have engaged in since the middle of the twentieth century. What this crusade represents is an intensification or exaggeration of an official teaching, the spillover effect of a militancy that already permeates vital political and social institutions.

The antifascist crusade is promoted through the deliberately indiscriminate use of the term "fascism," a tendency that George Orwell warned against in his *Tribune* article of 1944. Although Orwell could not possibly be identified as a fascist and, in fact, fought in the Spanish Civil War on the side of the Republican Left, he balked at the misuse of the word:

> By "Fascism" they mean, roughly speaking, something cruel, unscrupulous, arrogant, obscurantist, anti-liberal and anti-working-class. Except for the relatively small number of Fascist sympathizers, almost any English person would accept 'bully' as a synonym for "Fascist." But Fascism is also a political and economic system. Why, then, cannot we have a clear and generally accepted definition of it?

Orwell concluded that it is "because it is impossible to define Fascism satisfactorily without making admissions which neither the Fascists themselves, nor the Conservatives, nor Socialists of any colour, are willing to make. All one can do for the moment is to use the word with a certain amount of circumspection and not, as is usually done, degrade it to the level of a swearword."[5]

It is certainly understandable that during a struggle against Nazi Germany, which was then allied to fascist Italy and a military dictatorship in Japan, fascism in England would have a blurred definition. More puzzling is the abuse of the word in the twenty-first century. Mark Bray, a chief theorist of Antifa, has repeatedly decried a ubiquitous fascist danger.[6] Bray sees fascists in various guises, as sexists, racists, and corporate capitalists. He helped mobilize the Occupy Wall Street protest in September 2011, and he promotes the activities of Antifa because he is supposedly resisting forces similar to those that took over Germany in the 1930s. Nonviolence did not work back then, he explained on *Meet the Press* on August 26, 2017, and so it is necessary, as explained in his *Antifa: The Anti-Fascist Handbook*, to carry the struggle to a different level.[7] Bray insists that Antifa's violence is "ethical." He and his comrades are proudly "illiberal." And they don't see fascism or white supremacy as a view with which they disagree or as a difference of opinion. "This is easier to understand when you remember that Antifa isn't concerned about free speech or other democratic liberal ideas."[8]

Illustrating the antifascist mood of our time is a broadside by Jacob Siegel of *Tablet* magazine (2016) targeting my scholarship. Siegel scolds me for suggesting that fascism is peculiar to interwar Europe and that generic fascism was less destructive in its effects than Nazism. Both these suppositions were once widely accepted and may still be by some members of the academic fraternity. One encounters my interpretation in the work of Stanley Payne, who was long the dean of fascism studies in the United States. Like other distinguished historians, Payne defines what he considers "generic fascism" in interwar Europe and distinguishes it from Nazism, without denying there were overlaps between the two movements.[9] The Nazis borrowed from a fascist reservoir of ideas but were highly selective about what they took. Extreme racism targeting Jews and Slavs, as well as the force of Hitler's personality, entered into what Ernst Nolte, another historian of political movements, styles "radical fascism."[10] Unlike Nolte, I stress the nihilistic, violent character of Hitler's "national revolution," which distinguishes it from the run-of-the-mill revolutionary Right. It is difficult for me to see how the Nazi orgy of killing was simply a variation on Latin fascism or similar in character to something as anodyne as Austrian clerical fascism.

My interpretation of the growing irrelevance of Marxist-Leninism to our current politics closely parallels my stated views about the irrelevance of fascism as a political danger. Certain movements and worldviews seem to be forces of the past that contemporary politicians and ideologues evoke to rally their bases. This strategy works in the case of fascism, although not so much for Communism, because people rightly or wrongly believe fascists are a genuine threat to their survival. Those who have read my books know that I stress differences between our late modern age and what our journalists and educators decry as the bad old times.[11] But this anachronistic use of terms ripped out of other ages and contexts to describe present grievances is often conveniently ignored. Inherited political labeling is stretched to cover the present moment, and so the failure of certain political actors to take the prescribed step toward building the desired future causes the term "fascist" to punctuate our discourse.

In September 2018 the Brookings Institution hosted a conversation with former secretary of state Madeleine Albright and former Brookings president Strobe Talbott on the "threat of fascism and how we can avoid the tragic errors of the past."[12] To her credit, Albright, who had just published her book, *Fascism: A Warning*,[13] managed to avoid calling Trump a fascist, but did refer to him as the "most un-democratic leader the United States has ever seen." Albright, however, let it be known that "fascism is a more virulent threat to peace and justice than at any time since the end of World War II." Here one might wonder whether countries that vote democratically for populist leaders are actively promoting fascism or merely causing offense to Albright and Brookings by making the wrong electoral choice.

My assumptions about fascism do not necessitate the belief that humanity is getting better because some old villains are becoming politically insignificant. There is no evidence that human nature has changed much in the last fifty to one hundred years. Governments still act rapaciously in much of the world, and individual and group violence remains a social problem. In the first two decades of the twenty-first century, a spate of mass killings have occurred in the United States. No one would question that the murderers who targeted innocent victims were evil, demented, or both. But should we call them "fascists" because they expressed prejudice against certain groups? Most of those evils that have raged in this world have not come from fascism. Racial and ethnic prejudices have existed quite independently of that movement, and not even all fascists were historically anti-Semites or admirers of Hitler.

What is being challenged here is the widespread tendency, particularly among academic, media, and political elites, to dismiss dissenters as "fascists." This tactic turns off unwanted conversation, as when A calls B, with whom A disagrees, a racist, sexist, or homophobe. A is not just reproaching or censoring B. The name-caller is taking over the mantle of victimhood from victims in the past, which allows him or her, according to onetime German Marxist theorist Peter Furth, "to assert power over us."[14] The Antifa theorist Mark Bray also lays claim to the moral high ground when he insists that he is engaging in an unfinished struggle for the downtrodden everywhere. Bray insists that he is renewing a grand struggle once waged by Anarchists and Marxist-Leninists against fascist bigotry. *Pace* Bray, Anarchists and Communists in the 1930s were not combating sexism and homophobia, and unlike Citibank and the Republican Party, the Nazis murdered their opponents.

This fixation in the United States is hardly limited to Antifa gangs running around with the slogan "Punch a Nazi." A distinguished Yale professor of history, Timothy Snyder published an attack on President Trump in the *New York Times* right after the clash between right- and left-wing groups at Charlottesville in August 1917. The accused president was not only faulted for failing to take sides with the Left unequivocally; Snyder also viewed Trump's reluctance to give a blank check to the Left as incontrovertible evidence that fascism, meaning Nazism, is now flourishing in the United States: "We might choose to forget these slogans and these events from the years before World War II, but American Nazis remember the history in their own way, and so does President Trump. The Confederate statues he admires are mostly artifacts of the early years of the 20th century, when Hitler admired the United States for its Jim Crow laws." Further, "the presidential slogan 'America First' is a summons to an alternative America, one that might have been real, one that did not fight the Nazis, one that stayed home when the world was aflame, one that failed its test."[15]

Snyder's statements indicate the contortions that antifascists engage in when attacking their opponents. The unwillingness to distinguish less destructive generic fascists from German Nazis serves ascertainable ideological ends. One weakens the power of an otherwise sweeping accusation as soon as one admits that not all fascism equals Hitler. By calling someone a "fascist," the speaker is trying to get the audience to believe that the object of this attack would have happily cheered on Nazi crimes.

Another form of the *argumentum ad Hitlerum* protesting the fascist tendencies in Trump's America comes from the historian Christopher R. Browning in the *New York Review of Books*. "Trump has been the beneficiary of long-term trends predating his presidency showing the decline of organized labor. To consolidate his dictatorship, Hitler had to abolish the independent unions in Germany in a single blow. Trump faces no such problem. In the first three postwar decades, workers and management effectively shared the increased wealth produced by the growth in productivity." Moreover, "since the 1970s that social contract has collapsed, union membership and influence have declined, wage growth has stagnated, and inequality in wealth has grown sharply." Somehow the weakening of labor unions in what is becoming a postindustrial America suggests that the contemporary United States is moving toward the Nazi policy of *Gleichschaltung*, namely forcing all social institutions into the framework of a Nazi dictatorship. Trump and his party are imagined to be the "beneficiary" of this development, although we are speaking about an economic trend that has nothing to do with fascist coercion. Even more misleading is the equation of German *Gewerkschaften,* which were labor unions in the traditional sense, with organizations of public sector employees.[16]

My study gives special attention to those forms of antifascism that developed in the United States since the 1930s. That is because whatever radical ideas arise on the Left have often migrated from this country to the Old World. Since the end of World War I, the United States has been the most powerful and influential Western country. In addition to being an economic and military leader, the United States furnishes the popular culture and dominant ideas that reach the European press and that are taught in European universities. This observation is not a value judgment but a recognition of the asymmetry that has resulted from our hegemonic position.

A view that I have occasionally considered but then rejected is that antifascist ideologies and movements have sprung up to some degree independently of each other, in accordance with prevalent political and cultural situations in different countries. What made me reconsider this view, as I explain in *The Strange Death of Marxism,* is the degree of influence exerted by things American on other societies. It is hard to believe that our present antifascist movements would have sprung up in Canada or Western Europe without an increasing American presence. This is not to say that the Red Brigades and other leftist terrorists would not have operated in Western Europe without our ideas. But these earlier and sometimes quite explosive antifascists did not prioritize intersectional politics, which defines the present antifascism.[17] They were anticolonial, opposed to the US military presence in Europe, and vocally anti-capitalist. The present form of antifascism reveals a sharp American imprint and a different emphasis.

It is often maintained, perhaps most conspicuously by Allan Bloom in his best-selling *The Closing of the American Mind*, that American academia and American culture were poisoned by a "German connection," one that went from Nietzsche down to the Frankfurt School.[18] Apparently, Americans absorbed more Teutonic toxicity than was good for our democracy. Only small details of this brief are true. The Frankfurt School arose in interwar Germany and from there migrated to the United States. But this school of thought flourished more in the United States than it had in interwar Germany. This happened in such a way that critical theory became profoundly and perhaps distinctively American and developed a long-lasting relationship to American political culture. Many of its core ideas about combating prejudice and the "authoritarian personality" became so profoundly Americanized that they informed American concepts of democracy and were used to reeducate the German people after World War II. Positions that emanated from this school of thought about fascism as an expression of psychic abnormality resonated so well on the American side of the Atlantic that they were immediately applied to uncovering fascist tendencies through tests administered to government workers and students. What started out as an offbeat experiment in radical social thinking in interwar Germany became mainstreamed in the United States to the point that it might be inaccurate to treat it as a German import. To do so may be as misleading as treating Western Christianity as simply a new form taken by a Middle Eastern cult. By the time that Allan Bloom in the 1980s was declaiming against the Frankfurt School as a dangerous import, what he was describing was a very American ideology.

This work devotes considerable space to Germany, because of the pioneering role of the Germans since World War II in developing an antifascist state and society. Just as interwar Italy became the case study for generic fascism being raised to a form of government, so too does Germany today exemplify the elevation of antifascism to a state philosophy and program of mass reeducation. After World War II, the conquered Germans had no option but to submit to their forced indoctrination. But at least since the 1970s they have gone well beyond what their former conquerors imposed on them and what Germans might have initially perceived as humiliation. We may wonder whether other nations or peoples would have submitted so readily to continuing national self-abasement. In any case many Germans now revel in their anti-German identity, and it would seem from their media, universities, and party preferences that they have decisively rejected the distinctive national identity that they possessed even before the Nazis came to power.

On January 23, 2020, German president Frank-Walter Steinmeier delivered a penitential speech at a Holocaust conference at Yad Vashem in Jerusalem. Steinmeier stressed his people's continuing "full responsibility" for Nazi murders and lamented that "the worst crime against humanity was committed by my country." According to Steinmeier, "today's Jew hatred in Europe is the same as during the Nazi era," and one particularly dangerous hotspot of this epidemic is Germany.[19] Steinmeier spoke in English, because he considers the German language to be implicated in Nazi hatefulness. An ongoing national self-rejection that highlights an evil past and that must be borne collectively has become a permanent characteristic of German life and politics.

Some readers may question my reasons for highlighting antifascism as an ideology. For example, why should one treat antifascism as being more basic than intersectional politics for understanding today's political and educational establishment? Why is antifascism a more useful description than other terms that those who pursue a more perfect equality or more perfect globalism might adopt for their stance? The answer I would give is that fascism, however vaguely defined, remains the great evil against which those who consider themselves enlightened are now aligned. It is impossible to understand today's Left unless we also grasp what it claims to be resisting. A perpetual adversary shapes its mission; whatever its objections to capitalism, its main enemy is not the corporation or the bank but "fascism." In addition, too much space has been devoted to defining the present Left as Marxism revisited, and not enough attention has been given to the non-Marxist character of the continuing war against "hate."

Although what is characterized here as the post-Marxist Left continues to invoke Marxist shibboleths, many of its partisans and most of its financial backers still embrace a corporate capitalist economy. Until quite recently, the wealthy supporters of the antifascist Left showed remarkably little concern about the socialist rhetoric of their favorite public figures. When Democratic congresswoman Alexandria Ocasio-Cortez spoke at a Bernie Sanders presidential campaign rally on December 24, 2019, she announced that "it's fascism" that defines the present nature of US society.[20] Although Ocasio-Cortez recycles both Marxist tags and economic collectivist policies, the main enemy for her, or so it would seem from her statement, is fascism. This is the term that encapsulates what the present Left and much of the established conservative movement claim to be combating.

When a campaign organizer for presidential candidate Bernie Sanders in Iowa, Kyle Jurek, described what he and his comrades would do after their candidate won, he called for "reeducating people not to be f—cking Nazis." Jurek went on to explain: "Like in Nazi Germany after the fall of the Nazi party there was a sh-t ton of the populace that was f-cking Nazified. Germany has to spend billions of dollars reeducating their f-cking people not to be Nazis."[21] Jurek also talked up the advantages of the Soviet gulags for "reeducation" if other less violent methods fail to achieve their purpose.[22] Senator Sanders's campaign worker managed to bring together some of the themes that this book covers: the call for extending post–World War II German reeducation to conservative Americans, the view of the Soviet gulag as a center for values training, and the glorification of violence as an indispensable means for combating social reactionaries. This book will highlight the political culture that has rendered such attitudes morally acceptable. It is this antifascist political culture, not a history of specific antifascist movements, that will be the focus of this study.

Chapter 1 will examine the development of Antifa in the United States as both a major political force and a continuing source of civil disturbance. It will look beyond the often simplistic explanation for this development provided by sympathetic media; namely, that in violent protests and rioting we are observing a natural, understandable response to the discovery of systemic racism in the United States. One can condemn the indefensible killing of George Floyd in Minneapolis and also note that Floyd was used as a pretext for mobilizing revolutionary forces to swing into action. The result of what in some cases were planned actions was to leave inner cities devastated; to abet the shooting of policemen like the black retired St. Louis police captain David Dorn, who was killed while trying to guard a neighborhood store; and to precipitate hundreds of murders in cities from which the police had withdrawn. Although some of this violence may have been spontaneous, Antifa and those acting in concert with it had their fingerprints on the devastation. Moreover, their demonstrations prompted similar protests, resulting in looting and the toppling of statues by antifascists in Western Europe.[23]

It would not be an overly suspicious reaction to assume extensive cooperation among Antifascists across borders, as well as across regions of the United States. We are speaking here about activist groups that in most cases have been around for some time. Explanations that focus on indignant individuals who just happen to appear in certain places at the same time are too silly to be taken seriously. Most antifascist protests seem too well orchestrated to be spontaneous events. Even more remarkable are other factors related to the spreading riots, such as the general sympathy for the rioters expressed in polling and the absence of pushback from the other side. Why are there so few counterprotests, and why do violent actions from the Left not generate a proportionate response from the Right? One explanation offered here is that the antifascist Left has bested its opponents and critics on a scale that even its partisans may not fully appreciate. But there is another reason for not giving recognition to the glaring imbalance of forces. It is sometimes strategically useful to exaggerate the resources of one's rivals to justify continued militancy.

Chapter 2 will move back in time to examine three types of critical responses to the emergence of fascism in interwar Europe. One was the response from Italian antifascists and from German and Austrian Marxists. According to the criticism that arose on the Marxist Left, fascism embraced the concepts of a corporate state and organic nationalism as a counterrevolutionary strategy. Fascists allegedly worked at the behest of anxious capitalists to defuse a growing economic crisis by diverting attention from real social ills with their bogus cures and calls for national solidarity. Another noteworthy response to the creation of a fascist state in Italy came from the classical liberal economist Ludwig von Mises, who stressed the almost natural transition from an elaborate administrative state to a fascist regime. According to Mises, the unchecked growth of the modern state paved the way for the authoritarian nationalism that gave birth to fascism. Although this leap into fascism did not necessarily take place in all administrative regimes, one should not be surprised, according to Mises, when such regimes ended in the destruction of liberty. To advance their interests, government administrators allied themselves with nationalist forces from time to time.

Another critical perspective on fascism came from liberal parliamentarians, particularly those who had lost out to the fascists. These antifascists focused on the failures of prefascist governments to defend established constitutional arrangements. In the 1920s and 1930s, liberal critics, looking back at the fascist takeover of the Italian state in 1922, were given to enumerating the personal and collective mistakes that culminated in an unwelcome regime. Finger-pointing at individual culprits, together with observations about the structural flaws of earlier Italian governments, characterized this examination of the collapse of Italy's parliamentary monarchy.

Despite the different angles from which these critics launched their briefs, they nonetheless agreed on certain premises. None of them assumed that the fascists who took power and those who supported them were psychologically repressed or driven by prejudice. All of them took for granted that their adversaries were rational actors who were pursuing personal and group advantage. They also examined social and political structures and (at least in the case of some antifascists' personal failures) to explain why their side lost. Naturally, they thought their enemies were hurting the working class and/or creating an oppressive form of public administration coupled with an aggressive foreign policy. But these early antifascists did not ascribe the unpleasant aspects of fascist rule to mental illness: they understood that it was possible for others to follow fascist leaders without betraying signs of mental disease. Fascist followers were being gulled or else benefited from the fascist government, but in neither case were the antifascists seen as speaking about a mental pathology that antifascist authorities were required to address once they took power.

A possible interpretive objection to my line of thought is that I am providing a cookie-cutter definition of fascism. It may seem that I am going too far as a terminological purist in denying later movements that may draw from fascist traditions an association with interwar fascism. Admittedly I am engaging in a restrictive usage, but this is what historians of fascism have done in differentiating their subject from other movements that were essentially different but did share some characteristics, such as nonfascist right-wing authoritarianism or nonfascist nationalism. Such distinctions are essential for separating distinctive political movements and ideologies; for example, Nazi and Soviet totalitarian governments, or East German Communist socialism and Swedish welfare state socialism. But even more important may be the need to keep the word "fascist" from falling into utter meaninglessness. This historically specific term is now being used as a weapon against anyone with whom a speaker may disagree politically. In the face of rhetorical hyperinflation, it pays to be particularly careful in how one applies the f-word.

In chapter 3 emphasis will be placed on the redefinition of fascism as a therapeutic problem. Although the activities of such leading representatives of the Frankfurt School as Theodor Adorno, Max Horkheimer, Herbert Marcuse, Eric Fromm, and Karen Horney would provide support for the struggle against the fascist mindset, what they promoted had already been prefigured by American Progressives. During World War I and then in the early stages of the New Deal, US government advisers and social reformers hoped to apply "scientific" administration to fighting authoritarianism from the Right. The Frankfurt School and its war against fascism could thrive in the United States because the groundwork had already been laid there.

The critical theory that emanated from Frankfurt School emigres and their American adherents had a relatively restricted focus. The main target in their denunciation of "pseudo-democrats" and the "authoritarian personality" was anti-Semitism. This focus was entirely understandable, given the Jewish origins of these refugee theorists. Although they did pass critical judgment on prejudice against homosexuals and women, their fight against fascism and their prescriptions for government policies centered on anti-Jewish prejudice. This was the main theme of the *Studies in Prejudice*, a project that Adorno and Horkheimer carried out for their sponsors in the American Jewish Committee in the 1940s. Anti-Semitism is clearly the pivotal point in the most widely circulated volume in this series, *The Authoritarian Personality*, which was published in 1950.

Another fact that one must keep in mind is that the Frankfurt School was unalterably socialist. Some of its members, especially Herbert Marcuse,[24] viewed themselves as hardcore Marxist-Leninists, as well as partisans of erotic self-expression. Unlike the antifascists of the present era, however, the first generation of critical theorists were concerned less with constructing lists of victims and calling for accommodating them than they were with creating their own kind of socialist economy. Also, unlike today's Left, these architects of the therapeutic Left were not allied to billionaires and large investment companies while professing to be against the system.

A key text for understanding the fusion of revolutionary socialism with Frankfurt School themes is *The Destruction of Reason* (1954), a work by the Hungarian Communist man of letters Georg Lukacs (1885–1971). Lukacs viewed socialism as the "rational" path toward which Western history had been moving since the early nineteenth century. According to this view, socialism inhered in the "dialectical thinking" that originated with the philosopher Hegel (1770–1831). Although a defender of the Prussian state, Hegel had explained modern history as a revolutionary process that was accessible to and in some sense determined by human reasoning. Fascism, according to Lukacs, was the response of those who wished to hold back revolutionary change. It was therefore inevitable that fascists would be locked in mortal combat with Communism, as the final stage of an historical dialectic. Those who wished to nip fascism in the bud were urged to commit themselves to building a revolutionary socialist society, a goal that the Soviets were supposedly already carrying out. Lukacs produced *The Destruction of Reason* as an unmistakable defender of orthodox Communist positions.[25] Unlike some of his latter-day admirers, he was not battling sexism and homophobia. But his view of modern history as a choice between leftist revolution and fascism continues to shape the mindset of antifascist militants.

The concluding section of chapter 3—on penitential historiography—may be viewed as a worthwhile digression. It deals with the use of written history as a tool for making readers aware of the sins of the politically incorrect past and thereby leading them toward both expiation and zeal for social reform. Although antifascism is not the only aspect of this plainly ideologically driven historical writing, it does feature prominently in the penitential historiography of German, Italian, and Spanish "revisionist" scholars. Particular attention is paid to the arguments advanced by Fritz Fischer and his acolytes regarding Germany's "sole responsibility" for the outbreak of World War I.

Fischerites emphasize the supposed continuities in the German leadership classes and in German political attitudes from the Second Empire through Hitler's accession to power. This emphasis on what has become the ever-deepening burden of German historical guilt, which aroused my interest as a graduate student in the mid-1960s, motivated this aside in chapter 3. I examine historiographical appeals to guilt in relation to the present crusade against a presumed fascist threat. I am not suggesting that penitential historiography lacks any scholarly merit. What I point out is that determining its worth has been rendered difficult because historical studies are treated as sacred political texts. Anyone who questions these received accounts becomes politically suspect and, finally, immoral.

Chapter 4 offers an overview of the major changes undergone by antifascist ideology since the 1960s. Among the changes examined are the growing list of prejudices and forbidden words that government and other public institutions are combating, the reduction of historic fascism to Hitler and his exterminationist policies, and the association of fascism with emotions and attitudes that displease influential journalists, academics, and civic leaders. At this point, concepts become increasingly detached from long-received understandings. They depend for their meaning on what authority figures tell us. This recalls Thomas Hobbes's assertion in *Leviathan* that words acquire fixed meaning through a sovereign. The Hobbesian leader becomes both the source of linguistic clarity and someone who exercises political authority. In the antifascist order of things, settled meanings are no longer available. Words and ideas are banned or redefined to accommodate moral censors, so that the "fixity" of meaning that Hobbes thought was a precondition for civic peace no longer exists.

Chapter 4 will explore closely the emerging culture of antifascism, which projects a uniform quality throughout the Western world. Fascism is the central evil against which all liberal democratic societies must perpetually mobilize themselves. In 2018, the centrist German government under Chancellor Angela Merkel spent 116 million euros in a *Kampf gegen rechts* (Struggle against the Right) that targeted the producers of right-wing ideas.[26] Although the Right—except for one isolated party that is made up largely of disaffected members of Merkel's transformed Christian Democratic Union—has virtually no electoral presence in Germany, a crusade against what seem to be hidden forms of fascism is of fundamental importance for the German regime. Failure to be sufficiently on guard against this evil, which allegedly invades minds as well as governments, could result in succumbing once again to Nazi tyranny. Although racism, anti-Semitism, Islamophobia, sexism, and homophobia are all anathema in the Western media, they are also thought to be expressions of fascism. What falls under this category is also inevitably paired with Nazism and the threat of Nazi genocide. Accordingly, the European Parliament has demanded that every member state ban neofascist and neo-Nazi groups as sources of xenophobia.[27] No comparable demand has issued from the same body to deal with the very real threat of Islamicist violence.

Chapter 5 features a discussion of the European populist Right seeking to take power in France, Germany, England, Sweden, and the Lowlands. Although this discussion does not consider long-run political prospects for populist success, it does put into relief the present anxiety of some Europeans that "fascist" populists may soon be ruling them. These predictions may be grossly exaggerated, as are statements that liken populists to interwar fascists or German Nazis. But neither the political establishment nor its antifascist allies in the media and academy may intend to deceive us when they express concern. At least some of these voices may be coming from those who are genuinely alarmed by what they consider a threat to their power.

Chapter 6 will concentrate on the antifascism of the American conservative establishment, which resembles its leftist variants. The conservative media parrot the Left's warnings about a fascist danger while trying to adapt that message to their own cause. Like the Left, conservative celebrities find a fascist threat in, among other things, a resurgent European nationalist Right and, more generally, white racism and anti-Semitism. In view of so-called conservative sponsors, which include defense industries, immigration-friendly corporate capitalists, and pro-Israeli, socially liberal donors like Sheldon Adelson and Paul Singer, it is not surprising that conservative media have never felt driven to break from certain antifascist stereotypes.

Instead the conservative media pin the fascist label on their opponents with the same abandon as their rivals. This practice reaches the point of parody in Jonah Goldberg's best-seller *Liberal Fascism*, a work that highlights the supposed fascist and Nazi template of Democratic Party politics. Moreover, Goldberg's ally Dinesh D'Souza has undertaken to demonstrate the racist and protofascist lineage of the opposing national party. Supposedly the Democratic Party is hiding its fascist past, with the help of the friendly media. Conservative celebrities also bring up the fascism allegedly hidden in the radical Left when they denounce uncongenial authors and political actors. We are led to believe that democracy is endangered because of the influence of French deconstructionists and such undemocratic German thinkers as Nietzsche and Heidegger. Republican celebrity Glenn Beck famously featured on his TV program an enlarged photo of the German existentialist Heidegger, who briefly served the Nazis, juxtaposed to a photograph of Hillary Clinton. The association could not have been clearer. All that was lacking was the image of a Nazi swastika above Hillary's head.

Chapter 7 presents an extended contrast between the fascist and antifascist models of the state and looks at the assumptions about human nature that each has highlighted. Whereas fascists exalt masculinity and a warrior ethic, antifascists fight against what they condemn as "toxic masculinity." Antifascists have called for and, where the opportunity exists, implemented measures to remove a specific masculine identity from the workplace, social organizations, and even family relations. Another feature of fascism and of all traditional conservative movements that antifascists combat is the notion of a fixed human identity based in false social ascriptions. Finally, in contrast to the fascist stress on integral nationalism, the antifascists advocate a borderless world. (There is often an apparent lack of interest in the illiberalism of non-Western countries, even those that rigorously control immigration.)

An excursus follows chapter 7 in which reference is made to the theory of knowledge presented by Thomas Hobbes in his magnum opus *Leviathan*. Hobbes was uncertain whether people who conversed with each other shared the same perception of reality. From his perspective, facts that depend on sensory knowledge are subject to the accidental movement of our brain particles and cannot be entirely relied on as a truth source. Because of this problem it seemed to Hobbes that sovereign authority was needed, and not only to prevent the "war of all against all": such authority would also have to intervene to explain what things signified. Otherwise we would face endless bickering over the meaning of words, which in some cases could lead to civil strife. In the contemporary world, it is argued in the excursus, the media and to a lesser extent the academy provide the "sovereign authority" that serves to "signify" what things mean. This applies particularly to political labeling, in which terms have come to mean what journalists, politicians, and academics say they mean.

The afterthoughts section of this book will explain why antifascism is likely to remain a critical element in our political culture. Large corporations have moved toward the cultural Left and promote the initiatives of antifascist activists. Capitalist interests now dovetail with antifascist ones; for example, expanding immigration from the Third World and bringing down national borders create larger consumer markets and reduce the cost of labor. One should not exaggerate the danger to global capitalism posed by Antifa demonstrators, not even the ones who organized the Occupy Wall Street protest. These apparent enemies share common views on the social and cultural front.

Antifascism is integral to a post-Marxist Left that today enjoys cultural support in much of the West and, not incidentally, in the United States. This now-surging Left rests on an alliance of government, a corporate capitalist economy, and, for want of a better term, what has been styled "cultural Marxism." In accordance with Frankfurt School thinking, the devil we are urged to combat is fascism, and the struggle will go on between the properly sensitized and the fascist evil until the latter is destroyed. The antifascist demonology draws on the Christian view of Satan, whereas the war to be waged against fascism calls to mind the struggle of Christ and his disciples. Furthermore, the antifascist crusade recycles older mythic archetypes. It embodies the polarity that is present in all dualistic religion,[28] and this may be one of its psychic strengths. Antifascism is the most recent form of a mythical prototype that has proved remarkably durable.

# Chapter 1

# Antifa and the Mainstreaming of Antifascism

On June 1, 2020, Jeremiah Ellison, the son of Minnesota attorney general Keith Ellison and a Minneapolis councilman himself, used Twitter to declare his support for Antifa. This was in response to Donald Trump's tweet of the same day that the United States would designate Antifa as a terrorist organization. Neither Jeremiah nor his father had previously made any secret of his sympathy for Antifa. Nor had they hidden their estimation of Trump as someone leading the United States into what they understand as fascism. A smiling Keith Ellison had earlier posed for pictures with Mark Bray's *Antifa: The Antifascist Handbook* in the radical Moon Palace Bookstore in Minneapolis.[1] We might note that millions of Minnesotans elected him to his present post in 2018, despite what were by then plausible charges that he had physically abused his girlfriend.[2]

In late May 2020 two progressive Democratic congresswomen Ayanna Presley and Alexandria Ocasio-Cortez were found raising money for Antifa, an action that was judged by leaders of their party to be somewhat imprudent.[3] Although it is one thing to sympathize with Antifa and to attack its opponents as fascists or worse, identifying with it too openly might have the effect of unsettling non-leftist voters. Politicians in most districts in the United States, outside of cities like New York, San Francisco, and Minneapolis, must still be careful about sounding like those academics and out-and-out partisans who have expressed support for Antifa. In 2017 Mark Bray, then lecturing at Dartmouth College, was criticized for advocating force in fighting what he and his comrades designated as the fascist Right and for calling for de-platforming the nonleftist opposition. Thereupon one hundred members of the college faculty signed a declaration of support for him.[4]

Far more characteristic of the indirect defense of Antifa that has come from the mainstream national media is an opinion piece on the *Washington Post* editorial page of June 3, 2020, written in response to President Trump's and Attorney General Bill Barr's decision to designate Antifa a terrorist organization. The article's headline reads, "Is It Time to Call Trump the F-Word?" to which its author Ishan Tharoor then provides a predictable response.[5] According to Tharoon, who quotes Adam Weinstein of the *New Republic*, Trump laid the groundwork for a fascist state, deploying "xenophobia" and "ultranationalist" rhetoric to establish what looks like a fascist order. Nowhere in the opinion piece do Tharoor, Weinstein, or Frederico Finchelstein, a professor from the New School, whom the editorial quotes, openly back Antifa. But their sentiments do paint a dire picture of a would-be fascist president appealing to ethnic hate while leaving it to the reader to draw the necessary conclusions. Whatever has been tried to stop the fascist juggernaut has from all evidence not worked, and therefore we may need to do more to save us from a fascist future. After Antifa was designated a terrorist organization, *New York Times* columnist Nicholas Kristof seemed particularly exercised by the "Antifa hysteria," noting it "hasn't killed anyone and appears to have been only a marginal presence in Black Lives Matter protests. None of those arrested on serious federal charges related to the unrest have been linked to antifa."[6]

Indeed, some politicians and commentators view Antifa as a shield against a fascist or Nazi threat. The eagerness of Democratic presidential candidate Joe Biden, his party, and much of the national media to present President Trump as a fascist or as leaning in that direction is grist for the mills of Antifa activists. The black civil rights attorney and lifetime Democrat Leo Terrell has complained bitterly that his own party is condoning terror by not opposing the group.[7] Trying to reinforce what may seem to be a necessary alliance, presidential candidate Biden's staffers bailed out Antifa activists arrested for allegedly committing particularly conspicuous acts of violence.[8]

Antifa activists, who swung into action after Donald Trump's election in 2016, have voiced the same concern as the Democratic opposition about what they consider to be America's first fascist administration. And they have not been sitting on their hands. A widely distributed film from Project Veritas[9] by someone who infiltrated a group of activists shows that, contrary to its depiction in the *New York Times* as a loose collection of idealistic antifascists,[10] Antifa is a well-organized national movement, even if it continues to be an conglomeration of semi-independent radical groups, that foreign and domestic backers and sympathizers and generous funding. Antifa expert Mark Bray was not telling us the full truth when he stated in the *Washington Post* on June 1, 2020, that "Antifa groups are loosely organized and they aren't large enough to cause everything Trump blames them for."[11]

After 2016, Antifa activists positioned themselves as the frontline defense against the alt-right, until doing so became a profitless pursuit. Media interest in the alt-right dwindled after Trump's election, when its representatives, along with those incorrectly labeled as such, experienced de-platforming. (The establishment conservative movement in what has become the predictable response took the lead in ostracizing its own "extremists" or anyone viewed as inappropriately right-wing.)[12] Antifa has had the option of targeting anyone who appears on the long, wide-ranging "hate" lists of left-wing organizations such as the Anti-Defamation League and the Southern Poverty Law Center.

The clash between Antifa and elements of the radical Right in Charlottesville in August 2017 boosted the former's reputation. From this street fighting, which Antifa helped instigate, the group gained public esteem. The fact that a protester was killed by a car driven by someone with neo-Nazi associations did wonders for the image of the Antifa activists. According to a prevalent narrative, the embattled antifascists had faced down neo-Nazis and the Ku Klux Klan. Although it may be hard to sympathize with either side in this confrontation,[13] the media and the political class generally depicted it as a showdown between neo-Nazis and valiant crusaders for human rights. Throughout its history, Antifa has been able to take advantage of such crises to create a reputation of protecting the vulnerable and victimized. It played on this image in 2017 by presenting itself, with media assistance, as the good side in Charlottesville. The killing of George Floyd on May 25, 2020, and the rioting that followed provided additional opportunities for Antifa to gain increased popularity.

Yet it is not the case that, *pace* Bray, Antifa merely responds to police violence.[14] University campuses and radical leftist bookstores and coffee houses are among the places where Antifa has stacked weapons, black hoods, and other accessories for their assaults. Those who have been wounded and blinded during violent protests, supposedly by accident, are well-chosen targets.[15] Loads of bricks have suddenly appeared in areas where Antifa, in conjunction with Black Lives Matter (BLM), has staged protests.[16] In my borough of Elizabethtown, Pennsylvania, a BLM demonstration was planned for June 6, 2020, allegedly to protest the killing of George Floyd. Local business leaders then learned to their consternation that Antifa had piled up bricks on the eastern edge of Elizabethtown on the evening before the protest. As soon as reports of this surfaced, merchants invited in regional antiterrorist militias to protect their establishments.[17] The demonstration went off peacefully.

It would be a mistake to confuse Antifa with either classical Anarchism or Marxist-Leninism. Although it borrows symbols and historical heroes from both, together with Anarchist black flags and clothing, Antifa is distinct from older leftist movements. It blends with whatever leftist cause is in the ascendant and treats whoever opposes it as fascist.

The Antifa theorist Alexander Reid-Ross, who teaches geography at Portland State University, has come closer than anyone else to making sense of this movement's targeting of certain enemies. In his book, which has been widely acclaimed among progressives, *Against the Fascist Creep*, Reid-Ross presents a picture of a fascist danger that never quite speaks its name, except for some indiscreet white nationalists who divulge their true goals. Other promoters of the fascist threat also supposedly hide behind misleading labels, which renders them particularly insidious in the struggle against bigotry.[18] It is precisely the cleverness with which fascists and their sympathizers disguise themselves that, according to Reid-Ross, necessitates the cleansing operation of antifascist groups. T. Keith Preston, an historian of anarchism, has noted that Reid-Ross and other defenders of Antifa usually sound like "John Birchers of the Left."[19] Like the Birchers who imagined that Communist agents were in disguise and had to be exposed, the antifascists have their own version of the hidden enemy, whom they are trying to combat.

Preston also observes that, although Reid-Ross and his followers are able to offer academic definitions of what fascism taught in the 1920s and 1930s, they stray from these definitions when describing their present all-pervasive enemy. Fascist now means whom or whatever the antifascists have decided to attack. Further, these activists have no interest in debating those who deny their opinions and offer evidence of a contrary position. For example, nowhere in *Against the Fascist Creep* does Reid-Ross deal with the argument that fascism lost most of its influence and power after World War II. Instead, those who do not agree with his interpretation are linked to an all-enveloping fascist conspiracy by virtue of having consorted with people on the political Right. Preston asks whether name-calling amounts to a serious refutation or is really a method of avoiding a necessary discussion. Clearly this distinction is in no way relevant for antifascist discourse.

In any case Reid-Ross has increased his appeal by being featured in both the Israeli newspaper left-wing *Haaretz* as an expert on the anti-Semitism that has been unleashed in the United States since Trump's election and in the Arab news agency Al Jazeera, where he writes on anti-Islamic prejudice. (For a teacher of introductory geography with an undergraduate's knowledge of historic fascism, Reid-Ross validates the exclamatory phrase that I heard from European immigrants as a child: "Only in America!") Arun Gupta, of *The Guardian* and a co-organizer with Mark Bray of the Occupy Wall Street movement, has lavishly praised Reid-Ross's analytic skills. In a widely quoted Amazon editorial review, Gupta offers this endorsement: "This book is good for smashing cockroaches and fascism, which may appear more similar after a careful reading."[20]

It is no surprise that universities have provided a receptive base from which to recruit radical activists. Career revolutionary Eric Mann, speaking in 2007 at the University of California, San Diego, alluded to the role of universities as breeding grounds for leftist activism. He told the students assembled there that "the university is both the place where I was radicalized. It is the place where Mao Zedong was radicalized. It is the place where Lenin and Fidel and Che were radicalized." Citing Howard Zinn's *A People's History of the United States*, he informed his young audience that their country "is what's called a 'white settler state. . . . The United States has basically been conquering land under a white Christian flag under a view of white supremacy."[21]

Mann is the director of the Labor/Community Strategy Center in Los Angeles, where BLM cofounder Patrisse Cullors was trained. (Mann's fellow Weather Underground member Susan Rosenberg has served on the board of directors of Thousand Currents, which provides financial support for the Black Lives Matter Global Network.[22]) In his lecture at UC San Diego, Mann said his work involved "organizing mainly young people that want to be revolutionaries," which includes "finding young people that want to go into the high schools as public school teachers." The Labor/Community Strategy Center "is trying to build an anti-racist, anti-imperialist, anti-fascist united front."[23]

The movement that Antifa may resemble most closely in its methods and in how it targets its adversaries is German Nazism while it was struggling to take power. Both movements have traded in organized street violence, the nature of which have been defined by their enemies; both have taken advantage of a vast network of support from public administration, universities, and the producers of public opinion.

Unlike generic fascism, Antifa is not patriotic: it seeks to destroy, not reinforce historic Western notions. It is also by far too irrational and nihilistic to be Marxist. The last part of a cry chanted by activists at a mass protest in Berkeley, California, on August 27, 2017, underscores the true nature of Antifa's politics: "No Trump, No Wall, No USA at All."[24] Attempts by Republican politicians and PR staff to treat Antifa as the latest distillation of Marxist socialism reflect partisan opportunism, historical ignorance, or possibly both. Except for its efforts to identify itself with other forms of the Left that operated at other times, Antifa through violence and its ability to create extensive support systems looks very much like early National Socialism.

Intermittent appeals by activists calling themselves antifascist to establish decentralized government do not clash with the view that these militants have something in common with the Nazis. What is meant by decentralization is both the removal of already radicalized urban areas from police control and the establishment of bases from which these antifascists can operate. Antifa activists, along with BLM and others, temporarily established an "autonomous zone" in Seattle from which the police withdrew.[25] The mayor only moved to dismantle the zone after there were reports of rape and multiple shootings that resulted in two teenagers being killed and three people wounded.[26]

Soeren Kern, in his articles, "A Brief History of Antifa: Parts I and II," examines in detail the funding sources available for his subject.[27] A major sponsor of Antifa has been the Alliance for Global Justice (AFGJ), which has stood financially behind Far Left organizations. In 2010 the AFGJ was a principal backer of the Occupy Wall Street movement, and since then it has tried to create a favorable view of Marxist-Leninist governments, most notably Castro's Cuba. The AFGJ is principally a distribution center for allocating funds, which collects money from like-minded organization, such as George Soros's Open Society Foundation, Tides Foundation, and Ben & Jerry Foundation; these groups work hard to present themselves as mainstream progressive organizations. AFCJ funding has also gone to Refuse Fascism, an organization formed after the 2016 election with the goal of removing Donald Trump from office. The slogan on the website of Refuse Fascism is, "In the Name of Humanity, We Refuse to Accept a Fascist America!" Members identify as antifascist, though they are not part of Antifa.

Any consideration of antifascist funding should factor in large corporations, such as PepsiCo, Citibank, Nike, Facebook, Ford Foundation, and Goldman Sachs, that contribute to BLM and other left-wing activist groups. These corporate giants have helped bail out militants who were arrested, including both Antifa and BLM activists. Movements that demonstrate, topple statues, and engage in violence together are also likely to share the same funders.[28] As Influence Watch, a fact-collecting agency with loose connections to the Right, demonstrates, a continuing strength of Antifa is its ability to combine its activities with those of other left-wing organizations, such as Showing up for Racial Justice and Black Lives Matter. The BLM Global Network, into which most of the funding for BLM is funneled, moreover, supports revolutionary groups, including Communist ones.[29] None of this, however, proves corporations that fund the Far Left have any interest in promoting socialism or Communism.

There is more than one reason for the cultural radicalization of the affluent that has led to their support by some for the activities of Antifa and other movements like it. Mercer Global Consultants, which monitors the hiring of minorities, has reported that major corporations have yet to address the problem that their workforces consist of 80 percent or more of white males.[30] Corporations may therefore be concerned about being the targets of boycotts and adverse publicity from the Left, goaded on by sympathetic media. Introducing politically correct forms of address and promoting the cultural Left with generous donations and expressions of support may therefore be regarded as necessary precautions against suffering leftist reprisals.

Corporate executives can serve the cultural Left without having to be concerned about pressure coming from the largely ineffective and even diminishing Right. White male Christians, who on average are the country's most conservative voting demographic, may be a dwindling presence in the corporate world, even if that presence is not fading as quickly as diversity officers might desire.[31]

A Rasmussen poll from early June 2020 indicated that Antifa had the support of 22 percent of the country.[32] A CNN poll conducted in the first week of June 2020 tells us that most Americans consider white racism to be a major problem, and many blame this affliction on Donald Trump. Moreover, 27 percent of those polled believe violence is an appropriate response to the present level of police brutality and racism.[33] These findings show that antifascist groups like Antifa are operating in a somewhat friendly environment, particularly in US cities. What that means for those cities remains to be seen.

The Left center or liberal establishment that has made an at least tacit alliance with the kind of antifascism exhibited by Antifa may be saddled with troublesome friends, just as the German nationalist Right was with a supposedly sympathetic paramilitary in the interwar years. Self-described European antifascists complicate the picture by showing up in strange spots in the political spectrum. In Germany, the revulsion of antifascists for their own country as permanently tainted by its Nazi and even nationalist past has led them to join Zionist demonstrations waving Israeli flags. One can also imagine these anti-German Germans defecting to the Palestinian side, if they view it as more of a break from their country's past. Hatred may be the most powerful emotion driving their movement.

The point of this comparison is not to smear Antifa with the Nazi label that US media have broadly applied to the Right, when they are not identifying it with bigoted gun owners living in flyover country. It is to showcase where Antifa fits most easily among the dominant ideologies of the last century: it resembles most closely the nihilistic, destructive movement that it claims to be fighting. Of course, we need not push this comparison too far and should recognize its obvious limits. Unlike the Nazis, Antifa claims to be fighting fascism.

Comparisons with Communist activists have also been made. Because Antifa, consisting of autonomous groups, is not a single organization, membership numbers are not available. The membership of the interwar Communist Party USA, even during the depths of the Depression, never rose above

65,000.[34] Earl Browder, the CPUSA presidential candidate obtained 83,000 votes in 1936, which was at the height of his party's popularity. The percentage of support expressed for Antifa indicates that these modest numbers could be easily surpassed by votes given to a self-declared candidate of the Antifascist Left at just a few state universities.

Undoubtedly the Communists also once had a vast network of fellow travelers, reaching into the government. In contrast, the present antifascist Left has advocates at all levels of government and throughout the media and educational system. It is not a conspiracy, like "Communist infiltrators," but an open revolutionary movement whose ubiquitous sympathizers justify or underplay antifascist violence. One need only contrast the public concern in the 1950s—that Communist sympathizers were supposedly and surreptitiously infiltrating the film industry—with the commanding power wielded by today's cultural Left, including Antifa apologists in the national press. Unlike Communists and Communist fellow travelers of an earlier generation, the Left today does not hide its efforts to control the entertainment industry. Leftist opinion makers do not hesitate to order HBO or Netflix to remove from circulation whatever runs contrary to their ideological agenda, and obliging capitalists typically do as they are told.[35] Government attempts to move against Antifa may work about as well as German chancellor Heinrich Brüning's efforts to ban the SS and SA in April 1932. By June of that year Brüning had been replaced by a new chancellor, Franz von Papen, who removed the ban on Nazi paramilitary formations while trying to cut a deal with Hitler.[36]

Antifa not only represents the militant anti-capitalist Left but, more significantly, also constitutes the opposition to Western civilization. In the vanguard of these revolutionary forces, the corporate sector, as noted earlier, is playing a critical role.[37] PayPal, Pepsi, Adobe, and other corporations have been working to get Facebook and related electronic media to de-platform dissenting voices on the Right.[38]

A German libertarian philosopher Roland Baader self-published in 2002 what became a classic among culturally conservative defenders of capitalism: *Totgedacht* is a study of how intellectuals are destroying civilization. Baader takes up complaints that cultural conservatives and German patriots have typically leveled at the antifascist war against tolerance and traditional cultural standards. He scolds the intelligentsia for changing the meaning of words in such a way as to make it morally impermissible to argue against leftist censors. Baader further advocates on behalf of the concepts of a free market and commercial competition against "globalists" and "fake capitalists." Those opportunists whom Baader condemns embrace the antifascist cultural revolution not as capitalists, but as allies of a leftist government and ruling class. Baader separates these actors from those noble souls who follow their true interests qua capitalists.

The question remains whether capitalist interests can be dissociated in the real world from how the capitalist system operates. How that system functions will necessarily depend on certain variables, such as who wields political power and what cultural values are being taught by leading institutions.[39] Constructing ideal models of a free-market economy, and contrasting it to how "crony" or corrupt capitalists operate, dodges the question of whether we are looking at real as opposed to imaginary capitalists. Historical contexts are not easily separated from historical actors when we consider how systems function. In any case, it is exceedingly hard to divorce capitalism in its present corporate phase from the political problem this book analyzes.

Attempts to depict the present struggle as one between capitalists and socialist revolutionaries have been greatly exaggerated, given the overwhelming presence of corporate capitalists among the revolutionaries. What may be closer to the truth is the burgeoning alliance of the political and economic establishment with BLM and Antifa. German political scientist and cultural historian Claus Wolfschlag has observed that, in his country, the Antifaschisten target not the powerful but the marginalized. Government officials and the dominant parties do not feel at all threatened by rioting antifascists who are going after an already intimidated opposition on the Right. Nonwhites have joined in the widening strife throughout the Anglosphere and Western Europe, but they operate in this struggle as expendable accessories. According to Pew Research, 46 percent of protesters and rioters on US streets in the spring of 2020 were white, and an even higher percentage were Democratic. Only 17 percent (one out of six protesters) were Black and 22 percent Hispanic.[40]

US Antifa has borrowed its name, colors, and much of its rhetoric from the German Antifaschisten, who have been active in Germany since the 1960s and who may be described as an exquisitely indulged feature of life in an antifascist society. Oppositional political movements may borrow the practices of their enemies; for example, it has been frequently noted that certain features of German Nazism, such as concentration camps and the use of a vast surveillance system, were taken from the chambers of Soviet Communism. Although both Antifaschisten and Antifa seem as single-mindedly driven as other totalitarians, they lack a cohesive social vision to go with their violence. But they have been lucky in their enemies, who have not countered with enough force to discourage rampaging aggression.

Antifa and its supporters are not going away. Those who have caused unrest in the name of combating fascism will not likely be satisfied. They will demand the right to control the streets and, as a first step, the removal of the police. Then they will likely demand a share in determining social and economic policies. It may then devolve on the Left to rein in its antifascist allies as best it can.

Chapter 2

# Origins of Antifascism

Antifascism arose initially as a reaction to Italy's fascist movement and to the government that fascist leader Benito Mussolini formed in October 1922. Had not such a movement taken power as a revolutionary nationalist government in a Western country, fascism might not have attracted the international acclaim or the international opposition that it aroused. Mussolini's movement had already stormed onto the historical stage in its confrontations with the revolutionary Left in the wake of World War I. Its partisans engaged in combat with militant socialists in 1919, after the latter seized and occupied factories in Tuscany, the Emilia Romagna, and elsewhere in northern Italy. Calling themselves "Fasci Italiani di Combattimento," the fascist militants battled the well-armed "revolutionary syndicalists" in a succession of bloody encounters. By the end of this strife, three hundred fascists and four hundred revolutionary socialists fell in what had become a virtual civil war.

Although it later became customary on the Left to view the fascists as instruments of large landowners (*latifondisti*) and major industrialists (*grandi industriali*), they thus entered world history as self-described revolutionaries.

When fascists put up candidates for office in Milan in March 1919—namely, Benito Mussolini and the Futurist literary figure Filippo Tommaso Marinetti—their activists favored programs of nationalization. Mussolini, future fascist duce, spent most of his early life as a socialist and for a time edited the socialist paper *Avanti*. Mussolini broke from the Socialist Party during World War I when he advocated war against the Central Powers to acquire "unredeemed lands" from the Austro-Hungarian Empire. His former comrades among the Arditi—raiding units that had been deployed on the Izonso Front against Austro-Hungarian forces—allied themselves provisionally with Mussolini's movement soon after the war.

The Arditi also took part in the seizure of Fiume under the command of the Italian poet Gabriele D'Annunzio in 1920, after the Italian and Yugoslav governments had agreed to declare this former Hungarian port a free city. The attempted takeover of Fiume by young Italian ultranationalists collapsed when Italian royal troops forced them to surrender in December 1920. Out of this adventure, however, came an ancient Greek battle cry that the fascists later adopted: "Eia, eia, alala!" Heard regularly at fascist rallies, this war cry invoked a Greek deity: "Up then, Alala!"

Although the Arditi came into conflict with the new Partito Nazionale Fascista (established in November 1921) and eventually was taken over by Mussolini and his partisans, they embodied the martial spirit that came to characterize the black-shirted fascist *squadristi*.[1] Both groups were made up of war veterans who were disappointed by the poor outcome of a costly struggle, particularly by Italy's failure to gain more territory at the expense of the defeated Central Powers. These veterans, moreover, found it hard to adjust to civilian life in a country that was attempting to demobilize but was being crushed economically by socialist revolutionaries. Although both the Arditi and *Fascisti* participated in the civil unrest following World War I on the side of the factory owners and landowners, they were not driven primarily by material concerns: they believed they were fighting against the internationalist enemies of their people. They were also working to restore production in a country that had been paralyzed by socialist strikes and the occupation of factories. Both groups of revolutionary nationalists favored this slogan, which epitomized their attitude: "*Me ne frego*." (In our time, this slogan, which translates as "I don't give a damn," graces the shirts of Italian soccer players.)

As Italian premier, Mussolini took steps in the early 1920s to consolidate his power and the centrality of his movement within the framework of the

Italian state. In 1923 he passed, with the support of fascist deputies, the Acerbo Law, which allowed his party to gain two-thirds of the seats in the Chamber of Deputies. Fascists could thereafter achieve control of the chamber by winning only 25 percent of the popular vote. Over time Mussolini also weakened nonfascist organizations of workers and began to use the public schools to teach fascist virtues of obedience to *Il Duce* and loyalty to the revolutionary nationalist state. *Il Popolo d'Italia*, which was founded in 1914, as a pro-Allies, socialist organ, remained the official government newspaper until 1943.

On June 30, 1924, *Il Duce*'s socialist enemy, Giacomo Matteotti, rose on the floor of Chamber of Deputies and denounced his rule in a long, impassioned tirade. On July 10, Matteotti was kidnapped and then assassinated by thugs with party connections, although it was never determined whether Mussolini had advance knowledge of their deed. As soon as information about the killing spread, 150 deputies from the Left and center withdrew from the Chamber in a dramatic protest against Mussolini's rule. This protest, known as the Aventine Secession (in memory of the action of the Roman plebeians who in the second century BC withdrew from the patrician-dominated Roman Tribal Assembly to obtain concessions), failed: the hope entertained by the opposition that King Victor Emmanuel would dismiss Mussolini's government and vindicate the secessionists was never realized. In fact, the king seemed almost relieved to be able to deal directly with his premier without having to negotiate with the troublesome opposition in the Chamber. Equally noteworthy, most of the populace quickly lost interest in the political assassination. Two years later, when a few secessionists tried to reenter the national assembly, the fascist majority kept them from being seated.

This failed secession also allowed Mussolini to move toward the fusion of the Italian royal state with his party. The Grand Fascist Council came to overshadow the parliamentary government as it assumed both the executive and legislative functions. Founded in 1922 and meeting during most of the years of fascist rule in the Palazzo Venezia, the Fascist Grand Council, according to its mandate of December 9, 1928, was "the supreme organ that coordinates and integrates all the activities of the regime emanating from the revolution of October 1922," which was the event preceding the King's appointment of Mussolini as Italian premier. From this "supreme organ" a "labor charter" was proclaimed in 1927 that imposed on the Italian economy a neo-medieval

corporate structure. Capitalists became "providers of labor," and their employees were turned into "recipients of employment"; both were slotted into
a hierarchy of producers of wealth and services that existed for the benefit of
the Italian state. The premier and his cabinet met with the Grand Council
and decided pressing political and economic questions with its members. The
Council's dignitaries all belonged to the party and had to be approved by
Mussolini. Ironically, it was this council that in 1943 relieved Mussolini of
his party leadership and was complicit in having him arrested.[2]

Although it is now widely believed that Mussolini and his authoritarian
regime were merely a front for corporate capitalists and monopolistic landowners, this was far from universally believed in the 1920s or even into the
1930s. The most diligent historian of Italian fascism, Renzo De Felice, who
produced a multivolume study of more than two thousand pages on Mussolini and his rule, draws a sharp distinction between fascism as a movement
and fascism as a regime.[3] According to De Felice, the movement that Mussolini shaped after World War I represented the nationalist sentiments of Italy's
rising bourgeoisie. It reflected disgust with "liberal" premiers like Luigi Facta
and Giovanni Giolitti, who were widely seen as rotating nullities spearhead-
ing a government that could not control Italy's economic stagnation and
collapse.

The fascist idealization of heroic action on behalf of the nation resonated
with an educated citizenry that was not necessarily in sync with the interests of bankers and industrialists. In fact, it was not even clear whether the
early fascist movement had any interest in preserving capitalism. As early as
1919 at a nationalist conference in Florence, the novelist Enrico Corradini
(1865–1931), an architect of the fascist worldview, coined the term "proletar-
ian nationalism." Although not an advocate of a socialist economy, Corradini
was aligning his country with those nations overshadowed by the "Northern European plutocrats," whom the fascists presented as the true victors of
World War I.[4] But Corradini and other advocates for "proletariat nations"
were making mostly rhetorical points about their proletariat status. Once
Mussolini seized power for himself, explains De Felice, he was free to mold
the regime in accordance with his wishes. Significantly, this proved to be
something less than a disaster, as Mussolini worked to accommodate various social classes and avoided getting Italy dragged into war.

This balancing act ended when *Il Duce* threw in his lot with Nazi Germany. Thereafter he went from enjoying a relatively benign international

press, which characterized him as a man of order who between 1934 and 1936 took a strong stand against Hitler, to being seen as the Devil's henchman. In the 1930s, Mussolini also took an increasingly authoritarian stand in domestic politics as he tried to concentrate more political power in his person. He began harassing the Catholic Church, with which he had made peace in the Lateran Pacts in 1929. De Felice notes the *dérapage* that marked the Italian fascist government in the 1930s and that would be accompanied by such foreign policy misadventures as the attack on Ethiopia in 1936 and Italy's support for Nazi Germany. Mussolini's adoption of anti-Semitism, as illustrated by his exclusion of Jews from the party and professions in 1938, also represented a sharp break from his earlier positions. *Il Duce*'s longtime lover and biographer Margherita Sarfatti was a Sephardic Jew, the fascist Grand Council had Jewish members, and the March on Rome that brought Mussolini to power abounded with Jewish participants. Up until 1936 *Il Duce* had repeatedly denounced Hitler's anti-Semitism and was viewed by Zionist groups (some of whose members deeply admired him) as an ally.

Despite this volte face, Italian fascism for many years found supporters on the Left, as well as on the Right. Ernst Nolte provides one reason with this situation: "of all movements on the right, fascism is the most leftist; just as communism may be the most rightist movement of the Left."[5] Fascism may, in fact, have looked sufficiently leftist to make it appealing to social reformers outside of Italy. Its well-wishers included FDR's brain-truster Rexford Tugwell and the editors of the *New Republic*, which then was very left of center. The late John P. Diggins devoted his first book to American progressive intellectuals who found in Italian fascism a model for their own projects.[6] In *Entfernte Verwandschaft* [Distant Affinities] German historian Wolfgang Schivelbusch explores the extent to which New Deal advisers to FDR took seriously Mussolini's measures to offset the global Depression of the 1930s.[7] No matter that Mussolini inflated the Italian currency and passed around devalued money to employers to keep their workforces in place. His image as a reformer was what counted for his foreign admirers. Mussolini ran an "activist" government during a period of economic misery, and he was emphatically anti-Nazi for more than two years, which gave him cachet among progressives.

Perhaps equally important for understanding the progressive aspect of fascism was its association with its premier exponent, the philosopher Giovanni

Gentile (1875–1944). A coauthor with Mussolini of *The Doctrine of Fascism*, the longtime fascist minister of education, and a persistent critic of the influence of Catholic clericalism on Italian institutions, Gentile viewed himself in the tradition of Italian democratic patriots of the nineteenth century. His biographer A. James Gregor treats his subject as someone who remained focused on fascism as a movement of the future and who viewed the fascist state as a child of the modern era.[8] Gentile's view (taken from Hegel) of History as a process that continues to unfold as the actualization of Absolute Spirit testifies to his forward-oriented thinking. Gentile was also conspicuously on what seemed to be the enlightened side of critical political issues: he opposed Mussolini's pact with the Catholic Church in 1929, particularly the formative power that this agreement conceded to the church in public education; he protested the alliance with Nazi Germany and the anti-Semitic legislation of 1938; and he tried to save Jewish colleagues from being rounded up by the Gestapo after northern Italy fell under German control in 1944. None of this, however, prevented his assassination by the leftist resistance in Florence before war's end.

Quite possibly if Mussolini had listened to his foreign minister in the early and mid-1930s, he would have staved off his eventual fall. Dino Grandi, who in 1921 had been his rival for the leadership of the National Fascist Party, favored closer ties to Britain and steering clear of cooperation with Hitler's Germany. Like Gentile, Grandi vehemently opposed the anti-Jewish Racial Laws of 1938.[9] By then, however, Mussolini had fallen under the influence of others; for example, the fascist advocate of the laboring class, Giuseppe Bottai, who supported Nazi Germany and tried to import its doctrines selectively into Italian fascism. Curiously, some of the most "socialist"-leaning fascists were also among the most anti-Semitic.

This oft-forgotten history should indicate that fascist Italy's reputation even by the mid-1930s was hardly a settled matter. Distinctions continued to be made between a brutal Nazi Germany and a less dictatorial anti-Communist regime in Italy that engaged in activities that generally were approved of by the Western press. Although Mussolini boasted of working to establish a "stato totalitario," in which "everything would be in the state and nothing outside of it," his rule looked strikingly different from that of his Teutonic neighbor.[10] Jewish refugees who fled Nazi Germany were given asylum in Italy, where civil society was far freer than in Nazi Germany or Stalin's Russia.

Renowned artistic celebrities, such as conductor Arturo Toscanini, poet Giuseppe Ungaretti, playwright Luigi Pirandello, Futurist Tommaso Marinetti, and Gabriele D'Annunzio, at times expressed sympathy for fascism, particularly during Mussolini's early rule. In 1924, Mussolini held meetings with opera composer Giacomo Puccini regarding their shared interest in creating an Italian national theater. Shortly before Puccini's death the following year, Mussolini accorded him the honor of Senator for Life. The "fascist revolution" also heavily patronized innovative architects, and Mussolini undertook a facelift of Rome that would correspond to the momentous occasion of the rebirth of his nation.[11] He also tried to inject artistic and literary creativity into fascist journalism. With *Il Duce*'s blessings *Il Popolo d'Italia* featured the crème de la crème of Italian cultural life. Mussolini might have even gotten away with his repressive politics and preserved his appearance as a social reformer if he had listened to those who warned him against charting a perilous foreign policy course in the late 1930s.

Perhaps most relevant for this study, only a minority of leftist journalists and politicians, as well as some European Communists, would have decried his democracy deficit if Mussolini had not joined the Axis and moved into Hitler's camp. In 1924 he established diplomatic relations with Soviet Russia and in 1933 concluded a Treaty of Friendship and Non-Aggression with Stalin. It is doubtful that most European Communist parties would have bothered to go after a fascist leader who maintained friendly relations with the Communist motherland.

While Mussolini was turning Italy into a fascist one-party state in the mid-1920s, the attention of most of his fellow citizens was trained on other developments. The country was hit then by a sudden destabilization of the lira, partly a consequence of the need to service war debts, and the stocks of its largest companies were fluctuating wildly. The association of Italian industrialists, Confindustria, viewed Mussolini as someone who could bring order out of economic chaos, something that he managed more or less to achieve by the late 1920s.[12] By 1925 there were also negotiations between the papacy and the Italian state to end the strife between them that began in 1870 when the Kingdom of Italy seized papal territories, including the city of Rome.[13] Although a pact was not concluded until 1929 and only over the protests of anticlerical Old Guard fascists, it was in the works for some time.

Once Mussolini placed himself on Hitler's side, however, he forfeited positive "world opinion." He lost even greater goodwill on the Left when he sent "volunteers" to fight with the Nationalist forces during the Spanish Civil War. This move had the effect of placing *Il Duce* in the company of the Catholic Right, who were the natural allies of the Nationalists and General Franco, given the violent anticlericalism unleashed by the other side. For better or worse, fascism thereafter became associated with the traditional Right as well as Nazi Germany. Moreover, the term "fascist" was applied preeminently to Hitler's Germany, which became the most significant representative of that ideology and form of government. Hitler and Mussolini exchanged visits to their capital cities, where they affirmed their shared ideological ground. Certain inconvenient facts went down the memory hole during these expressions of mutual admiration—that the early fascists were fanatically hostile to Germany and Austria and that Mussolini, while celebrating "Latinity," had often mocked Germans and their government as the "barbarians across the Alps."

## Clericalist and Liberal Opposition

Not all of fascism's early enemies were on the Left; in the 1920s and even thereafter, Mussolini had to contend with traditional liberal and Catholic clericalist opposition. One of his longest and most relentless opponents was Luigi Sturzo (1871–1959), the priest who organized the Partito Popolare Italiano (PPI; a distant predecessor of the Christian Democrats) in 1919. Sturzo was known (probably incorrectly) as a "clerical socialist" who tried to fashion a party that would ally the church to the Italian working class and impoverished peasants, particularly in his Sicilian homeland. His creation of the PPI caused the papacy to remove "*non expedit*" instructions for Italian Catholics, who had previously been prohibited from voting in Italian elections. The instructions against voting for Catholics had been in force since the period of Italian unification. Thereafter clerical authorities allowed Catholics to vote, presumably to support Sturzo's party. Much to the Vatican's displeasure, however, the priest became a pesky adversary of Mussolini. In 1924, as a member of the Chamber of Deputies, Sturzo voted against the Acerbo Law, which allowed the Fascist Party to gain two-thirds of the seats in the Chamber of Deputies. Thereupon the Vatican, through its emissary to the Italian state Cardinal Pietro Gasparri, in an effort to stabilize relations with Mussolini's government, agreed to send Sturzo out of the country. The unruly priest was assigned to an Italian monastery and from there to several residences in London, before he moved on to the United States, where he remained in exile until the end of World War II.

Sturzo did not return to his native land until 1946 when he was received as a hero by the Republican, postfascist government. The president, Luigi Einaudi, and the premier, Alcide De Gasperi, claimed to be aligned with Sturzo's political thought. In 1953 this apparent spiritual progenitor of the postwar government was raised with papal permission to the post of Senator for Life.

But this recognition and honor did not keep Sturzo from lacing into Italy's Christian Democratic establishment with the fury he had vented against Mussolini's regime.[14] Gasperi, who had been concerned that Sturzo would sabotage his own pro-American political course, had managed to delay his return to his native land after the war.[15] The sulfurous Sicilian priest uttered this sarcastic observation when he learned of Gasperi's action: "The fault of fascism is great but that of antifascism no less great." Significantly one of Sturzo's complaints about fascism—that it taught a pagan worship of the state— became a standard Catholic position during his lifetime. So too did Sturzo's attacks on fascism for denying the Christian view of the person. Augusto Del Noce, Gabriele De Rosa, Emilio Gentile, and various contributors to the Catholic-leaning journal *Review of Politics* reiterated and recycled Sturzo's critical view of fascism.[16] In November 2017 the priest who never minced words underwent beatification by the Vatican and is now on his way to sainthood.

A liberal reaction by Italian constitutionalists and opponents of Mussolini's efforts to centralize power was also perceptible in the 1920s, and for a while, it found a voice in Italy in the cultural historian and philosopher Benedetto Croce (1866–1952). A onetime collaborator of Giovanni Gentile and a fellow Italian Hegelian, Croce later moved in a different political direction from Gentile and in the 1920s became the tolerated voice of the opposition. Although Croce made no bones about his objections to Mussolini's transformation of the Italian parliamentary monarchy, he also hoped that, by remaining in Italy as a public figure, he would be able to moderate the regime. Periodically Croce would urge *Il Duce* to restore freedom of the press and a multiparty electoral system. But the prospect for these proposals became extremely dim after a referendum was approved in March 1929 restricting membership in the Chamber of Deputies to those on a single list provided by the Grand Council.

At the time of this plebiscite, an avowedly liberal booklet "Nuova Liberta" was circulated throughout Italy that urged all Italian parties to work together to restore constitutional liberties. This polemic may have been more instructive for what it indicated about the inherited defects of the Italian parliamentary government than for what it advocated as an alternative to the fascist regime. Only 30 to 40 percent of eligible Italian voters, we are told, bothered to cast ballots between 1860 and 1924; large party blocs locked national politics in a *partitocrazia* [party politics], and those parties that Mussolini drove out of the Chamber seem to have feared each other at least as intensely as they opposed the fascists. From 1919 until 1922 the Socialists had "sabotaged every attempt to bring order to the government lest the Communists on their left accuse them of being 'traitors to the proletariat.'" "Nuova Liberta" raises doubts about whether the Socialists could free themselves sufficiently from their Communist allies to unite with bourgeois parties against the fascist dictatorship. It concluded, "In order to explain the condition to which we have been reduced, it is not enough to say that the fascists have divested us of liberty. This is only part of the truth. The other more important part of the truth is that we've made bad use of our liberty."

A more comprehensive liberal critique of fascism issued from the free-market Austrian economist Ludwig von Mises (1881–1973), who wrote about the fascist regime in Italy and later, with far more concern, about the Nazi takeover in Germany.[17] Despite Mises's reservations about the state as "an apparatus of compulsion and suppression,"[18] albeit one that protects its citizens and their property from violence and enforces contracts, he was not entirely hostile to Italian fascism. This seems to have remained Mises's view in 1927, when he published a defense of his preferred political and economic order, *Liberalismus.* Like Croce, Mises did not regard Latin fascism as a sustainable experiment that would lead to a stable regime. He considered it to be a noisy, unruly antidote to socialism that would eventually be replaced by less frenetic rule: it was a temporary expedient to deal with the radical Left's threat to life and property. To their credit, the fascists were temporarily providing "forces for a civil war in which the side with the larger numbers will prevail." The real threat that fascism represents is "that its adherents and admirers value violent conduct for its own sake." These activists turned their conviction that "war is the natural condition of countries into a justification for perpetual strife." In addition, the fascists could not supply "the intellectual weapons" that in the end would allow the liberal side to prevail:

> When the vivid impression of the shameful deeds of the Bolsheviks fades from memory, then the socialist program will exert its attraction on the masses once again. Fascism cannot accomplish more in this struggle than wage war on those who spread these ideas. If we are serious about combatting socialist ideas, then we must confront them with other ideas. There is only one idea than can effectively counter socialism, which is liberalism."[19]

In his native Austria, Mises reacted favorably to the clerical fascist regime of Engelbert Dollfuss, which was established in 1931 as a force against both the Nazis and revolutionary socialists. Mises regarded Dollfuss's authoritarian government, as he did Italian fascism, as a time-limited expedient for dealing with sinister threats to civic life from the Left. But the coming to power of Hitler in Germany and his own subsequent flight from Central Europe (because of his Jewish background) caused Mises to think critically about the brutal dictatorship that had established itself in Germany.

Those problems that Mises associated with Italian fascism became far more unsettling in the case of the Nazis. Italian fascists, according to Mises, had the "merit that would live after them" of having lent "emergency help" against dangerous forces on the Left.[20] With the German Nazis, however, violence became a totally destructive way of life. Certain defects in Germany's political history, according to Mises, helped explain the country's turn toward totalitarian solutions. Not surprisingly, his list of defects is similar to what other refugee scholars were then compiling in response to the Nazi cataclysm. Germans, we are told, pursued a narrowly nationalist course in their cultural and academic life. They were less open to liberal ideas than the English and Americans and overemphasized the centrality of the state in their evolution as a nation and in the development of their industrial economy. But together with this criticism of a German *Sonderweg* (a particularistic, illiberal path to political and economic modernity), which today is a veritable fixation among German academics and journalists, Mises focused on the German penchant for state bureaucracy as a precondition for Nazi dictatorship.

In a later book, *Bureaucracy*, published in English by Yale University Press in 1944, Mises identifies German National Socialism as a particularly virulent form of socialism. National Socialists embraced a worldview and economic policy deeply rooted in the Prussian glorification of public administration. Mises insisted that private ownership of the means of production existed *in name only* under the Nazis and that true ownership of the means of production resided in the German government. It was thus no longer nominal private owners but the German government that exercised the *substantive powers of ownership* in the Third Reich. No longer did private owners have the power to decide what was to be produced, in what quantity, by what methods, and to whom it was to be distributed, as well as the prices to be charged and the wages to be paid. They, according Mises, were reduced to government pensioners. He further insisted that officials in the proliferating, strangling state bureaucracy that thrived under the Nazis were entirely different from those who worked in the private sector. Even in large corporations, private employees were answerable to stockholders and market forces. This was not true of bureaucrats under the state socialism that after January 1933 prevailed in Nazi Germany.

The pro-welfare state or socialist Left responded to such broadsides by pointing out that "democratic" states produced expansive public administrations without experiencing the horrors that drove Mises into exile. Mises might have countered that a vast state bureaucracy may not be a sufficient cause of centralized dictatorship but can most definitely contribute to it. One could also argue that an unopposed administrative behemoth works against inherited freedoms, even if it does do so less destructively than Nazism.[21] A final point: Nazism would have been far less dangerous internally and internationally if it had not enjoyed state power. No matter how unpleasant an ideology may seem to us, absent state power it cannot crush all opposition, let alone engage in mass murder.

## The Marxist Response

In the 1930s and during World War II, a systematic Marxist critique of Nazism and, more generally, of fascism crystallized among Central European Jewish intellectuals.[22] Members of this group dealt critically not only with capitalism as a social and economic phenomenon but also with Mises's distinction between private corporations and public administration. Franz Neumann (1900–1954) stands out among those German Marxists who paid special attention to classical liberal positions as an alternative to his socialist thinking. Neumann knew Mises's work well and makes references to it in his classic *Behemoth*, which was published in the United States in 1944.[23] Not surprisingly, *Behemoth* found admirers on the Left as soon as it appeared. Herbert Marcuse, who then was already a prominent spokesman for the Frankfurt School, was drawn to Neumann's work because it explored the connection between corporate industrial power and the Nazi government. Like Marcuse, Neumann spent much of his life as a Far Left activist who developed close ties to the Communist Party. Despite this engagement, Neumann's compelling analysis did not reflect Communist partisanship. In key points, his analysis overlaps that of Mises and the Austrian Marxists Karl Kautsky and Rudolf Hilferding. Like these figures, Neumann viewed the consolidation of state power as basic for understanding the Nazis' seizure of power and their success in destroying adversaries.

According to Neumann, the Nazis, like the less violent Italian fascists, forged a fateful alliance among corporate capitalists, government administrators, the army, and assorted nationalist groups. From that came the appearance of a highly centralized state, resembling Thomas Hobbes's "mortal deity," an early image for a sovereign state that absorbs into itself all human associations. As a Marxist, Neumann emphasized the crisis of advanced capitalism as propelling this alliance, but he also looked at the role of state power and other forces that helped build the "Nazi Behemoth." In Neumann's formulation, the political-economic coalition that resulted in the Nazi state could only lead to an aggresive foreign policy and continuing internal repression. The capitalist class required such actions to prevent an internal economic crisis that would otherwise lead to a workers' revolution and the reorganization of society in accordance with rational socialist principles. Faithful to the Marxist view that fascism, especially in its Nazi form, was an attempt to upend and suppress socialist revolution, Neumann insisted on a Marxist revolutionary solution.

Curiously, his argument met dogged resistance from another Frankfurt School aficionado, Friedrich Pollock (1894–1970), who scandalized his circle by insisting that Neumann's "behemoth" could assume relatively benign forms in some Western societies. Pollock observed that the government bureaucracy and corporate capitalists could work together in a way that gave the appearance of being democratic and that could attract majority support in advanced industrial countries. Pollock cited the United States as an example of the effectiveness of this new political order based on managerial cooperation and without the militaristic features of Nazi Germany.[24] His analysis, which was mostly confined to commentaries, easily segued into examinations of the managerial revolution, a theme that pervaded the work of such disaffected Trotskyites as Bruno Rizzi and James Burnham.[25] These erstwhile Marxist thinkers understood fascism as a particular form of managerial organization that stressed national cohesion. For geopolitical reasons that did not affect the United States as a great continental power, managerial states in Europe felt driven to engage in risky military adventures, a tendency that became truly explosive with the advent of fascist regimes.

In his correspondence with Max Horkheimer, another member of the Frankfurt School, Neumann argued furiously against Pollock's concept of a self-stabilizing state capitalism. He indicated that one of the reasons he undertook *Behemoth* was to demonstrate that there was no future to the existing economic system once it had reached the stage of "totalitarian monopoly capitalism." According to Neumann, "the contradictions of capitalism in Germany have become effective at a higher and therefore more perilous level, even if the existing contradictions were disguised through a bureaucratic apparatus and the ideology of a people's community." Pollock's theory supposedly created an overly positive picture of capitalism as it presently existed or was imagined existing in certain Western countries. This interpretation, according to Neumann, would be dangerous, if a flawed economic model were presented as an alternative to the Nazi state. Neumann finally castigated Pollock for denying the raison d'être of the transplanted Institute for Social Research, by "departing unmistakably from its Marxist purpose."[26]

The conceptualization of the Nazi dictatorship as a hypertrophied modern state can likewise be found in the posthumously edited and published writings of Karl Kautsky (1854–1938), who was a leading Austrian Marxist theorist and was often referred to as "the Pope of Marxism." Kautsky's devotion to Marx's views of history and capitalism shaped much of his scholarly oeuvre and his longtime editorship of *Die Neue Zeit*, a journal of high socialist theory founded in Stuttgart in 1883. After the Bolshevik takeover of Russia, Kautsky engaged in a prolonged conflict with the pro-Soviet wing of European socialism, and as is well documented, he and Lenin became implacable enemies.[27] As early as 1919 Kautsky published a blistering attack on Soviet Bolshevism as an exercise in "terrorism" and "a new form of Tartar dictatorship" that Western socialists should emphatically repudiate. He

characterized Lenin's rule as representing a "regression into barbaric conditions, and the Alpha and Omega of its ruling strategy is simply to shoot people."[28] After years of battling the pro-Soviet wing of European socialism,
Kautsky moved to the Netherlands, where he later died, in forced exile from
a Nazi-controlled Germany. There he watched the transformation of the
modern state into whatever grotesque forms it assumed under the Nazis and
Soviets.

The exiled socialist expressed concerns about these totalitarian developments without ever fully abandoning his Marxist premises. He went on believing that a crisis of monopoly capitalism had led to both imperialism and
political dictatorship. Nonetheless, it is possible to trace a line of descent from
Kautsky's perceptions about uncontrolled public administration to later, more
systematically developed interpretations of totalitarianism. Franz Borkenau,
Rudolf Hilferding,[29] Hannah Arendt, and other witnesses to the Nazi and
Soviet dictatorships who came out of Central European Marxist circles eventually shifted their focus from the contradictions of capitalism to studies
about operationally similar totalitarian regimes. These observers recognized
there were extensive structural and ideological links between the German
catastrophe and what they saw happening in the Soviet state.

They also meditated on why a socialist revolution of the kind that Marx
had predicted did not occur or seem likely to take place. They began to view
a runaway modern state as a principal actor in establishing a new kind of
regime. Nazi and Bolshevik leaders managed to erect their own collectivist
governments, while making a fetish out of denouncing "liberal capitalism."
But they treated economic relations as a tool for increasing personal control
by those who took charge of the political apparatus. In such centralized governments, the political did not conform to the classical Marxist analysis, as a
development of secondary importance. Rather the state became the driving
force that shaped human wills and suppressed its declared enemies.

Although there were admittedly Marxist interpreters of fascism and Nazism outside of Central Europe, those who came from this region were particularly rigorous and scholarly in their thinking. They were not just reacting
to leading events, in the way Italian socialists periodically denounced the fascist government from Paris or New York.[30] They started with a social theory
that they then tried to apply to a political crisis—and despite their initial
dedication to Marxist theory, these theorists were able to modify their conceptual framework to bring it into line with available facts. The same atti-

tude obtained among economic liberals, who examined events based on their understanding of power relations and the operation of public administration.

Italian antifascists may have been less systematic at least partly because they were fighting what looked mostly like a run-of-the-mill dictatorship. It was a government that, according to its critics, featured clever demagogues who promised the gullible material benefits in return for abandoning their liberties. In a famous letter to the exile newspaper published in Paris *Corriere degli Italiani* in March 1927, longtime head of the Italian Socialist Party, Pietro Nenni (1891–1980), compared Mussolini to Napoleon III, the nephew of the great Napoleon who elevated himself through a plebiscite in 1853 to the rank of emperor of the French. Louis Napoleon achieved this by appearing to be all things to all people. Marx, Nenni reminds us, had written perceptively about this political adventurer, who rose to political prominence after the French Revolution of 1848.

Nenni's response was to add a call to action in which his allies would be

> drawing over to the antifascist side international public opinion, inundating Italy with clandestine newspapers, and extending ties to antifascists over the Alps as well as on the Italian side of them. . . . Even if the tyranny that the masses seek to overthrow makes concessions when confronted by the turmoil of the public place, History will not save Mussolini any more than it saved Napoleon III. . . . This will be the response of events even sooner once we organize for the struggle that lies ahead. We can do this by relying on concrete positive elements, ceasing to fight among ourselves and uniting against the enemy that tramples on (*calpesta*) and humiliates us.[31]

Nenni's call to action seemed to appeal to whatever was needed to overthrow a personal dictatorship, and there was good reason for this. Italian fascism looked far less sinister in 1927 than Nazism did after Hitler took power in January 1933.

"Fascism as a government," to use De Felice's phrase, was generally far less brutal and totalitarian than its German counterpart, and unlike Nazi rule, *Il Duce* could have applied the brakes in the 1930s before he slid into disaster. His regime therefore offered a far less grim target than the government of his future Axis partner over the Alps. During most of Mussolini's rule, his opponents in Paris had difficulty even keeping their adversarial press afloat. The editor of *Corriere degli Italiani* and Sturzo's devotee in the PPI,

Giuseppe Donati, worked overtime to preserve a united antifascist front, even without the Communists. Socialists and the bourgeois parties bickered constantly with each other, and it seemed to Donati that a new "democratic citizen" may have been necessary to combat fascism.[32] The German situation caused greater alarm and generally more thoughtfulness among its enemies. Opponents of the Nazis were dealing with a far more deadly and more aggressive enemy than Mussolini's government and therefore felt compelled to provide a detailed, systematic study of this historical problem. The fact that most of them were Jewish and subject to special mistreatment may have made them even more determined to understand the new political reality in Germany.

One of the most impressive studies of this kind came from German legal theorist and longtime German labor lawyer Ernst Fraenkel (1898–1975), who in *The Dual State* (1941) famously distinguished between two political entities that were both present in the Nazi regime: a normative state and a prerogative one. The first kind of state adhered to those laws it enacted and treated all German citizens as legal equals. The other state, which was subject to the Nazi Party, broke established legal arrangements whenever it suited its purposes. It was the second state that began to overshadow the first from the very day the Nazis took power.[33] Fraenkel associated himself with Marxists, but his critical examination of the prerogative state (*Maßnahmenstaat*) was clearly not of Marxist origin. One finds evidence of the famous interwar debate between the normativist theorist Hans Kelsen and the brilliant defender of authoritarian government Carl Schmitt in the works of Fraenkel and in those of a likeminded colleague, Otto Kirchheimer (1900–1965). Although the events-driven studies produced by Fraenkel, Kirchheimer, and others of their background took varied forms, a Marxist materialist worldview would not have been foundational for their arguments.

There was, however, one constant Marxist reference point in the work of these thinkers; namely, a belief that political actors were pursuing their ends rationally. They attributed to those fascists or Nazis whom they critically studied Max Weber's concept of *Zweckrationalität*.[34] Without fully unpacking this complicated sociological concept in Weber's work, let me note that this great social thinker argued strenuously that the choice of adequate, carefully considered means to achieve an end could be "rational," even if one disputed the morality or soundness of an actor's goal. The rational person was making a decision after having established a causal connection between his means and the ends he wished to reach. For Marxist scholars in interwar Europe, the ends being sought were also rational to the extent that they conformed to the fascists' material or political interests. Their critics presented those who came to power in Germany in the 1930s as rational beings, to the extent they were consciously and methodically pursuing their interests. These interests and how certain people pursued them were far from admirable, but they were understandable in terms of their pursuit of power or the desire to hold onto their fortunes. Those found in these positions predictably formed alliances with or worked to create governments that would enable them to advance their goals. But Frankfurt School luminaries, like Eric Fromm, Theodor Adorno, and Wilhelm Reich, criticized the narrowness of this approach. They insisted that sexual repression and sadomasochistic abnormalities had to be factored in to grasp the appeal of Nazism and fascism in general. German Jewish Marxists in American exile became preoccupied with the psychological underpinnings of anti-Semitism; eventually they produced the *Studies in Prejudice* series for the American Jewish Committee that highlighted the morbid, repressed aspect of the Nazi "mentality."

There was also a noticeable division of interests in how German refugees analyzed the fascist or Nazi problem. Neumann wrote *Behemoth* as a structural and economic interpretation of the Nazi state, but this did not prevent him from engaging simultaneously in his own speculations about anti-Semitism. It is also clear that not all studies about anti-Semitism as a historic problem emphasize psychic abnormalities. They also address cultural, social, and religious circumstances that engendered and sustained anti-Jewish sentiments. This was certainly true of Neumann's preoccupation with the roots of anti-Jewish feelings that he believed fueled Nazi anti-Semitism. Neumann's devotee Marcuse, however, evinced no special interest in anti-Jewish prejudice as a long-standing evil.[35] And though Marcuse wrote voluminously on the erotic deprivation caused by advanced capitalist society, he was attracted to Neumann's work primarily because of its analysis of the alliance between industrial capitalism and the German military and governing classes.

Other views on the irrationality of Nazism circulated outside the psychic interpretations advanced by members of the Frankfurt School and their US votaries. Although not without merit, these views do not directly bear on this study and are only noted in passing. They include those who stressed the mythic elements that informed Nazi ideology, investigators of Nazism as a form of modern nihilism, and interpreters of the Gnostic, counter-Orthodox Christian currents in the Nazi apocalypse. Authors who raised these interpretations—for example, Mircea Eliade, Hermann Rauschning, Eric Voegelin, and Hans Jonas[36]—were serious observers of their time, and their writings can still be read with considerable profit. But their views were never the dominant academic or political ones cited to explain fascism or Nazism. Whether these interpretations have become entertainment on today's History Channel or the central theme of cult leaders, they do not fit into the historiographical mainstream—nor have they affected politics in any significant way. It is equally extraneous for this book to consider the speculations of psychologists that Hitler was mentally sick or suffering from syphilis. Although such conjectures may be worth pondering, they do not affect the mainstream discussions among "experts." And we are looking here at how academics, journalists, and others who have been deemed significant intellectuals have understood fascism and Nazism since the 1920s.

The other assumption that warrants mention is that the movement or movements in question were historically specific. Fascism and Nazism are not free-floating concepts but are anchored in a well-defined temporospatial framework and refer to ascertainable actors and events. The most cogent critics of fascism and Nazism studied the object of their investigation through an intensive examination of economic, cultural, and institutional arrangements. They related their studies to concrete historical contexts and avoided speculation about an eternal fascist enemy. An alternative mindset eventually prevailed, but that happened mostly after the Axis powers were defeated.

Critical analysis of fascist actors in interwar Europe gave way to a novel enterprise. Fascism became, among other things, the favored term of political scolds and those who sought to trample on the historical liberties of those who offended them. Surveying an earlier stage of this continuing process, Italian filmmaker (and longtime enemy of both fascism and the Catholic Church) Pier Paolo Pasolini memorably observed in 1974, "Nulla di peggio del fascismo degli antifascisti" (Nothing about fascism seems quite as bad as the antifascists).[37]

Chapter 3

# Post–World War II Antifascism

The following survey of the major trends in antifascism after World War II focuses on three intersecting defensive strategies that the movement deployed against what it saw as fascism. Each represented a departure from the more analytic approaches that were characteristic of interwar examinations of fascist thought and practice. At times these strategies were applied jointly in the attempt to cleanse the political culture of fascist legacies. All three were predicated on the belief that what was targeted was a deeply embedded evil that, despite the defeat of the Axis powers in 1945, still endangered the survival of democracy. Not surprisingly, the advocates of all three strategies saw the state and massive social engineering as essential for making their work possible. Although antifascist reformers opposed the statist authoritarianism practiced by the Right, they readily endorsed coercive methods, providing they helped keep at bay a putative fascist danger.

The three strategies were forced reeducation of the German people, the treatment of fascism as a form of pathology that required prolonged therapeutic treatment, and the production and distribution of pedagogical (that is to

say, penitential) historiography emphasizing the disastrous results of living under a reactionary social order. Antifascists have typically favored using more
than one of these three approaches. The evil they wish to combat is seen as so
pervasive that countering it may require every available resource. Whichever
the method to be applied, however, guilt and penance are the necessary ac-
companiments of the mind formation that antifascists are intent on fostering.

## German Reeducation as a Template

A former Yale professor of philosophy who is now associated with the Free
University in Berlin, Susan Neiman wrote an entire book, *Learning from the
Germans*, about what she considers one of antifascism's greatest moral achievements since 1945.[1] Neiman lauds the reeducation of the Germans under
Allied supervision and the subsequent antifascist atonement of the Germans
as approaches that Americans would do well to imitate. Although she stops
short of calling Trump another Hitler, she stresses the similarity between
these two "evil" leaders in fomenting bigotry. Neiman sees the German example of "overcoming the past" as one that her own country should follow,
once it manages to free itself from its racist and authoritarian ruler.

Neiman also has kind words in her book and in an interview with *The
Guardian* for the now dissolved East German Communist regime, for which
antifascism was a continuing political and educational mission. Under the
Communists, there was no chance that the German people would ever re-
vive their fascist legacy, although the price for this protection was a regime
that curtailed civil liberties. Quite possibly, we are led to believe, the United
States as we battle white supremacy will have to pay a similar price.[2] In any
case Neiman is insisting that we look at Germany's "path toward the West,"
to use a favorite phrase of antinational German academics, to better understand the example we should be emulating. Much of this path was imposed
by Germany's conquerors from across the Atlantic, but it became in time the
model of antifascist reeducation and social engineering for non-Germanic
countries and may now help Americans overcome their past. Yet Neiman's
path toward the West does not have much to do with Western civilization
before recent times. Plato, Aquinas, Luther, Hobbes, Pascal, Machiavelli,
Hegel, and other Western thinkers would not qualify as members of Neiman's late-modern notion of the West.

May 8, 1945, is the official date in the West for the defeat of Nazi Germany (in Russia it is May 9). The end of World War II in Europe is still an occasion for celebration and not only for the four major victors: the United States, Russia, Great Britain, and France. Equally noteworthy, the government, media, and educational institutions of the defeated Germans celebrate May 8 as a "day of liberation" from their previous tyrannical regime. This overlooks the fact that after that date the defeated Germans were exposed to harsh treatment from their conquerors. For months after the war, the Western Allies limited food supplies to the starving Germans to about 1,250 calories per day. (Inhabitants of what were deemed "friendly countries" were at that time allowed 2,000 calories in daily food supplies.) The caloric intake for Germans who did not farm their own food was finally raised to about 1,500 calories by the beginning of 1946. Even more appallingly, hundreds of thousands of Germans were kept in detention camps well into 1946, where many were maltreated.[3] The inhabitants of central or eastern Germany who remained within a German state fell under a Soviet dictatorship thereafter known as the German Democratic Republic.[4]

The four major belligerent powers (France had been added by then) formally arranged for the occupation of a soon-to-be-defeated Germany in February 1945, putting on paper plans for an Allied Control Council. By the time of Germany's unconditional surrender in May, the Council was ready to begin its work. Yet plans for the occupation of Germany were hatched years earlier. In the United States both military and civilian officials were instructed on how they would administer the Germans, after they were defeated, at the University of Virginia as early as 1942. A plan put forth by Secretary of the Treasury Henry Morgenthau and Undersecretary Harry Dexter White called for harsh treatment of the defeated population in order to avoid World War III. These proposals gained acceptance in principle from FDR and (more tentatively) from Churchill at the Second Quebec Conference in September 1944.

Although the more vindictive features of the Morgenthau Plan—fragmenting Germany into multiple, separately administered regions, turning the country into a subsistence-level rural society, and destroying German industry or transferring it to Soviet Russia—were softened, it is possible to recognize an aspect of the original plan in the policies implemented during the occupation of Germany. White, who turned out to be a Soviet informant, called for Russian access to Germany's Ruhr region, which was heavily industrialized and full of iron ore, but his proposal was given short shrift. One aspect of the Morgenthau-White proposals, however, was implemented, casting a long shadow on postwar Germany: it offered a detailed blueprint for the forced instruction of the impoverished German population in antifascist teachings.

More trials awaited the vanquished side. From July 17 through August 2, 1945, a conference in Potsdam held by the victorious powers resulted in punitive decisions regarding the defeated Germans. A proposal put forth by Eastern European countries to expel their ethnic Germans was approved in Potsdam by the major powers. Before this resettlement ended, close to fifteen million Volks- and Reichsdeutsche (Germans from former German territory and those from countries where they were minorities) were driven from their ancestral lands,[5] with hundreds of thousands dying during what was described by the Allies as a population exchange. Arrangements were also made at Potsdam to allow the Poles to annex lands in central Germany east of the Oder-Neisse Rivers. Meanwhile Poland's eastern territories (with their mixed Polish-Ukrainian populations) were given to the Soviet Union, which was then expanding westward.

Perhaps equally important for Germany's postwar political culture, plans were worked out at Potsdam to hold war trials, the purpose of which was to demonstrate to the world the evil character of the regime that the Allies had just defeated. The major phase of these trials lasted from November 20, 1945 until October 1, 1946. and featured notorious war criminals brought before an International Military Tribunal. Nazi leaders who were put on trial were either executed (if they did not anticipate the hangman by committing suicide) or condemned to spend decades or lifetimes in prison.

Worthwhile questions were raised at this time and during the trials of lesser malefactors concerning the procedures' legality and, most importantly, whether they furnished a dubious precedent for other extralegal international trials.[6] In the United States, Senator Robert Taft caused an uproar by raising such questions in defiance of both national parties, and in England Winston Churchill expressed reservations about what became the Nuremberg Trials, when he learned about plans for them devised as early as 1943. Churchill suggested that Nazi leaders who had committed particularly heinous crimes should be summarily shot. A legal irregularity, that is, criminal charges that were manufactured in an ad hoc fashion and which became a precedent, argued Churchill, might have worse results than meting out ex post facto justice.[7] Some charges against the eventual defendants, such as "conspiring against the peace," were in fact manufactured for the occasion.

Eventually it became clear that Soviet-appointed judges at Nuremberg were punishing German leaders for acts that their government had been equally complicit in, such as attacking Poland in September 1939 while party to the Soviet-Nazi Pact. The main Soviet judge at the trials, Iona Nitichenko, had previously presided over the show trials conducted by Stalin between 1936 and 1938, which provided the legal justification for the Soviet tyrant's decision to turn on and execute his former Communist associates.[8] Her presence and the judgments handed down gave the trials an appearance of hypocrisy that its critics were all too willing to bring up. Then there were the questions of the terror bombing of civilians conducted during the war by the Americans and British and the rapes and murders of German civilians committed by the invading Russian armies in the winter of 1945.[9] Although it would be foolish to compare such deeds to the acts of mass extermination carried out by the Third Reich, the role of moral judges assumed by the Allied Powers may not look as convincing in retrospect as it did immediately after the war. One may reach this conclusion without in any way condoning truly shocking Nazi atrocities, which befell my own relatives who failed to leave Europe in time. Despite these reservations, the trials were enormously effective in changing cultural and political attitudes; their impact on German society can still be discerned in the country's self-absorbed atonement for its national past.

Contrary to certain misconceptions, many would be surprise to learn that the trials went on for years after the most-publicized phase ended in October 1946. Anyone whose name came up in reference to Nazi-related activities was forced to fill out detailed questionnaires (*Fragebogen*) concerning his contacts with the previous government.[10] Authors and thinkers who were linked to the prewar national Right or any anti-Communist movement were forbidden to set up or write for Allied-approved publications and sometimes were interned. This was even true for opponents of the Nazis who were burdened by insufficiently antifascist affiliations.[11] Although the non-Soviet-controlled parts of Germany were allowed to form a constitutional government in 1949 (under Allied supervision), the Allied High Commission oversaw German affairs until 1955.[12]

It is important to process these details, because they help qualify the view that, by the onset of the Cold War, efforts at reeducating the Germans had largely stopped. The need to contain the Soviets and to reindustrialize and eventually rearm Germany supposedly came to overshadow the initial determination of the Allied High Commission and their advisers to combat the fascist spirit. But in fact no sudden about-face took place in how the commission addressed the task of reeducation or forcing the Germans to overcome their past (*Vergangenheitsbewältigung* [overcoming the past]).

Into the 1950s the occupation government still determined who would be allowed to receive a license to publish and distribute printed material. The educational curricula of the German Länder and the social studies and history textbooks adopted for German public school reflected the obligatory universalist, antifascist outlook of Germany's post-Nazi government. German courts routinely banned political parties that were held to be threats to democracy, even though not all such banned parties constituted a threat to the constitutional order. Some of these banned parties, like those attracting regionalist and monarchists in Bavaria, were outlawed because they generated unwanted competition for the mainstream parties—namely, those that were organized under Allied supervision and that were charged with constructing the popular will in an approved political direction.

It is, however, true that under the Christian Democratic governments of Konrad Adenauer and his successor Ludwig Erhard in the 1950s and 1960s, more emphasis was placed on economic growth and resisting the Soviet bloc than atoning for the Nazi past. Moreover, the postwar electoral victories of anti-Communist Republicans in the United States and the shift of West European politics toward the Right with the onset of the Cold War helped soften Western attitudes toward the defeated Germans. But under the Social Democratic government of Willy Brandt, who was chancellor from 1969 to 1974, making restitution for Germany's history under the Third Reich again became a priority.

The Social Democratic chancellor became a transformational figure, negotiating peace agreements with Communist states in Eastern Europe, in which he ceded already lost German territory and apologized for Nazi crimes, and ostentatiously embracing cosmopolitanism, He was widely acclaimed for breaking from the business-as-usual attitude of Germany's anti-Communist Christian Democrats and for moving toward the more self-consciously antifascist Germany that exists today. The Sixty-Eighters, who led student revolts in the late 1960s, were a complementary force in establishing a more contrite, antinationalist Germany. These rebels, some of whom attained high places in the German government and in journalism, always warned against German fascism and regarded West Germany's alliance with the Americans as tantamount to a return to the Nazi past.

After reunification in 1991, Germans moved ever more directly toward antifascism as a state ideology. The remark by a former foreign affairs minister and violent socialist revolutionary Josef Fischer that Auschwitz is the founding myth of the German Federal Republic has become more, not less, true since German unification. The vital center of German parliamentary politics is found today on the multicultural Left, and the boast of Chancellor Angela Merkel that in Germany no right-of-center party will be allowed to govern may, for better or worse, be true. The only German party that is openly patriotic, Alternative für Deutschland (AfD), polls between 11 and 13 percent nationwide, and no German coalition will consider allowing this deviationist party into a government. The AfD is made up mostly of disaffected Christian Democrats who challenge Angela Merkel's immigration policy. The self-image of Germans as antifascist cosmopolites is now embedded; this is an image that their conquerors labored mightily to instill in the conquered country.

Illustrating the power of this negative picture of the national past were the mobs of young enthusiasts who swelled the streets of major German cities in 1996 to welcome Daniel Goldhagen, the controversial historian who had recently published a remarkably anti-German tract. In *Hitler's Willing Executioners*, Goldhagen claims, with less-than-convincing evidence, that the German people at least since the nineteenth century had yearned to murder their Jewish fellow citizens.[13] And so when Hitler implemented an already widely endorsed "eliminationist anti-Semitism," the German masses endorsed it demonstratively. The notorious attack of anti-Semitism against Jewish businesses and synagogues known as Kristallnacht, on November 9 and 10, 1938, according to Goldhagen, was a murderous rampage that attracted more than Nazi street gangs: ordinary German citizens, who had been imbued with the German anti-Semitic culture, allegedly joined in the violence. Significantly, historians who made their reputations as critics of German nationalism, like Hans Mommsen, Richard Evans, Ian Kershaw, and Fritz Stern, challenged the credibility of these charges. But among younger Germans raised in an antifascist, antinational culture, Goldhagen's perspective is popular.

Equally indicative of the antifascist mood in Germany since unification is the elevation of the anniversary of the country's surrender in 1945 to a rigorously enforced day of celebration. This practice began in the former East

German Communist regime, which declared May 8 to be a "day of liberation." Until 1966 the German Democratic Republic treated May 8 as a workers' holiday and even afterward, when it became necessary to work on that day, held annual festivities on what is known as *Befreiungstag*. Celebrating Germany's unconditional surrender as a "day of liberation" was turned into a litmus test for antifascist feelings. Never mind the fact that such paradigmatic German leftists as Willy Brandt and Rudolf Augstein, then editor of *Der Spiegel*, ridiculed this proposal.

Among the numerous attacks against those who continue to view the anniversary of Germany's unconditional surrender as a source of sorrow is an invective by Ignaz Bubis, a former director of the Central Committee for Jews in Germany. Opponents of this antifascist celebration, according to Bubis, are people living in the past, who wish to continue what happened in Germany between 1933 and 1945.[14] Although Bubis qualified this charge by describing his opponents as Nazi sympathizers who want a "perhaps more moderate version" of Hitler's tyranny, his accusation has a now-familiar tone. It resembles our own antifascist rhetoric, which equates insufficiently progressive views with nostalgia for the Third Reich.

Also exemplifying the attempts of German elites since unification to incorporate Eastern German Communist antifascist attitudes has been the showcasing of Communists in paying tributes to anti-Nazi resistance. Until the mid-1990s the annual commemoration of the resistance movement centered on a ceremony held on July 20, honoring the abortive attempt by the martyred Claus von Stauffenberg and others to assassinate Hitler and overthrow the Nazi government. Although the conspirators represented a wide range of views from monarchists to social democrats, antifascist Germans, particularly academic and journalists, have balked at this commemoration and even demonstrated against it. Most of the conspirators against Hitler, they have charged, were German nationalists of one sort or another, and even their social democratic allies were thought to hold views that were reactionary by current antifascist standards.

In 1995 the federal government agreed to include the Communist resistance to the Nazis as an integral part of the annual celebration. Two arguments were advanced for this change, most prominently by antinationalist historians Heinrich Winkler and Hans Mommsen.[15] One, the East German population would feel offended if Communist opponents to Hitler were not included in festivities and exhibits honoring the German resistance. Two, the celebrations were taking place not to honor the German people but to pay tribute to wartime German antifascists. The first argument was largely specious, because there was no reason to believe that Germans who had suffered under Communist tyranny were yearning to celebrate Communist antifascists. But the second argument advanced by its proponents may carry more weight. For those who have tried to elevate antifascism to a German state religion, including Communist functionaries in the celebratory rituals made perfectly good sense.

Historian Rainer Zitelmann correctly observes that the attempt to draw Communists, including former Stasi informants in Brandenburg, into an antifascist front was a clever flanking move by pro-Communist leftists.[16] After German unification, lurid reports about Communist brutality began pouring in from the East. These revelations caused Germans to move back toward the formerly widespread template of the 1950s, when West Germany stood in the frontline against totalitarian Communism. From that perspective Communism was the enemy of those who valued personal liberties. Like Nazism it was a form of totalitarianism, and that category encompassed both Communists and Nazis who threatened a liberal constitutional order: "In the place of anti-totalitarianism there now emerged a purer anti-fascism combined with fashionable anti-anti-Communism. As a result of this development any anti-Communist position was deemed to be reactionary or primitive."[17]

A missing observation in Zitelmann's otherwise perceptive analysis is the major reason why German antifascists were and still are attracted to the now-fallen German Communist dictatorship. It is not because they are orthodox Marxist-Leninists. These fans of the fallen Communist dictatorship viewed the East German state as an appropriate punishment for a nation that they hope would ultimately disappear, through Third World immigration and/or absorption into an international body. Much of Germany's intelligentsia opposed the reunification of Germany because they felt the Germans did not deserve to have a unified country, given their guilt for starting those twentieth-century wars and given the devastation that accompanied these conflicts.[18] Leaders of Germany's Greens, like Jürgen Trittin and Claudia Roth, have expressed such opinions repeatedly, and the parents of Angela Merkel chose to live in Communist East Germany because they considered

Communist oppression a fitting fate for their morally contaminated nation.[19] Inherent in these attitudes is a post-Marxist form of antifascism. Those who embody and implement it are critical of traditional social relations and cultural values, and they made common cause with the Marxist Left to finish off a world that disgusts them.

German reeducation has become a model for the reconstruction of other Western societies. Some of the measures that social psychologists and public administrators imposed on a defeated Germany in an earlier crusade against fascism have now been applied elsewhere. It is hardly accidental that this form of democracy makes citizens subject to a coordinated antifascist social experiment. In this program of socialization, the media, culture industry, public administration, and state-controlled education all play pivotal roles. It is noteworthy that a remark by the Christian Democratic federal deputy, Friedrich Merz, to the effect that Muslim migrants, in addition to the German Right, were also spreading anti-Semitic sentiments brought down the wrath of Merz's supposedly conservative party. His Christian Democratic colleagues rushed to remind the deputy that on the seventy-fifth anniversary of Auschwitz it was inexcusable that this political leader should be arousing "xenophobia" instead of focusing on the right-wing nationalist danger in Germany.

A more robust democracy and true constitutional freedoms, it is feared, might open the door to a renewal of fascism. Therefore, self-government for the people must remain a closely monitored process, until enlightened rulers can be sure their population has been immunized against fascist impulses. One might contrast this attitude to the hope expressed by Antonio Gramsci, the theoretical father of the Italian Communist Party, that the intelligentsia (*il ceto intelletuale*) would never distance themselves from the laboring masses. Intellectuals, according to Gramsci, could only justify their existence by serving as a vehicle for the material betterment of the proletariat.[20] But in Germany's reeducation model, which has now spread to other liberal democracies, the working masses are viewed as the bearers of deep-seated fascist and authoritarian attitudes. It therefore behooves the intelligentsia in alliance with the state to keep the ignorant and impulsive from exercising their unguided will. The success of democracy depends on acting illiberally in the short and middle term to prevent a fascist recrudescence. An unredeemed false-democratic man became the target for, if necessary, forced conversion when the antifascist project arrived on Germany's shores.

## Antifascism as Psychological Reconditioning

The Frankfurt School had been operating for eleven years in Germany before it migrated to New York City, by way of Geneva, in 1935. Soon after its relocation, it was renamed the Institute for Social Research and acquired a structural relationship to Columbia University. Later, as part of the process of Americanization, its German periodical, *Zeitschrift für Sozialforschung*, became a widely respected English-language journal, *Studies in Psychological and Social Science*. There are two ways of understanding the Frankfurt School's evolution in the United States: as a prolonged existence in exile occasioned by the Nazi takeover of Germany or as a fusion of a radical ideology (one that was radical by interwar German standards) with changing American fashions. Although much of its early work on the connection between fascism and sexual repression was published in German, most would eventually become available in English. In 1950 the School was reestablished with American support and encouragement in Frankfurt as part of a new German university. Max Horkheimer returned to Germany to direct this operation and then lured Theodor Adorno into helping him manage the restored German institute.[21]

Despite the Frankfurt School's return to its place of origin in 1950, critical theorists, who imaginatively blended Freudian and Marxist ideas, continued to exert a powerful influence on American political culture.[22] While the School was being reestablished in Germany, the American Jewish Committee brought out *The Authoritarian Personality*, a gargantuan installment of its *Studies in Prejudice* series.[23] A project that had been in the works since 1944 when Horkheimer was asked to head it, this study would strongly influence social psychology and other social sciences in the United States. Horkheimer and his companions undertook a task of great importance for its adherents, as well as for those who managed to wade through its convoluted English prose. The contributors claimed to be demonstrating the deep-seated psychological problems that caused the "authoritarian personality" to make possible the horrors of fascist tyranny.

After World War II ended, critical theorists Adorno and Herbert Marcuse believed that the United States, far more than Germany, was falling prey to fascist temptations. In an oft-cited letter that Marcuse wrote to his longtime collaborator in February 1947, he explained that the world was then divided into two blocs: one led by an "imperfect" socialistic state and the other embracing the "neofascist" West under American leadership. According to Marcuse, the states in which the old ruling class had survived the war politically and economically would soon become fascist. Furthermore, "the neofascist and Soviet societies are economically and in terms of class structure enemies, and a war between them is inevitable. Both, however, are in their forms of domination antirevolutionary and opposed to socialist development." In view of this dire situation Marcuse called for defining a revolutionary theory that would "resist both systems and represent orthodox Marxist teachings without compromise."[24]

Such thoughts raise persistent questions about whether the critical theorists ever represented orthodox Marxist teachings as opposed to Freudian-tinged cultural criticism. Every major European Communist party together with Soviet party theorists had railed since the 1920s against the fusion of those two streams of thought. From an orthodox Marxist and certainly a Marxist-Leninist perspective, that critical theorists placed far more emphasis on erotic gratification than on economic transformation and identified fascism with sexual dysfunctionality, which meant theirs was an idiosyncratic leftist position. European Communist regimes were understandably offended by this unsettling invention.

Equally interesting is another belief that Marcuse shared with Adorno; namely, that if the Institute for Social Research could devise a proper revolutionary theory, it would change the nature of history, starting with the confrontation then taking place between the imperfectly socialist Soviet Union and the neofascist United States. Although this claim was undoubtedly far-fetched, it was not completely out of place. After all, the war waged by the Frankfurt School in exile against fascist or fascist-like prejudice had an impact in the United States during World War II when social psychologists and academics steeped in critical theory were helping the US government plan for the reeducation of the Germans.[25]

Other forms of antifascism preceded, overlapped, and sometimes competed with the antifascist views propagated in the United States by the critical theorists. In the interwar period journalists and academics expressed concern about the appeal of the Italian and German models of government to certain sectors of US society. Concern was likewise raised about a US variety of fascism, one that might come wrapped in an American flag, as represented by the populist style and folksy message of "Share the Wealth"

Huey Long, who was governor of Louisiana from 1928 to 1932.[26] Alarm would also be generated by an unusual critic of the New Deal, Father Charles Edward Coughlin, who inveighed against Jews and Wall Street on a weekly radio program from suburban Detroit.[27] Rightly or wrongly Coughlin for years became the face and voice of fascism in the United States.

After World War I, to the consternation of some, books began appearing that glorified the Aryan race; for example, T. Lothrop Stoddard's *The Rising Tide of Color* (1920).[28] Stoddard, a brilliant polemicist and New England blueblood, became by the 1930s an outspoken advocate for Nazi Germany and its eugenic planning. In reaction to what the writer Sinclair Lewis viewed as surging profascist sentiment in the United States, he published in 1935 his popular novel *It Can't Happen Here*, a 400-page exploration of a US government takeover by fascist leaders.[29] Lewis's wife Dorothy Thompson, a prominent journalist of the time, was particularly unsettled by the spread of fascist thought. Like her husband, she believed this ideology was gaining momentum on this side of the Atlantic and warned against it in her columns.[30]

Another form of antifascism that clearly overlapped the spread of cultural Marxism in the United States and sometimes mingled with it was the identification of US industrial and military power with fascism. This is the subgenus of antifascism that I encountered as a graduate student at Yale University in the 1960s, as a frequently turbulent opposition to the war in Vietnam erupted. Fascism became synonymous with US military activity directed against Communist insurgencies and the extension of Soviet control. Although those who made this argument may not have been aware of its provenance, their critique of fascism was at the heart of Franz Neumann's investigation of Nazism, and it was reflected in some of the antifascist rhetoric of Neumann's close friend, Herbert Marcuse. A later statement of similar views could be found in Bertram Gross's *Friendly Fascism: The New Face of Power in America* (1980), which emphatically associates fascism with the US military-industrial complex.[31] Although Gross examines the ideological manipulation that he identifies with this behemoth, he focuses mostly on the structural and material preconditions of a fascist state. Gross also wrote critically about the proliferating public bureaucracy and the difficulties of gaining control of this managerialized modern state and economy.[32] His voluminous study of management recalls James Burnham's examination of the managerial revolution and the writings of a post–World War II leftist analyst of American power relations, C. Wright Mills.

These competing or intermingling forms of antifascism in the United States were not, however, the models that led to the present antifascist ideology, except in a very derivative way. The Frankfurt School and its disciples provide the bridge between critiques of prewar fascism and Nazism in Europe and the contemporary imperative for cultural and emotional transformation. Reaching its apogee long after the age of European fascism and Nazism, today's triumphant antifascism is a reaction not to the spread of self-described fascist regimes but to the breakthrough of a Left that must be understood in terms of its own morality and mandate for power. After World War II, both the psychology profession and social theorists assigned prominence to emigre critical theorists and to those whom they trained. If critical theorists Theodor Adorno, Max Horkheimer, Herbert Marcuse, Eric Fromm, Karen Harney, and Ilse Frenkel could not change Russia's imperfect socialism, they nonetheless hoped to sell their market brand of antifascism to New World inhabitants. *The Authoritarian Personality (TAP)* unveils the "pseudo-democratic personality," which Adorno in his chapter identifies with Republican voters and those who express reservations about socialism. According to the contributors to *TAP*, those afflicted with dangerous emotional difficulties—a condition that they often attributed to overbearing fathers—tried to hide their disorder by appearing moderate and tolerant. It was therefore necessary for the specialist to probe deeper and discover what lay beneath the surface. The contributors also hastened to make certain connections that for them seemed self-evident. Being anti-Semitic, antisocialist, and expressing disagreement with FDR's New Deal were all considered highly indicative of the "authoritarian personality."[33]

Although this antifascist analysis would seem to clash with American patriotism, Christopher Lasch in *The True and Only Heaven* notes the wide appeal enjoyed by *TAP* in postwar America, and not only on the far Left.[34] As early as 1947 Adorno and his associates created the California F-Scale Test to evaluate the proneness of applicants for state employment to "fascist attitudes." This test was eventually administered across the nation to, among others, candidates for police work and public-school students: it was thought to be necessary for screening out or treating socially threatening personalities.[35] It has continued to be used in personality assessments for adolescents and job applicants throughout the US, and elements of the F-Scale Test have been incorporated into psychology inventories in, among other states, California and Minnesota (with the California Psychological Inventory and the

Minnesota Multiphasic Personality Inventory). In the 1980s Canadian professor of psychology Bob Altemeyer constructed a new model for F-scale testing that removed the vaguely worded questions in the older form. This too was subsequently given to applicants for public employment.[36] All such testing have a clear relationship to those measures proposed in the final section of *TAP* for dealing with the fascist mindset in modern Western democracies.

Although such a project never won over the anti–New Deal Right, the work commissioned by the American Jewish Committee nonetheless attracted anti-Soviet progressives.[37] The US supports the critical theorists, who established *Commentary* magazine in 1951, were staunch Truman Democrats and also quite anxious about anti-Jewish prejudice. A leading American sociologist and a paradigmatic Cold War liberal, S. M. Lipset, lavished praise on *TAP* but also felt its authors should have connected those psychic disorders they examined to Soviet Communism. Lipset, who published his relevant comments in *American Sociological Review* in 1959, was particularly impressed by Adorno's investigation of so-called working-class authoritarianism, a problem that Lipset was then engaging as well.[38]

An obvious connection between Lipset's politics and the Frankfurt School in exile, and one extensively discussed by Lasch, was a shared distrust for the working class. Ironically or problematically, this was the class the Left claimed to be serving. But Lipset and the contributors to *TAP* were looking elsewhere for support—to an administrative class that enlisted social scientists to address emotional disorders in the general population.[39] Of course, the critical theorists pursued other goals than just spreading their variation of Freudian depth psychology. They also hoped to reduce economic inequality while combating the fascist personality and other evils of late capitalist repression. Significantly the Far Left politics espoused by Adorno and other contributors, who may have been less anti-Soviet than they were opposed to the Western alliance, eventually faded from mainstream interpretations. For a while this allowed their findings to fit into the struggle against an undemocratic Communism just as it had earlier provided ammunition against a fascist enemy.

Another development brought about by the Frankfurt School and its epigones was the theoretical and rhetorical fusion of fascism with "right-wing extremism." Because the Frankfurt School equated right-wing extremism with a susceptibility to or espousal of fascism, labeling someone an extremist of the Right implied that this targeted individual might indeed be an undetected fascist.

This linkage may also be observed in how some admirers of Mussolini's regime were grouped in the same category as American nativists and anti-Black racists. In a study of right-wing extremists and fascists in Pennsylvania between 1925 and 1950, religious historian Philip Jenkins includes both the Ku Klux Klan and Italian Americans who felt pride in Mussolini's restoration of honor to their ancestral land.[40] The more Jenkins delved into this time period in his book, the less likely it seemed that all his subjects belonged in the same ideological camp. It is not even clear that Mussolini's admirers in the United States were all right-wing extremists; they could have been just southern Italian immigrants living in South Philadelphia who were cheering something of significance back home in Italy.

## Penitential History: A Digression

One aspect of reeducating the defeated Germans after World War II that has influenced the United States and much of the rest of the Western world was its use of historical studies to reconstruct national character. Contrary to the intentions of the Morgenthau Plan, Germany was not reduced permanently to a fragmented, deindustrialized country, nor was its economy totally socialized in the way that Franz Neumann and other Marxists advised the occupying powers to do. But the Germans, it was believed, could be pedagogically reconditioned through the creation of new faculties and new disciplines; for example, political science. In addition, meticulously revised textbooks, particularly those explaining the German past, could help turn them into good democrats.

The German state of Hessen was among the earliest and most dedicated of the Länder to implement this educational project. By the summer of 1945 both the Socialists and Communists in Hessen gained the approval of the occupying powers to be reconstituted as democratic political parties; at the same time, local authorities began preparing textbooks suitable for weaning younger Germans away from their nation's past. University faculty were also summoned, with the assistance of, among others, critical theorists, to push German higher education in a new direction. In 1950 a young associate of Adorno reestablished the Institute for Social Research in Frankfurt. Jürgen Habermas was tasked with carrying out a survey of German students intended to indicate where they stood on the scale between democratization and exhibiting traits of an authoritarian personality. Although the initial study, which came out in 1957, only involved 150 students (it was eventually expanded to 550), Habermas drew portentous conclusions from this limited sample. He asserted that German students would require considerably more pedagogical instruction to be able to resist residual fascist influences.[41] In the decades that followed, Habermas became one of the West's most zealous critics of the German past and of any road that might lead back into Europe's ethnocentric or anti-cosmopolitan past.

An historical work that enjoyed acclaim for being fully consistent with efforts to overcome the German fascist past was Fritz Fischer's 1961 book, *Griff nach der Weltmacht* (published in English in 1967 under the title *Germany's Aims in the First World War*). This revisionist work immediately gained the approval of a mostly younger generation of postwar German journalists and academics. Fischer was a dedicated Nazi during the Third Reich and, after the war, was forced to undergo denazification. Fortunately for his career, he gave the impression of having undergone a change of heart.[42] As a professor at the University of Hamburg, where he had previously worked as an informer for the Third Reich, he championed German reeducation and called for a definitive break from Germany's tainted past.

In the 1950s Fischer received invitations to attend conferences at Oxford University that explored the need for a critical revision of his country's historiography. At the same time, he worked to establish friendly relations with the East German Communist government. Along with a gaggle of progressive German researchers, he gained access to archives in Potsdam that contained historical records captured by the Red Army in 1945, which subsequently handed them over to the German Democratic Republic. Fischer's now-famous work, in which he contends that the German imperial government launched World War I to achieve world domination, was only made possible by his political views, which accorded him special status and access: he was granted permission to look at certain documents, which had been denied to less progressive historians, such as Gerhard Ritter, his staunch critic and a firm supporter of the government of Chancellor Adenauer.

Fischer's magnum opus and the support it elicited from historians Immanuel Geiss, Wolfgang Mommsen (the brother of Hans), and Heinrich Winkler and from most of the German media both reflected and accelerated changes in the larger German culture. His panoramic second book on the outbreak of World War I, *The War of Illusions* published in 1969, dwelled on the aggressive mindset of all German classes in 1914. It was also the mindset, he reminded his readers, that lay behind the catastrophe of 1933.[43] Fischer's last book, which was published in 1988 and was predictably titled *Hitler Was No Operational Accident*, echoed the antifascist tone of all his writing since the early 1960s.[44] In this work Fischer set out to demonstrate one last time the lines of continuity between the German Second Empire and Hitler's dictatorship. Fischer and his disciples left no stone unturned in driving home their frequently repeated pedagogical lessons.

Yet it is easy to pick out the weaknesses in these books' arguments, which lie just beneath the surface of their depiction of Germany's role in World War I. Fischer decided to ignore the war aims pursued by other belligerents, which were at least as scandalous as those of the Germans.[45] He also failed to consider that the German Empire was indeed encircled by a hostile Franco-Russian alliance in 1914, that the Russians were fully mobilized on Germany's and Austria's border before the Germans declared war on them,[46] and that rival nationalisms and entangling secret alliances, more than inherent German aggressiveness, were responsible for starting the war. Fischer and his disciples also had a tendency to cite supposedly incriminating sources in a deliberately abbreviated fashion; for example, a memorandum written by the German chief of the General Staff, Helmuth von Moltke, in December 1911, which allegedly made clear that Germany would inevitably have to go to war, given the international situation. Yet this memorandum also provides evidence that Moltke hoped the Germans and their Austrian allies would evade the pervasive belligerent mood of the time and not allow tensions to boil over into a European-wide war.[47]

In addition, the so-called reactionary nationalist historians whom Fischer and the Fischerites claimed to be opposing did not really fit their description. A major target, Gerhard Ritter, strongly criticized the reliance of Imperial Germany on unworkable military solutions. He lambasted Erich Ludendorff and other German commanders for holding dangerously unrealistic views of Germany's power in 1914 and for sinking back periodically into unwise fatalism.[48] But he also castigated the Fischerites for their reductionist accounts of the past. Ritter complained that his opponents were driven not so much by a desire to understand the past as by a fixation to locate all the essential elements of Nazi tyranny in the German Second Empire. Long after Ritter's death in 1967, it is still difficult to find any unabashed critic of

Fischer's thesis who has been allowed to advance in the German or Austrian academic world.

Fischer's works do, however, offer a prototype of what is characterized as "penitential history." He claimed to have unearthed compelling new evidence for why Germans were required to expiate their collective past. One such piece of evidence, which was stored in East German archives until the late 1950s, was a document outlining the extensive war aims of German chancellor Theobald Bethmann-Hollweg. Those aims included economic control over Eastern Europe and the Second Empire's incorporation of conquered territory in the West. These annexationist aims, which were dated September 9, 1914, were drawn up during the Battle of the Marne, about six weeks after the beginning of the hostilities. The memorandum was then sent from Koblenz, where the chancellor was then living, to the German Minister of the Interior, Clemens von Delbrück, in Berlin.

Fischer assumed that Bethmann-Hollweg formulated his aims before the war started, but that is not the only conclusion one could reach.[49] Nor are these aims any more alarming than those produced by the French and other Allied powers at about the same time. In their analysis of this memorandum, East German Communist historians attributed what should be seen as provisional war aims to a program of conquest devised by German finance capitalists. In general, although East German historians initially hailed Fischer's achievement, they pointed out its shortcomings, in particular that his work did not examine World War I within a broad framework of rival capitalist elites competing on an international stage.[50] This was hardly surprising, because Fischer and his circle were not really aiming to confirm any Marxist-Leninist interpretation. Rather they were seeking to profit from the imposition of a guilt trip on their countrymen. Not surprisingly, much of Fischer's support came from antifascist historians in the United States, like Fritz Stern at Columbia and Hajo Holborn at Yale, who extolled Fischer's mission in reminding his wayward nation of its collective culpability for causing two world wars.[51]

Fischer's call for collective German penance, according to his disciple Wolfgang Mommsen, "showed the complicity not only of German leadership but of all social classes in these annexationist aims."[52] Unlike Marxist accounts of the world wars, which examine war aims within the context of an economic system, Fischer and the Fischerites purported to be revealing the true extent of shared German guilt for the crimes of the twentieth century. A celebration in *Der Spiegel* of the fortieth anniversary of Fischer's magnum opus extols him for exposing a longtimelie, one that treated the outbreak of World War I as the fault of both sides by proving indisputably that the Germans were guilty of starting World War I. Not surprisingly, *Der Spiegel* had been saying the same thing for the preceding forty years, during which time it attributed opposing views to right-wing German nationalists.[53]

Because of their uniformly evil past, according to the Fischerites, Germans had to accept the permanent division of their country (until the fall of the Berlin Wall changed the situation). To become reconciled to this deserved loss, Germans were urged to read *Griff nach der Weltmacht*, presumably with the proper mindset. Fischer's disciple Immanuel Geiss explicitly linked his teacher's historical narratives to its intended political goals. If Germans were taught "that Germany must bear most of the guilt for the First World War, that this war in the case of the Germans was not a defensive struggle, and that the ruling classes launched this war in order to obtain new markets and raw materials [in Eastern Europe]," then they would recognize Poland's Western border and renounce any right to a reunified Germany.[54]

Moreover, the word "definitive" (in German, *maßgeblich*) crops up each time the Fischerites defend their teacher's thought.[55] For them history is not a contentious discipline but a form of moral and social therapy, which must be applied to attain its salvific effect. Fischer's disciple Helmut Lindemann underscores in now familiar terms the purpose of *Griff nach der Weltmacht*. The book was produced "out of patriotic concern, as an invitation to Germans to revise their history, to confess their guilt and to draw the necessary consequences after Fischer has proved the illusions of grandeur that once possessed the German people." According to Lindemann "one may criticize or question certain aspects of Fischer's work. That however does not lessen its eminent political value to which great weight must be assigned for setting right and enlightening our political consciousness."[56] The emphasis is placed on reading accounts of the past that will make the reader more willing to feel collective guilt and engage in collective political atonement. Such accounts are definitive because any attempt to challenge them betokens a deficient moral consciousness.[57]

This approach to the historical past is often presented as "revisionism," but this characterization only applies if the intended revision is to be considered in a free and open marketplace of ideas. Fischer and his disciples were not engaging in a discussion that was open to scholars with diverse judgments about a specific area of investigation. Nor were these revisionists engaging in what nineteenth-century German historians, who defined their discipline, regarded as "Wissenschaft"; that is, a methodical study of relevant documents yielding tentative conclusions about the past. This is not the interpretive approach that penitential historians have in mind. Their approach is distinguished from mere investigations of data by offering an intended moral uplift. Further, it is no longer allowable under the new dispensation to believe that the study of the past, properly understood, should lead to an open-ended discussion among researchers. Herbert Butterfield, who defended the view that the discipline of history should foster free and open discussion, noted that even though historians in practice did not always consistently meet that high standard, they were expected to aim at it.[58]

Fischer's penitential history also differs from the conventional historicist approach, which is perhaps best represented by Hans-Georg Gadamer. Such a historically minded approach recognizes that there are idiosyncratic, personal, and time-dependent circumstances of the times in which a historical work is created that affect its perspective. Engaging in the discipline of history necessarily entails some bias and time-centeredness. This, according to Gadamer, may create a problem as well as an incentive for the researcher. What pushes us toward our project may also distort our judgment, and therefore, we must be on guard against bias even while profiting from those personal reactions that have driven us toward our object of research.[59]

The present revisionism, however, seeks a different end: teaching us to deplore the reactionary forces and collective injustices of an earlier era. Therefore, those who render politically unacceptable judgments about historical works that perform this function are typically accused of working against an enlightened political consciousness. Only ecstatic approval seems to be the appropriate response to such didactic writings. Let us look, for example, at how the US journalistic and academic world greeted Eric Foner's *Reconstruction: An Unfinished Revolution, 1865–1877*. When this revisionist work on post–Civil War Reconstruction was published in 1988, critical assessments or even measured praise seemed unsuitable. Compliments were heaped on Foner's penitential writing in the national press as a "heroic synthesis,"[60] and he was called the preeminent historian of Reconstruction.[61]

Foner's work has been praised as having superseded all earlier studies on Reconstruction, most importantly, the two-volume work by W. A. Dunning that appeared in 1907. Although Dunning came from an antislavery Republican background, Foner and his votaries condemn him for not having gone far enough in defending the Reconstruction government. Dunning noted that most Southern whites had been excluded from political power during the military occupation of the post–Civil War South. Evidently, he focused too much on this fact and on Republican corruption during the occupation.

Foner states *his* purpose quite straightforwardly in the preface to his book. His publication "required, however, not simply the evolution of scholarship but a profound change in the nation's politics and racial attitudes to deal the final blow to the Dunning school. If the traditional interpretation reflected and helped to legitimize the racial order of a society in which blacks were disenfranchised and subjected to discrimination in every aspect of their lives, Reconstruction revisionism bore the mark of the modern civil rights movement."[62] Not surprisingly, this moralist has also labored to update those narratives present at Civil War battle sites. In line with his commitment, Foner has promoted our "Second Reconstruction" by calling for the removal of statues and memorial plaques celebrating the Confederate commander Robert E. Lee.[63]

In an incident that should have caused more scandal than it did, two shots were fired across the bow by the widely respected historian Eugene D. Genovese against Foner, his erstwhile fellow Marxist revolutionary. These attacks, published in the social democratic publication *Dissent*, called attention to Foner's deliberate use of professional associations to pursue various political objectives that had nothing to do with scholarship.[64] According to Genovese, a fuller evaluation of Foner's contributions to scholarship would have noted this ideological commitment that spilled into his published work. Of course, Foner might have responded by indicating that his study of Reconstruction should be considered independently of his defenses of Communist regimes.

A far more striking case of historiography being used to arouse guilt and a call for collective penance is Howard Zinn's *A People's History of the United States*. Although Zinn rarely describes what he portrays as "fascist," he misses few opportunities to rage against the wickedness of the American past, starting with Columbus's genocidal campaigns against the Arawak Amerindians, the rape of the New World through the establishment of slavery and racism, and then US wars of aggression against anticolonial countries. In a revealing monograph, Mary Grabar points out the numerous factual errors and plagiarisms that mar Zinn's popular history.[65] Grabar notes that Zinn garnered multiple awards during his lifetime and even posthumously as a result of his one renowned book. She quotes Eugene Genovese who described how Zinn moved from being an old-fashioned Brooklyn Jewish Communist to a "rock star" of the New Left by the 1960s.[66] Zinn, who died at the age of eighty-seven in 2010, also lived long enough to become a hero of the multicultural Left, as shown by his continued popularity among the current generation of progressives.

What may distinguish his *livre de succès* from some of the other examples of penitential historiography mentioned in this section is its simplistic, sermonic style. Zinn's work reads like a stump speech given by a member of the Democratic Left, and as Grabar shows, his scholarship has elicited negative evaluations even from those who like Eric Foner share his eagerness to write history from the bottom up but who are shocked by his bloopers and unproven generalizations.[67]. Perhaps most strikingly, according to Grabar, Zinn imagines that the United States is committing genocidal acts on a regular basis. "One reason these atrocities are still with us," as Zinn explains in *A People's History*, "is that we have learned to bury them in a mass of other facts, as radioactive wastes are buried in containers in the earth."[68] Perhaps the most astonishing part of this statement is Zinn's implied boast that no one would be writing about America's sins if he were not doing so himself. A veritable industry now exists to perform this task.

A perhaps more respectable form of guilt-tripping in historical writing can be found in Spanish historiography since the end of the Franco regime. Books on Spain's fascist legacy come out almost daily, while monuments erected by the Franco regime are torn down and school textbooks are rewritten to glorify the antifascist side in the Spanish Civil War.[69] Pio Moa in Spain and Stanley Payne in the United States have both written extensively about the exaggerations and distortions to which this rewriting of history has led.[70] A noteworthy aspect of anti-Franco and, more generally, antifascist Spanish revisionism is the portrayal of Moorish Spain (Al Andalus) as an oasis of tolerance surrounded by Spanish Catholic bigotry. Spanish Arab linguist Serafín Fanjul has produced two massive volumes since 2000 that examine variations on this ideologically driven myth.[71] Looking at the views of medieval Spain that are found in the works of such fashionable authors as Juan Goytisolo,[72] Americo Castro, and Claudio Sanchez Albornoz, Fanjul dissects their pro-Muslim, anti-Spanish Catholic positions.

Given that Fanjul is an avowed freethinker who made a reputation as a translator of Arabic texts, it is hard to depict him plausibly as a Spanish Catholic zealot. In his book he distinguishes innocent exaggerations—overstating the Arab influence on the Spanish language and Spanish architecture or resurrecting the nineteenth-century romantic images of Al Andalus in Spanish literature—from the more tendentious and deliberate misinterpretations of the Spanish past. Among the latter are accounts that overstate Catholic sins while sweeping under the rug the brutal treatment inflicted on Christians and Jews under Muslim rule in medieval Spain. Fanjul likewise notes that anti-Catholic historians typically omit the crushing of non-Muslim communities by Almohade rulers in the eleventh century and the periodic outbursts of violence against religious minorities during the Kingdom of Grenada from 1238 until 1492.

Equally misleading, according to Fanjul, is the presentation of Muslims and Jews as two of the three nations that helped produce a Spanish people. Catholic religious affiliation was once a necessary aspect of Spanish identity, and neither the Jews nor the Muslims, both of whom had their own qualifications for group membership, met that requirement.[73] According to Fanjul, there is also no compelling evidence to believe that Spain crumbled economically or politically because it expelled Jews in 1492 and then converted the Moors in 1609, after a series of Muslim revolts. Unlike the Jews, who enjoyed wealth and, in some cases, high social position, the Muslims who remained after the consolidation of Catholic Spain in 1492 were rural and poor. But there is also no indication that, however unfortunate and unjust the expulsion of the Spanish Jews had been, the country fell apart afterward. The Spanish government made other more disastrous mistakes, such as colonial overexpansion and wasteful spending, that led to the country's decline as a great power.[74]

According to Fanjul, the criticized writings represent resistance to the integral Spanish nationalism of the Franco era and the growing presence of Muslim immigrants in today's multicultural Spain. Most easily forgotten, notes Fanjul, is the inconvenient fact that the Muslim conquest of Spain in 711 brought about an "orgy of bloodshed" against the Latin and Visigothic inhabitants, one that lasted well into the 750s. Older residents who did not convert to Islam (*muladis*) were often callously massacred, unless they fled north to Asturias, where the Christians managed to hold onto their territory.[75] Moreover, the attacks on the Reconquista from the antifascist Left, according to Fanjul and Stanley Payne,[76] are designed to shatter the center-piece of traditional Spanish identity. Although those who pursue this work might claim they have other aims, it is hard not to observe their single-minded dedication to destroying the pride once felt by Spaniards in their Catholic national past.

Yet another relevant example of penitential history is the interpretation of fascist Italy as the inescapable endpoint of a wicked, corrupt national history. The most famous and perhaps most prolific historian to emphasize that view was the late Englishman Denis Mack Smith. Beginning with his first book *Cavour and Garibaldi 1860* (1954), Mack Smith treated Italian unification with conspicuous disfavor. Characteristic of his long list of books, including a biography of Mussolini, are attacks on Italy's reactionary parliamentary government that supposedly led later to dictatorship. Members of Mack Smith's rogues' gallery are Italy's founding father Count Camillo di Cavour and the monarch whom he served, Victor Immanuel, the ruler of Piedmont-Savoy who later became king of Italy. Mack Smith also attacked Italian parliamentary leaders from Italian unification forward, including D'Agostino Depretis, Francesco Crispi, and Giovanni Giolitti.[77] In contrast to his teacher George M. Trevelyan, with whom he studied at Oxford, and who viewed Italian unification as a nineteenth-century liberal achievement, Trevelyan's former student raged at how an Italian nation-state came about. According to Italian historian Guido Pescosolido, "Mack Smith turned the older discourse about Italian national unification into its negative opposite. Not only did he trace the causes for the emergence of fascism back to the birth of a unitary Italian state. He also delineated a history of the Risorgimento [the movement in the nineteenth century leading toward Italian national unification] and the liberal state which is devoid in its fundamental components of any positive aspect."[78]

Pescosolido distinguished Mack Smith from other Italian thinkers whom the Englishman intermittently praised, particularly the liberal Italian patriot and neo-Hegelian philosopher Croce. Although Croce once befriended Mack Smith, he would have distanced himself from the decidedly antinational direction in which the younger writer took his work.[79] According to the *New York Review of Books*, Mack Smith was not really like Gramsci, a Marxist, but rather was some kind of liberal. Another historian who has vigorously commented on the roots of fascism, Jonathan Steinberg, argues that Mack Smith's major accomplishment was telling historians what they did not want to hear.[80]

Few historians of Italy have been more lionized than Mack Smith. Indeed, his counterattacks on Rosario Romeo, Renzo De Felice, and other historians who pointed out his *"strafalcioni"* (gross mistakes) emphasize jealousy as the reason for their lack of appreciation. Mack Smith, as he himself noted, was more widely read than his rivals, even in Italian translation. His books continue to sell more briskly than Romeo's three-volume biography of Cavour,[81] which is densely documented. Also, unlike these other historians, Mack Smith has been honored for supposedly daring to expose the roots of fascism. High-brow publications in the United States have complimented him for besting De Felice when the two sparred over the origins and character of Italian fascism. In this debate Mack Smith accused De Felice of trying to minimize the criminal nature of fascism, an evil that Mack Smith worked tirelessly to expose, to the applause of other progressive historians.[82]

No one is denying that these authors I discuss in this section had merit. Their studies in history covered many hundreds of pages. In particular the books of Denis Mack Smith could fill entire library shelves with highly stimulating reading. He exhibited a literary brilliance that a less adroit scholar might feel egalitarian envy on encountering. But I am not interested here in how these representative authors express themselves. More relevant for this study is the glowing description of them as truth-tellers. Even when they engage in questionable generalizations, very few with influence in their field have called them to account.

The next chapter examines current calls to arms against a reemerging fascist danger. Again, antifascists evoke past confrontations between fascism and antifascism as they work to insert present engagements into a meaningful past. But the established conventions of historical scholarship—the use of footnotes and the documentation of problematic statements—have become propagandistically less relevant as the fight against fascism gains in intensity.[83] We are therefore encountering what are mostly antifascist polemics, rather than older forms of penitential historiography presented in a traditional scholarly guise. Zinn's focus on the United States' burden of historical guilt may foreshadow this new model of antifascist writing, which is a style of discourse that is more inflammatory and more sentential than most of the works discussed in this chapter.

# Chapter 4

# Defining and Redefining Fascism

Frank Böckelmann, a onetime Marxist theorist, has expressed both shock and wonder at how his fellow Germans obsess over Nazi dangers, doing so with ever more intensity the more the twelve years of Hitler's rule recede in the past. Every church or school gathering, academic conference, and book fair in Germany now routinely rails against fascism and Nazism. Meanwhile the German government has poured many hundreds of millions of dollars into various enterprises intended to "fight fascism." For instance, a gathering of German historians at Munster in 2018 was devoted to finding new ways to combat a supposedly ubiquitous Right. When contemporary historian Axel Schildt delivered a speech at the conference calling for the banning of certain words that might encourage fascist attitudes—for example, words containing the noun "Volk"—the audience went wild applauding. At the Frankfurt Book Fair in 2018, a leader of *Aufstehen gegen Rassismus* (Stand up against Racism) demanded that the government take vigorous action against the Alternative für Deutschland, Germany's right-of-center party, which the speaker described as "the parliamentary arm of Nazism." The assembled crowd cheered loudly, although one might have had trouble distinguishing genuine enthusiasm from the fear felt by some that they might have appeared insufficiently antifascist.[1]

Böckelmann notes an obvious weakness in this antifascist crusade, which continues to be sustained in Germany by the government, the media, educators, churches, and the entire culture industry: "It depends on the materialization of evil. Those who imagine that they are resistance fighters need Nazis around." Every now and then Germans can point to the real thing: people wearing Hitler shirts kicking up a row at a soccer game or anarchists trying to offend the easily intimidated public. Antifascists in Germany are in all probability "grateful for these isolated embodiments," for without them it would be harder to show that the antifascists are bravely resisting an imminent "return to 1933." This, after all, is the disaster against which Germans are urged to be on guard.[2]

The antifascist grand spectacle, according to Böckelmann, requires a bit of improvisation. "A Germany that has actually forgotten its own past deposits the years 1933 to 1945 into the immediate present and delights in acting as the conscience of humanity."[3] Playing this role requires the continuing modification of what Nazism was to make it fit current political concerns. Thus, anyone who openly opposes admitting more Third World Muslims into Germany or advocates making German the official language may be depicted by German politicians and media barons as talking the same language as the Nazis or leading the country in that direction. What counts as fascism or neo-Nazism, argues Böckelmann, is easily shifted, according to need, despite the chronological and conceptual distance that exists between those characterizations and what the Third Reich actually did and taught. Aggressive racialism, the conquest of neighboring countries, the cult of the leader, the ruthless suppression of dissent, and (especially in the German case) virulent anti-Semitism—none of these elements seems widespread among most Germans today. Indeed, if there is a threat to liberty in present-day Germany, it is coming mostly from those who are waging a crusade against an arbitrarily defined fascist enemy.

It is possible to see how a demonization of undesirable people may persist after these groups have dwindled numerically or even vanished. For example, Spanish Catholic nationalists feared the presence of hidden Jewish forces in Spain long after those Jews who were unconverted were forced to leave in 1492. But those who feared Jewish influence (or the influence of Jewish *con-*

*versos* after 1492) did not simply attribute Jewishness to anyone who offended them. The rage and organizational élan that have accompanied crusades against fascism are particularly remarkable given their often randomly chosen targets. This randomness is related to another problem: definitions of fascism are based at least as much on free association as on confirmable evidence of real fascism.

The earlier chapters in this book demonstrate that, in the 1920s and 1930s and even into the 1940s, those who spoke about fascism had a specific phenomenon in mind. Those who read or listened to them knew what that phenomenon was, and perhaps most importantly, fascists or Nazis identified themselves as such. This is not the process of identification that is currently taking place. Now, a Russian Jew in Germany or a Moroccan Jew in France who votes for a right-of-center nationalist party because he has observed that Jews have been frequently assaulted by Muslim youth and because he wishes to limit the number of young male Muslims coming into the country, may be linked through a process of increasingly free associations to the Third Reich.[4]

One typical element of this antifascist process is pointing to the presence of a style of speech that allegedly was used by the Nazis and interwar fascists. For example, when a Social Democratic deputy in the German Federal Diet, Martin Schulz, who had been a high-ranking EU official, responded to a speech about migrants by AfD chief Alexander Gauland in December 2018, he denounced a "style of communication" that linked Gauland's remarks to "what had been previously heard in this assembly." This was an obvious allusion to Nazi deputies who had been elected to the Reichstag in the interwar period. Schulz then went on to stress that "democracy must guard against such people, who belong on the dung heap of history."[5] For Schulz, the evidence that Gauland was a Nazi sympathizer was not the content of his speech—unchecked immigration, a subject that should not be off-limits in a parliamentary assembly—but his style of communication that allegedly resembled that favored by the Nazi Party. What made this style (*Stilmittel*) so offensive was not so much the words that Gauland chose to use for his speech but his audacity in raising a subject that the German Left did not want discussed.

Another manifestation of surging antifascism in Germany was the reaction to the election of a minister president (the head of the provincial government) in the Thuringian provincial assembly in February 2020. Initially this position was to go to the head of the centrist Free Democrats, Thomas Kemmerich. But Kemmerich could only obtain the votes needed for his election by receiving support from the AfD, which had garnered 23 percent of the vote in a recent provincial election. An outcry then went out from the German media that Kemmerich had dared to solicit votes from Nazis and Nazi-sympathizers.

At this point Chancellor Merkel stepped in and condemned the "inexcusable behavior" of Kemmerich and the Thuringian assembly for negotiating with a party that she too apparently believed or at least intimated resembled Hitler's party. Merkel then proceeded without any constitutional authority to impose her own choice of minister president for Thuringia, after forcing Kemmerich to withdraw his candidacy.[6] The German chancellor selected a decidedly leftist candidate Bodo Ramelow, whom the cowed assembly dutifully confirmed, whereupon Antifa groups swung into action and threatened Kemmerich and his family. At the same time German journalists simultaneously condemned Kemmerich for wishing to collaborate in something "inexcusable" (*unverzeihlich*) that would have permitted the AfD to restart the Nazi Holocaust. The head of the Thuringian AfD, Björn Höcke, who is now considered in the English-speaking press to be the "firebrand of the German Far Right," has been repeatedly likened to Hitler and stands accused of making speeches that "are riddled with words and phrases 'confusingly similar' to those used by the Nazis."[7]

One need not be a supporter of the AfD or of any other German party to see that these accusations verge on hysteria. They are intended to keep German voters in the antinational, antifascist, and pro-immigration lane where media and educational leaders wish them to stay. Even the brash Höcke, who hardly minces words on the hustings, bears little resemblance to an interwar Nazi demagogue. However provocatively he has warned against more Third World immigration, unchecked immigration was hardly a signature Hitlerian position. Höcke's exhortation that Germans "reverse direction" and cease cultivating a politics of guilt hardly demonstrates that he is a Nazi.

Least of all is there justification for the view that Kemmerich's decision to accept AfD votes to become minister president would have endangered the lives of groups that had suffered under the Nazis. This attack is unfortunately typical of the direction taken by antifascist activists.[8] An East German novelist, Uwe Tellkamp, has spoken mockingly of the "disposition corridor" (*Gesinnungskorridor*) into which the German leadership class has forced German public opinion.[9] Tellkamp, who grew up under a Communist regime in Dresden, is amazed by how easily the antifascist Federal Republic of Germany has taken over repressive Communist practices. Tellkamp's fellow East German, the writer Daniela Krien, explained in an interview with the *Tagesspiegel* why she decided to move back to her former land: "In the East something has been preserved and remained, a German identity that has been lost in the West, which has fused with the identity of its Allied Occupiers. That never happened in the East in relation to the Soviets. I think that may be the reason for the strengthening of national conservative forces here."[10] Particularly upsetting for German patriots, who seem to be found mostly in the East, is this statement made by Merkel to *Die Welt*; "Germans are whoever decides to come to us."[11]

## The Antifascist Academy

An equally interesting example of wielding the f-word can be found in Timothy Snyder's denunciation of Donald Trump in *The Guardian* published October 30, 2018. According to Snyder, both President Trump and "the Nazis claimed a monopoly of victimhood." Like the fascists, "Trump and some of his supporters mount a strategy of deterrence by narcissism: if you note our debts to fascism, we will up the pitch of the whining."[12] All Snyder manages to prove here is that Trump behaves like other presidents when he is beset by a hostile press. It is difficult to see how Trump has been more fascist in this respect than FDR, who denounced and tried to ban abrasive Republican journalists from press conferences.[13] How does Trump compare as a fascist to Harry Truman, who as president wrote a letter to *Washington Post* music critic Paul Hume threatening to punch him in the nose because Hume panned a singing performance by Truman's daughter?[14]

An equally glaring misuse of the charge of fascism shows up in a commentary on Senator Bernie Sanders by *National Review* columnist Kevin Williamson. According to Williamson, Sanders "may call himself a socialist, but so did Mussolini for a long time."[15] Sanders's earlier opposition to immigration, we are told, indicates that he was "all too happy to appropriate the rhetorical scheme of the altright knuckleheads." Williamson seems not to know that both the European Left and US labor unions were long on record opposing unskilled or low-skilled immigrants moving into their countries. One wonders why such a policy should be regarded as peculiarly characteristic of Italian fascism.

Examples of such antifascist free association abound in academic literature in the United States. One is a widely discussed polemic, *How Fascism Works: The Politics of Us against Them* (2018), by Jason Stanley, the Jacob Urowsky Professor of Philosophy at Yale University. In this book Stanley dwells on certain ominous tendencies that he identifies with fascism, some of which he may have drawn from *The Authoritarian Personality*. Among those tendencies that offend are appeals to "a mythic past," "anti-intellectualism," and "sexual anxiety" when "the patriarchal hierarchy is threatened by growing gender equity." Stanley confesses to being especially sensitive to these traits for personal reasons. In 1939 his father left Nazi Germany only to enter an America then beset by its own fascist danger. The United States that awaited Manfred Stanley was tainted by the "America First" movement and other forms of antiwar isolationism. These threats to tolerance and equality came back with a vengeance in 2016 when "Donald Trump revived 'America First' as one of his slogans, and from his first week in office, his administration has ceaselessly pursued travel bans on immigration, including refugees, specifically singling out Arab countries."[16]

Throughout this account of Trump's apparent embrace of Nazism are questionable historical statements. America First, *pace* Stanley, had nothing to do with pro-Nazi advocates, as demonstrated by the works of Wayne Cole, Justus Doenecke, and other historians.[17] The 1924 Immigration Act was not legislation devised exclusively by xenophobes. This law that restricted immigration had a broad range of support, including the American Federation of Labor.[18] Stanley's father, who like my own family escaped from the Nazis in the late 1930s, certainly experienced material and emotional hardships. But the catastrophe from which Stanley Senior escaped was something far worse than what his son is lamenting—Donald Trump's decision to do what his predecessors had already attempted, by enacting a limited travel ban.

Almost all attempts to depict President Trump and other leaders whom antifascists dislike as Nazi tyrants lapse into fantasy. This tendency is basic to redefinitions of antifascism in which demonization is dressed up as historical analysis. Jason Stanley works especially hard to create a fit between fascism and Donald Trump's connections to entrepreneurial capitalism. According to Stanley, "in fascism, the *state* is an enemy; it is to be replaced by the nation, which consists of self-sufficient individuals"; "fascist ideology involves

something at least superficially akin to the libertarian ideal of self-sufficiency and freedom from the state." Supposedly fascists share with other social
Darwinists the ideals of "hard work, private enterprise and self-sufficiency."[19]
They also follow in the path of Mussolini "who denounces the world's great
cities, such as New York, for their teeming populations of nonwhites."[20]
Stanley's book offers unverified historical statements that in some cases are
patently false. Italian fascism famously glorified the state and taught "*tutto
nello stato, niente fuori dello stato.*" Yet it was German Nazism, which Stanley
never bothers to distinguish from Italian fascism, that placed *das Volk* above
the state. Neither movement followed libertarian teachings nor pretended
to. Christian journalist Ron Dreher is correct when he suggests that Stanley's
real intent is to stifle any discussion he disapproves of.[21] Like his colleague at
Yale, Timothy Snyder, Stanley moves quickly from what he finds politically
distasteful to ascriptions of fascist intolerance and, finally, calls for protective
measures against a perceived enemy.

## Fascism just around the Corner

Stanley's colleague at Yale and fellow antifascist, Timothy Snyder, has not
only fulminated in newspaper articles against the Trump presidency but has
also provided more historically oriented warnings that allegedly emanate
from his reflections as a research scholar. In *On Tyranny: Twenty Lessons from
the Twentieth Century*, Snyder explains,

> Both fascism and communism were responses to globalization: to the real and
> perceived inequalities it created and the apparent helplessness of the democ-
> racies in addressing them. Fascists rejected reason in the name of will, deny-
> ing objective truth in favor of glorious myth articulated by leaders who claimed
> to give voice to the people. They put a face on globalization, arguing that its
> complex challenges were a result of a conspiracy against the nation. Fascists
> ruled for a decade or two, leaving behind an intact intellectual legacy that
> grows more relevant by the day.[22]

In the prologue, Snyder makes key assumptions about the oppositional Right
that are essential to his view of fascism. For example, he asserts that fascism
has bequeathed to it an "intact intellectual legacy," which (to say the least) is

a contestable point. Do we really see Western governments calling for a fascist-type corporatist economy? Do our national media advertise a philosophy of the will of the kind that fascist authors of the interwar era were promoting? What about a call for wars, to furnish the dominant nationality with *Lebensraum*, or to restore the glory of the Roman Empire?

Snyder tries to validate his argument by making fascism fit a tailor-made definition: it is an authoritarian alternative to "globalization" that treats "complex challenges" as "a conspiracy against the nation." According to Snyder, Donald Trump's attempt to renegotiate international trade agreements for US workers indicates fascist tendencies. We are urged to resist the adversaries of globalization, because "anticipatory obedience" to fascist and Nazi tyranny allowed evil acts to occur in Germany and Austria.[23] One need not excuse such terrible occurrences in the 1930s as Kristallnacht to ask a highly relevant question: What do Nazi crimes have to do with globalization and its critics? Snyder offers for our physical and moral protection a medley of not very original maxims—"contribute to good causes," "believe in truth," "learn from peers in other countries," "make eye contact and small talk," "remember professional ethics," "defend institutions," and "make a private life"—that are intended to prepare us for the impending struggle. Snyder highlights incidents and events from the struggle against Nazi Germany to prepare us for the worst.

Mark Bray has expressed most of the same views as Stanley and Snyder about a fascist menace. He also finds considerable overlap between what happened in Europe in the 1930s and "Trump's America." Unlike other antifascists, however, Bray is not writing principally for the academic community or for what today passes for the world of letters. Less than two years after the demonstrations of September 2011, Bray published a book, *Translating Anarchy: The Anarchism of Occupy Wall Street*, that describes such activism as the first stage of an anarchist struggle against fascist-tinged capitalism.[24] As demonstrations against this system mount and become increasingly disruptive, capitalism, it is hoped, will collapse and be replaced by a people's economy.

Unlike more garden-variety academic antifascists, Bray is consciously reclaiming the socialist antifascist tradition of the interwar years. He points admiringly to the German and Spanish Communists of an earlier era and repeats their calls for an end to capitalism and the downfall of its fascist supporters. In his *Anti-Fascist Handbook*, Bray retells the history of fascism from the 1920s to the present.[25] There is nothing in this presentation that has not already been said by the traditional Far Left, and clearly Bray is reaching back to connect with this older, pure leftist tradition. He depicts the struggle between fascists and everyone on the Left, including the Communists, as the great battle between evil and good to which we are now being forced to return. This romance of the Left, which Bray traces back to the interwar period, is woven throughout his narrative.

In his third chapter, we do find some of the same scenes that illustrate Snyder's discussion, such as neo-Nazis attacking Syrian refugees.[26] Bray dwells on the victory of, among other villains, the Golden Dawn, which became a leading parliamentary party in Greece in 2012. While Bray was then visiting Greece, Golden Dawn, which does proudly flaunt fascist symbols, was gaining adherents in response to a growing refugee problem. It remained Greece's third- most popular party as late as 2017.[27] Given the generally poor living conditions in most of sub-Saharan Africa and the likelihood that the population of Africa, which has now reached more than a billion, will quadruple, according to UN figures, in less than a century,[28] and given the perpetual civic turmoil in the Middle East, it seems likely that a refugee problem will continue to bedevil Europe.

Bray even spots fascism in some unlikely situations, such as when members of Merkel's Christian Democratic coalition "aggressively pursued the swelling AfD electorate by proposing a ban on burkas in public and a new Integration Law that would control where refugees can live and force them to learn German language, culture, and history."[29] This proposed Integration Law would not have the effect of segregating Syrian refugees in Germany, but it would have pushed them into learning the German language. Requiring this minimal standard of assimilation does not represent a return to Nazism.

Like other antifascist polemicists, Bray searches for his enemy among those who would appear to have little to do with real fascists. He trots out, for example, "Pinstripe Nazis," who supported the "white backlash" that put Donald Trump into the presidency and who rallied in France to the National Front (which has been renamed the Rassemblement National). Steve Bannon, Milo Yiannopolous, and various others are all painted with the same fascist brush. Bray has not only organized Antifa units in the United States but in 2015 also helped create in Kurdish Rojava an International Freedom Battalion that incorporates Communist and anarchist activists from across

Europe. He even pulled into this enterprise supplementary volunteers from Turkey and Kurdistan.[30] With obvious pride Bray informs us that he modeled his antifascist coalition on the International Brigades that fought for the Left in the Spanish Civil War.[31]

To his credit, however, he does address two questions that less inquisitive antifascists typically eschew. The first is whether there is a fit between current expressions of fascism and whatever forms that movement took in interwar Europe. Although both were devised to serve the ruling class and exploit impoverished minorities, they nonetheless have palpable differences. For example, the older fascism was primarily an interwar Central European phenomenon, whereas the fascism that Bray decries has now spread everywhere in the West. Moreover, the older form of fascism was more explicitly militaristic and less friendly toward a global economy. Despite such variations, Bray assures us, there is enough of a likeness between the old and new forms of fascisms to make it a family resemblance. And the comparison being drawn has strategic value: the enemy whom the antifascists have in their crosshairs generates solidarity for the protestors.[32]

The second question is whether the antifascist struggle can accept free speech or in any way tolerate the opposition. For Bray, this question is mostly an irrelevant distraction from revolutionary activities. "The antiauthoritarian principle of individual and collective autonomy promotes a vision of human diversity and plurality at odds with the stifling homogeneity of capitalist consumer culture. If fascists were to start organizing in such a society, antiauthoritarian anti-fascists would still organize to shut them down, but they would not construct massive prisons to lock them up as the American government has done to countless political prisoner over the generations." Further, Bray explains, "even if you agree that shutting down fascist organizing constitutes an infringement upon the free speech of fascists, it is still patently obvious that anti-fascists advocate for far more free speech in society than liberals, both quantitatively and qualitatively."[33]

To fully understand such statements, it is essential to recognize that, for Bray, the antifascists are in mortal combat with institutions that depend on a capitalist ruling class: "militant anti-fascism challenges the state monopoly on political legitimacy by making a political case for popular sovereignty from below." Bray reports that antifascists do not subscribe to the "liberal notion that all political 'opinions' are equal," and they "unabashedly attack the legitimacy of fascism and institutions that support it."[34] His underlying assumption is that we are already deep into a civil war between fascists and antifascists; therefore, the question of providing a platform for one's adversary is no longer worth considering. We are warned against "the liberal alternative to militant anti-fascism," which "is to have faith in the power of rational discourse, the police, and the institutions of government to prevent the ascension of a fascist regime," and he points to "the failure of the allied strategy of appeasement leading up to World War II."[35]

Bray's contentions raise multiple questions. What precisely in our present situation corresponds to the one that allowed Hitler to take power in Germany? How are those who favor an open debate of political differences practicing the appeasement politics of those who failed to stop Hitler? We are also not told who exactly were the "liberal" antifascists who tried to appease the Nazis. Is that a reference to those European leaders who wished to avoid another war with Germany? There was nothing specifically liberal about figures like Lord Halifax and Edward VIII in England or Mussolini in 1938 who opposed military confrontation with Nazi Germany. European Communist parties also favored appeasement between September 1939 and March 1941 while Nazi Germany and Soviet Russia were allied. Even murkier are Bray's references to the fascists who benefit from "rational discourse."

On one point, I do agree with Bray and my own former professor Herbert Marcuse. We are now dealing with an artificial "tolerance" that is manipulated by those in high places for their own benefit. For a confirmation of this assertion, one need only read the perfunctory point–counterpoint debates in the newspaper or the typical Republican versus Democrat staged discussions to see the strenuously maintained limits of public political discussion. Yet it is difficult to comprehend how these staged debates between often vacuous alternatives are allowing a fascist will to prevail.

One can no longer even be surprised to find conservative publications depicting Trump's America careening toward fascism in attacks that are every bit as hyperbolic as Bray's rhetoric. Thus the "conservative realist" *National Interest* published a feature essay by Amitai Etzioni on August 1, 2020, about how "Donald Trump is changing the country in ways that should have all Americans concerned." Etzioni's title asks, "Is America on the Road to Becoming an Authoritarian State?" The narrative centers on the connections between growing up as a Jew in Nazi Germany and having to watch Donald Trump take the United States down an eerily similar path toward a racist dictatorship.[36] As neoconservative-aligned publications and websites, particularly *Bulwark*, have moved strategically into the Democratic camp, they sound more and more like the subjects of this chapter when assailing Trump's "fascism."[37]

The post-Marxist Left plays loosely with antifascist labels; certainly, Bray's work raises the question about who is a true Marxist. Neither Kautsky nor Hilferding nor Rosa Luxemburg would have recognized in his complaints about prejudice a Marxist analysis of capitalism in crisis. Bray fails to analyze the corporate capitalist power that he assures us is behind the fascist superstructure of ideas that is catapulting fascist politicians into power. The fact that German citizens are concerned about the arrival of 1.5 million Muslim migrants from the Third World proves neither the existence of a fascist threat nor the operation of a repressive capitalist structure. Large corporations are among the last actors to incite xenophobia in the contemporary West. Furthermore, there is nothing peculiarly capitalistic about the resistance to dramatic demographic change, which would be equally understandable in a socialist country.

## South American "Fascism"

A precedent for the indiscriminate use of fascism that this chapter explores may be found in descriptions of twentieth-century South American governments by US educators and political journalists. Among such supposedly fascist governments were the semi-authoritarian rule of Getulio Vargas in Brazil from 1930 to 1945,[38] the various incarnations of Juan Peron in Argentina from the late 1930s until his death in 1974, and the dictatorial presidency of Augusto Pinochet in collaboration with the Chilean military from 1973 to 1990. At least some shadow of evidence can be furnished for this charge from the now-distant past. Vargas, who was an industrial modernizer with a populist flair, did sidle up to Nazi Germany until 1940, partly because his country sold a great deal of Brazilian coffee and cotton to the Germans and partly because Vargas was thumbing his nose at the *Norteamericanos*. But this Brazilian leader then turned around and supported the Americans both because he was appalled by Nazi tyranny and FDR's government worked to win his support. Peron expressed a political affinity for Mussolini in the late 1930s but later backed the Americans in World War II because he assumed they would win that struggle. He also did not become president of Argentina until after the war ended, in 1946, after having served in several earlier governments.[39]

Both Vargas and Peron did adopt some of the theatrical features of Latin fascism (like gaudy uniforms and mass rallies) and cobbled together and then disposed of their own versions of a corporate "new state." Yet South American leaders who temporarily took on fascist trappings were never full-fledged fascists and were happy to change their styles. Peron by the end of his political career was linking his makeshift economic policies (which proved disastrous for his country) to expressions of admiration for Maoist China. Since 1946, ten Argentine presidents, some with radically different economic policies, have belonged to the Justicialist Party founded by Peron. Vargas in his last phase as Brazilian president in the early 1950s was an unmistakable technocrat, returning to his persona when he assumed power in 1930. Pinochet was an anti-Communist general who established a military government after overthrowing a Marxist president, Salvador Allende, whom the Chilean middle class thought had gone too far in nationalizing the economy and in establishing a one-party leftist government. Military dictatorship also came to Argentina between 1976 and 1983, and it treated the Left brutally.

But this does not prove that either Pinochet or his Argentine counterparts were fascists as opposed to anti-Communist generals. (The two are not the same.) What happened, quite predictably, was that military juntas took over countries wracked by civil discord. The Argentine *golpe de estado* in 1976 occurred after the right-wing and left-wing Peronistas began fighting each other in the streets of Buenos Aires after Peron's death. Juan Linz, Amos Perlmutter, and Stanley Payne have all stressed that authoritarian governments have been the rule in Latin American countries.[40] Further, these scholars relate the authoritarianism to a social structure in which the bourgeoisie never really came to power. Whether one approves of these regimes, it would be stretching the f-word (albeit not for the first time) to apply it to them, even the ones that are anti-Marxist.

References to South American fascism usually mean that military rule has prevailed somewhere south of the US border. Sometimes these regimes involve a charismatic leader who promises economic reform. But military coups were not an exclusively interwar phenomenon, nor did they show the revolutionary nationalism revolutionary nationalism or the quest to restore lost empires that marked European fascism. Despite these differences, *Merriam-Webster Dictionary* and the *Times Literary Supplement* have both identified the Justicialist Party in Argentina, and presumably all the presidents who belonged to it, as fascist.[41] Fascism is now being used to refer to Jair Bolsonaro, the president of Brazil who is trying to modernize the Brazilian economy and fight administrative corruption.[42] Since Bolsonaro succeeded a leftist government and is known for his populist style, he too is tarred with the fascist label. The assignment of that label is by now a frequent practice among the Western media, and its application to South American governments has a venerable genealogy.

Chapter 5

# Antifascism versus Populism

Antifascists have mounted a crusade against a feared enemy, but not necessarily the one they claim to be combating. In November 2018 French president Emmanuel Macron compared the current political unrest to the crisis that existed on the European continent in the 1930s: "in a Europe that is divided by fears, retreat into nationalism, and the consequences of economic crisis, one sees almost methodically articulating itself all that punctuated the life of Europe from the post-World War One era up to the crisis of 1929."[1] On the centenary of Italian fascism's birth in 2019, the television channel Europe 1 informed viewers that "fascism has now revived under the form of 'populism.'"[2] Developments like the creation of a ruling coalition in Italy allied with the right-of-center Lega Nord's Matteo Salvini and the emergence of a populist Right throughout the West supposedly prove a fascist resurgence. Today fascist ideology "has become once again an instrument that treats as normal the virility of the strong man and the brutality of simplistic thinking." And "indeed, democracy can die with a small fire or else go up in flames all at once." A menace embodied by the old and new forms of fascism alike is "the determination to educate generations that would not resemble those of the past." Presumably, antifascist efforts to monitor cultural and educational resources have been aimed at keeping neofascists from returning to a past that will not pass.2

Perhaps second only to President Trump as an object of attack as a fascist has been Vladimir Putin. The Russian president has evoked shared comments from the likes of the mainstream news magazine *Newsweek*[3] and the neoconservative *National Interest*, with the latter definitively pronouncing Russia to be "an unconsolidated fascist state."[4] George Will upped the rhetoric of his neoconservative colleagues in 2014 when he announced that "Putin's fascist revival carries echoes of Hitler."[5] His seemingly hastily thrown together brief suggests that Putin has not only also ruled in an authoritarian fashion—which is undisputed—but has also acted aggressively to regain territory lost by his country during the collapse of the Soviet Empire. But more qualified critical perspectives are needed.[6] One does not have to approve of Putin to observe that he is a nationalist who appeals to Christian traditionalists.

As mentioned, antifascism in its present form relates to a configuration of ideas and policies that belong to the post-Marxist Left.[7] Unlike the traditional Marxist Left and its more moderate variations, the post-Marxist Left emphasizes the need for cultural transformation to be brought about by making war on traditional social and gender identities. This activist Left, as indicated earlier in the words of former Weather Underground member Eric Mann,[8] associates the evil that needs to be removed with white Christian men and with the oppressive civilization that this group has produced. The Left in both France and Germany has also accused the generic Right of being linked to the Third Reich and, however circuitously, to Nazi atrocities. German journalists and politicians seem to be particularly eager to charge those on their own real or imaginary Right with minimizing or trivializing Nazi crimes and ignoring the history of the German people leading up to Hitler's reign of terror.

Giving voice to these German antifascist concerns, Thomas Haldenwang, president of the Office for the Protection of the Constitution (*Bundesamt für Verfassungsschutz*), an agency that oversees "extremist" dangers to Germany's democratic order, warned Berliners in May 2019 against a surging Far Right. Haldenwang designated as a public danger those German citizens who view the historical past differently from his own agency, singling out those unredeemable reactionaries who regard May 8, 1945, as the day of Germany's catastrophic defeat. He also scolded those who dwell on a fact that is not meant to be noticed: about a half-million German civilians were killed in aerial bombing toward the end of World War II. Noticing these things puts the offender in the same category as Muslim terrorists; namely, as threats to German democracy.[9] Moreover, "extremists" who have stated inconvenient but demonstrable historical facts too emphatically have been subject to police searches and threats of detention as fascist sympathizers.

What makes this antifascism in its most recent manifestations stand out is its increasingly frenetic nature.[10] In Germany, for example, the government has singled out the Alternative für Deutschland (AfD) from among a medley of political parties as an antidemocratic threat.[11] AfD members are being forced out of public posts while the Left engages in assaults and vandalism against party officials. often with impunity.[12] The admission of more than 1.5 migrants into Germany since 2016 has led to intense criticism in some quarters, bringing reprisals against those who express unwelcome opinions. No right-of-center German party is safe from government prosecution or from mayhem, which is often incited by the media. Entirely typical of the program and dominant views of AfD is *Widerworte*, a work by Alice Weidel, the co-chairman of the AfD faction in the German Upper House (Bundestag). Save for brief references to the German war of liberation during the Napoleonic Wars and the celebration of German democrats and liberals in previous times, one finds nothing even remotely nationalist in Weidel's critique of her government's spending, educational, and immigration policies. Thinkers whom she holds up for praise are the English classical liberal John Locke and defenders of the free market like Friedrich Hayek. Indeed, there is nothing in Weidel's book that would not turn up in a discussion of German politics by an American center-right newspaper like the *Wall Street Journal*.[13]

Another feature of present-day antifascism is its top-down character: it is an elitist ideology that claims to represent the alien and oppressed. Politicians like Macron, who are beholden to international bankers and multinational industrialists, are rushing to join French antinationalists, like Bernard-Henri Lévy[14] and the editorial board of *Libération*, in protesting a rising fascist tide. This threat supposedly goes beyond those resisting the Left's cultural, administrative, and/or educational dominance. The establishment, which has taken up antifascist rhetoric, is facing an obstreperous, politically organized opposition to its concept of liberal democracy. Most frighteningly for the power elites, the "fascists" are now raising what seems to be the banner of revolution and claiming to speak for "the people."

Contrary to what its defenders may think, liberal democracy is held to be a closed system by those who do not enjoy its advantages. For the French who reside in the peripheries of their country, rather than in urban or suburban areas, liberal democracy is a spoils system that benefits migrants, foreigners on social welfare, government employees, tenured professors, and LGBTQ supporters. Sixty-seven percent of French interviewees in a 2018 survey object strenuously to the generous government support given to the Third World migrant population streaming into France.[15] Forty-one percent of those interviewed define themselves specifically as "French nationalists," as compared to only 20 percent among their German neighbors.[16] Seventy-two percent believe that immigration has engendered "disquieting problems for our country," and 54 percent consider immigration to be "a political project aimed at replacing one civilization by another deliberately organized by our intellectual and media elites."[17] Only 11 percent of those French interviewed believe that immigrants can be "integrated into French society." These responses should not surprise us.

A great deal of research correlates immigration from Africa and the Near East with the rise of a populist Right. According to Roger Eatwell and Matthew Goodwin in *National Populism and the Revolt against Liberal Democracy*, these anti-elitist protests have produced a snowball effect and typically attract a mélange of protesting groups, from traditional patriots and Christian traditionalists to alienated members of the older socialist Left. Eatwell and Goodwin argue persuasively that the association of the new populism with a down-and-out working class overlooks the presence of better-educated traditional conservatives. Eighty-one percent of Donald Trump's vote in 2016 came not from a financially battered, semi-literate working class, which may have been the target of Hillary Clinton's "basket of deplorables" remark. Most of Trump's voters were in fact white-bread Republicans who viewed the Democrats as unpatriotic and culturally hostile.[18] Among populist groups in every Western country, one finds a passionate revulsion for the culturally leftist media and the professoriate. The same groups manifest a dislike for global financial elites who are thought to be antagonistic to national members of the working class.

Those who view themselves as cultural radicals or progressives are discovering they have no real standing among the populists as true revolutionaries. The populists scorn their rulers as elitists. Branding populists as fascists may represent an attempt by the cultural Left to reclaim the moral high ground. Antifascist intellectuals and the verbalizing class are stuck in a strange alliance with plutocrats and government administrators against an old leftist constituency that is gravitating toward the populist Right. It is therefore strategically imperative for the antifascists to bring back to honor liberal democratic cosmopolites as the only recognized Left. This has required the construction of an historic confrontation between themselves and would-be followers of Hitler, Mussolini, and Franco. This quest for the appearance of the moral high ground has necessitated an orchestrated struggle between "tolerance" and "intolerance," in which the enemies of "fascism" stand for progress and cosmopolitanism.

According to Eatwell and Goodwin, although liberal democracy is visibly under attack, the accusation that their opponents are "fascists" is overblown. Calling for referenda on immigration or opposing LGBTQ initiatives may be a good or bad thing, but there is nothing fascist about holding views on these subjects that do not accord with those of political and cultural elites. Nor does the fact that populist leaders come forth to speak for likeminded followers mean that we are on the path to fascist authoritarian rule.[19] But some opponents of this populist wave may in fact think that the Western world is returning to an ominous interwar past. Typical of this last group are left-leaning intellectuals who protest passionately against Viktor Orban's "fascist" government in Hungary and the AfD in Germany. Some of these critics may be genuinely worried about a return to those conditions that allowed the Nazis and their allies to wreak havoc in the 1930s. But this antifascist anxiety sometimes verges on the hysterical; for example, when the venerable Board of Deputies of British Jews in March 2019 castigated a former Conservative minister of Indian descent (married to a Jewish husband) for referring to the Labour Far Left as "cultural Marxists."[20]

The problem is that "cultural Marxism" (which is admittedly not the best term to designate what is meant here) is charged with anti-Semitic and possibly Nazi connotations.[21] The term actually describes a particular movement for change that combines some elements of Marxist socialism with a call for sexual and cultural revolution. Among critics of this effort to transform Marxism into cultural revolutionary doctrine have been both traditional Marxists and members of the interwar Far Right. But this onetime association of the term with the Far Right hardly indicates that designating cultural radicals as cultural Marxists is a peculiarly Nazi practice.[22] Such signature cultural Marxist positions as attacking traditional gender roles and Western national identities first surfaced among interwar cultural radicals with Marxist leanings and later became integral to the antifascist Left. To recognize this lineage is to note the obvious, and so is the perception that what is described as "cultural Marxism" is only distantly related to traditional Marxism and therefore should be qualified with the adjective "cultural."

Among the "fascist" symptoms that antifascists decry are, curiously enough, features of an older Left that the populists have revived. A resistance to Third World immigration that might have a negative impact on the native-born workforce was for generations a characteristically leftist position. The American Federation of Labor under its founder Samuel Gompers mobilized its members to support the Immigration Act of 1924, which decisively reduced immigration levels to the United States. The head of the United Farm Workers, Cesar Chavez. railed against illegal immigration in the 1960s, particularly the practice of replacing union members with cheap foreign labor.[23] One of the most vigorous anti-immigration activists in the United States in the 1970s was a black Democratic congresswoman from Texas, Barbara Jordan, who served from 1936 to 1996. Jordan's once-resolute stand as a champion of vulnerable workers has now vanished from the historical record.[24] Moreover, a critical stance toward immigration was by no means unique to the American working-class Left and its advocates. The French Communist Party strongly opposed the immigration of North Africans lest they take jobs away from Frenchmen. As late as 1982, Georges Marchais, who headed the party, published an editorial in the French Communist newspaper *l'Humanité* that denounced the use of immigration by the capitalist class to displace French workers.[25]

The open borders position of today's Left stands in glaring contrast to what were once traditional leftist views. Members of the Left through most of the twentieth century would have denounced the move toward open borders as a "neoliberal" trick intended to increase capitalist fortunes at the expense of low-paid workers. They would have also been disconcerted by the antifascist Left's unwillingness to allow Western peoples to preserve their national identities: the antifascist assault on Western identities would have reduced the Old Guard to utter bemusement. The longtime editor of the Communist journal *L'Humanité*, Georges Cogniat, argued for the value of rooting Marxist-Leninism in a strong national consciousness. In a widely read book *Réalité de la nation: L'attrape-nigaud du cosmpolitisme* (1950), he denounced the war against national borders as a tool by which neoliberal capitalists were robbing French laborers of their just wages.[26] Cogniat and other French Communists even praised the virtue of *enracinement*—rootedness in an ethnic and national group—as a working-class strength. In addition, antifascist hostility to displays of solidarity among European nations would have even shocked an older, less multicultural Left.[27]

Eatwell and Goodwin believe that populist leaders have benefited by invoking the "Four Ds" when addressing their followers. They have appealed to "a more 'direct' model of democracy" because of "anxieties about the *destruction* of the nation that have been sharpened by rapid immigration," strong concerns about "relative *deprivation* resulting from the shift towards an increasingly unequal economic settlement," "*distrust* of the increasingly elitist nature of liberal democracy," and "*de-alignment* from the traditional parties, which have rendered our political systems more volatile."[28]

The head of the old Hungarian Communist Party (*Magyar Szocialista Munkáspárt*; Hungarian Socialist Workers' Party) since 1989, Gyula Thuermer, has now redefined himself as a National Communist. Thuermer expresses concern about the effects of immigration on the Hungarian working class and appeals to Hungarian national identity, like the nationalist government of Viktor Orban. This Communist leader is as hostile as Orban is to George Soros, whom he regards as a vulture global capitalist. Thuermer does complain, however, that Orban has made too many concessions to the EU, so that Hungarians "buy German milk" while their own dairy farmers languish.[29] He has also dwelled on the overpowering sense of sadness he felt as he stood in the Hall of Trianon outside Paris, where the treaty was signed that stripped the Hungarian nation of more than half its territory after World War I.[30] Thuermer reproaches the "ruling elite" in Hungary since 1989 for neither "getting back Transylvania" from Romania nor doing anything to relieve the disabilities of the Hungarian minorities still living there. It is unimaginable that any German statesman would similarly lament his own country's loss of territory in any past war without being attacked in the media as an unreconstructed fascist.

The liberal democratic establishment in the West, unlike the head of the Hungarian Communist Party, has catered to groups that have nothing in common with the native-born working class, the Left's historic base that it now often condemns as bigoted and unenlightened. The establishment eagerly promotes leftist identity politics, as well as Third World immigration, which has created a reservoir of cheap labor. It also seeks to break free of national attachments that an older, traditional Left in varying degrees affirmed. In this new friend–enemy alignment, the populists are free to incorporate positions that were once uniquely leftist; social conflict no longer rages, as in an earlier era, between the owners of the means of production and their workers. This inveterate conflict has been replaced by a new one—between antifascists and those accused of fascist sentiments. And behind these labels is a new class conflict, in which economic and media elites are allied to Third World immigrants and the underclass against both the traditional working class and surviving critics of leftist identity politics.

We might cite here the more optimistic view of this confrontation offered by Eatwell, Goodwin, and Markus Wagner, leader of the AfD in North Rhine-Westphalia. According to their interpretation of current events, the struggle between the populists and members of the liberal democratic establishment, who are now attacking their adversaries as fascists, may not culminate in the defeat of either side. After the present strife, a post-populist deal may take place in which the warring sides will be partly accommodated.[31] Evidence for this deal is supposedly already available. The supporters of Brexit have won, and the UK government is removing the country from the EU, albeit on terms that will not imperil the English economy. Although the Rassemblement National in France (aka Front National) has not been able to rise against the combined force of the other parties in presidential races beyond the low thirtieth percentile, the government of Emanuel Macron has already taken preliminary measures to tighten immigration requirements. Members of the European Community, moreover, have imposed restrictions on migrants who are seeking asylum, and these displaced people will have to be approved at the EU borders before being allowed to settle anywhere among member states. Wagner, a professor at the University of Vienna who has spoken at AfD gatherings in Germany, believes things may be looking up for his still-ostracized party. The vote totals for AfD are increasing, particularly in elections being held in the former East Germany.[32] According to Eatwell and Goodwin, the liberal democratic establishment may soon be inclined to make piecemeal accommodations to the populist opposition, and as in Austria and Italy, coalitions may be formed to include those whom our elites are now stigmatizing as fascists.

## A Limited Populist Challenge and the Crusade against Fascism

This positive outcome marked by mutual recognition of once-warring parties may not, however, come to pass, because the contending sides described here are not at all evenly matched. The antifascist liberal democratic establishment holds almost all the useful resources—ranging from the government bureaucracy, the educational system, and donations from large corporations and funders like George Soros to a swelling immigrant electorate and the culture industry. Is there any evidence for this assertion made by the founder of the French New Right, Alain de Benoit? "All of the political parties of the traditional type are in the process of being swept away by the force of these unprecedented and atypical movements." Indeed "the resentment and hate of the political class as well as of their media and financial faithful are explained by the fact that they are like a bear on an ice block about to melt."[33]

While the crusade against fascism has accelerated, the stand-in for fascism—namely, populism—is stumbling in its ascent to power. There is no evidence that what Benoist is describing is happening in most of Western Europe. The liberal democratic establishment has handed its rival a fait accompli in the form of a large Third World immigrant population and a vast panoply of programs intended to serve this clientele. Thilo Sarrazin's *Deutschland schafft sich ab* (Germany Abolishes Itself) and Laurent Obertone's *La France Interdite* (Forbidden France) both show that there is overwhelming support for Third World immigration from the media in Germany and France, together with widespread media defenses of the programs earmarked for immigrants.[34] In 2016, the year that Obertone's study highlights, the French government spent 756 billion euros on social programs that disproportionately served an immigrant clientele. Although Macron referred to this amount as "a nutty sum" (*pognon dingue*), he and his government are not likely to reduce it.[35] Nor would the media likely tolerate such cuts. Further, the number of native-born women in Western Europe who choose to bear children continues to decline, while the number of Third World immigrant women giving birth to children has stayed the same. In 2016 the native-born French made up 80 percent of the population but less than 60 percent of births. Of the 783,640 registered births in France in 2016, 30.9 percent were to immigrant mothers, who were mostly from Africa and who constituted only 9.7 percent of the French population. We may doubt that much has changed in these matters since Obertone's research was completed.

French scholar Jérôme Fourquet demonstrates in *L'Archipel français* (The French Archipelago)[36] that the populist strategy of forging an alliance between the socially traditional bourgeois and an insecure working class may be less and less workable in his country. According to Fourquet, the native-born French (*Francais de souche*) are divided into three very distinct groups: urban bourgeoisie who identify socially with the Left, the Catholic bourgeoisie who are economically pro-interventionist but socially conservative, and a vast undifferentiated mass of French inhabitants who are culturally and politically shaped by American fashions and values. Fourquet asks whether these heterogeneous groups could be brought together to form a French populist majority, given that even the children of the Catholic bourgeoisie have been gravitating toward a profoundly secularized youth culture.

There is also little evidence that German voters are challenging the system to the degree that both antifascists and populists suggest. One might think from recent efforts by Thomas Haldenwang and his federal intelligence agency (*Bundesamt für Verfassungsschutz*) to ban the AfD as a "hate party" that the AfD is romping to victory.[37] In point of fact less than 10 percent of German voters support that party, which is the only German national party that is emphatically critical of immigration. Further, the AfD's support lies disproportionately in eastern regions of the country that were under Soviet control. A nationwide poll in Germany in June 2019 revealed that the party regarded as the best suited to solve political and social problems was the pro-immigration, outspokenly antifascist Greens (*die Grünen*). In contrast to the AfD, which received no more than 4 percent support from those answering questions about Germany's desired future, the Greens registered as high as 27 percent.[38]

A commentator who is sympathetic to the AfD, Benedikt Kaiser has stated that the poor showing by the AfD in a regional election in Hamburg in February 2020, in which it won only 5.3 percent of the vote,[39] was a deserved "rejection" for a party that failed to campaign adequately. Although a long-awaited "lurch toward the Right" (*Rechtsrutsch*) among the affluent did not took place, it might still be possible, according to Kaiser, for the AfD to capture the support of the working class, particularly in areas affected by Third World immigration.[40] Indeed, in Hamburg's deteriorating neighborhoods, the AfD captured 20 percent or more of the registered vote. But even so, why should we believe the cordon sanitaire against Kaiser's party would come down if its candidates won 20 percent of the vote throughout Germany? More likely that situation would lead to an increased mobilization among government bureaucrats and the media against a looming fascist danger.

The German response to a supposed fascist threat is so extreme that we can only understand it in relation to the country's growing preoccupation with the Nazi past. By now that Nazi past has been made to encompass almost the entire course of German history, as shown by the section on penitential historiography in chapter 3. This German response is actually part of an internalized consciousness, according to three post–World War II antifascist critics, Alexander and Margarete Mitscherlich and Franco-German journalist Géraldine Schwarz.[41] Antifascist authors, particularly the ones writing from and about Germany, treat the ideology they oppose as a suppressed impulse and a buried memory from the Nazi–fascist era. Continuing external control is therefore needed to keep the fascist mentality from repossessing European societies. The German Federal Agency for Civil Education (*Bundeszentrale für politische Bildung*) was created to provide "political education" in German schools; in accordance with the wishes of antifascist critics, it maintains public awareness of German guilt for the nation's fascist past, while focusing on the dangers to German democratic institutions supposedly coming overwhelmingly from the nationalist Right.

The German novelist Uwe Tellkamp, who grew up in Dresden in Communist East Germany, has noted the similarities and differences between Communist antifascism and the kind of antifascism that now reigns in the German Federal Republic. Although both forms relentlessly target freedom of thought, they do so through different means. Communist dictatorships feature authoritarian governments that intimidate their critics through physical force or professional ostracism. The liberal democratic form of antifascism is physically less brutal but also more insidious: it takes over people's lives internally until it swallows up "civil society."[42] Because of its ever-tightening control of cultural and educational institutions, liberal democratic antifascism in Germany may have become unstoppable. It is perpetually at war with a never-defeated fascist enemy, which the instigators identify as those who resist the never-ending antifascist campaign. And rather than raising questions about this crazed project, universities, churches, and the mass media all rush in to participate.

A closer look at populist parties in Western Europe will allow us to see more clearly the disproportion between their electoral strength and the fear they arouse, and whether the response to these parties confirms Natalia Antonova's lament in *The Guardian*, "From Britain to Ukraine, the Far Right is thriving on shared emotion."[43] At this point, it is no longer necessary to determine whether European journalists and administrators are correct in their equation of populism with fascism or Nazism; let us examine the Right's electoral and governing potential, which is under fire from the antifascist establishment. Although their vote shares may be occasionally higher, populist parties in Belgium, Holland, and Sweden typically garner about 15 percent of the votes; in France Marine Le Pen's party has never received more than 33 percent, and the right populist Austrian Freedom Party won nearly 26 percent of the vote in 2017. From September 2017 until November 2020, support for the AfD in Germany, according to polls, has fallen from 12.6 to 9.5 percent. This is hardly evidence of a thriving German electorate on the right.[44] A book that relates the fate of the AfD and other right-of-center parties in Germany to the design of the occupying powers after World War Two is Josef Schüsslburner's *Scheitert die AfD?*[45]

No matter what percentage of the votes these parties gain, their opponents on the Left carefully maneuver block them from entering governing coalitions. In France the Rassemblement National and its predecessor the Front National have managed to send only one delegate to the National Assembly since the Front's founding in 1972. Although France's populist Right has entered the second round of elections, the parties of the Left and center have predictably united to keep its candidates from winning electoral districts. In French presidential runoffs, for example, the Left and center have cooperated to keep the French populist candidate, most recently Marine Le Pen, from rising above a fixed percentage in the low thirties.

In Austria a leader of the populist right-wing Austrian Freedom Party, Heinz Christian Strache, was able to enter a coalition with the centrist People's Party, after his party had won 25.97 percent of the vote in an Austrian national election in September 2017. But when the media revealed that Strache, who was then Austrian vice chancellor, was entangled in a financial scandal, support for his party plummeted to about 16.17 percent by September 2019. The fact that Strache's party could drop ten points in support within two years, indicated how precarious that base of support was. According to Die (Wiener) Presse, he was caught embezzling money and subsequently expelled from his party.[46]

Thereafter the Austrian Freedom Party was thrown out of the ruling coalition.[47] The populist Swedish Democrats have constituted the third largest party in the multiparty Riksdag since 2015, and their share of the vote has generally ranged from 12 to 15 percent. Not surprisingly, the ruling parties have kept the Swedish Democrats out of the ruling cabinet. Although these data cited may go back a few years, the electoral and demographic trends and exclusionary practices they describe are not likely to change any time soon.

The Anglo-American world would seem to represent an exception to this quarantining of the populist Right that has taken place in other Western societies. A closer look at this apparent exception, however, suggests the deviation is not as great as one might first think. Boris Johnson's landslide victory as Tory leader in the parliamentary election of December 2019 was a dream come true for the 52 percent of the British electorate who in June 2016 voted to leave the European Union. A bit of research would uncover, however, that it was not the Tories but the United Kingdom Independence Party (UKIP) that since 1993 has carried the torch for British independence from the EU. In 2015 this anti-EU party managed to elect deputies to the National Assembly of Wales and placed its members on municipal councils throughout England. But party officials could do nothing to change England's "first through the gate" electoral system, which provides the Conservatives and Labour with a near monopoly of seats in the House of Commons and nearly exclusive power to form governments. Even in 2015 when UKIP attracted 3.8 million votes, it landed up with only two seats in the House of Commons, while its party head Nigel Farage lost his own district. It was only after a Brexit champion, Boris Johnson, gained control of the Tories' party machinery that England's departure from the EU would be earnestly pursued.

The question that might be asked, however, is whether Johnson's successes represent a clear victory for the populist Right. One can easily believe that a lackluster Labour campaign and an accommodation of the anti-Semitic Left by Johnson's opponent Jeremy Corbyn contributed to Labour's recent electoral disaster. Other issues, in addition to the delayed implementation of Brexit and the opposition of England's globalist elites, added to Johnson's favorable position. In addition, part of his attraction for British voters may have been his willingness to fit in with a progressive culture. During his campaign he conspicuously invoked the ideal of diversity[48] and enthusiastically endorsed gay marriage[49] and other social positions associated with the Left. Descriptions of Johnson in the US conservative press as a leader who combines social conservatism with economic populism were quite inaccurate.[50] Nearer to the truth, Johnson may be the closest to an electable candidate that the political Right can field in our present Anglo-American society.

But this qualified statement is different from portraying Johnson as the standard-bearer of the socially conservative Right. Although hardly a favorite of the globalist establishment, Johnson promotes an exceedingly modest populist agenda, certainly in comparison to the more robust populism that one finds in Eastern Europe or even in the Rassemblement National in France. Johnson's populism is limited to statements of determination to leave the EU in the name of national sovereignty and to taking occasional swipes against illegal immigration.[51] The English prime minister may be close ideologically to Geert Wilders, the head of Holland's Party for Freedom. A socially progressive critic of Muslim immigration who defends Zionism, feminism, and gay rights, Wilders mixes his criticism of Third World immigration with views that would play well among most establishment Democrats in the United States. One would never confuse Wilders or Johnson's stance on social issues with those of more traditionalist populists such as Victor Orban, Matteo Salvini, or (perhaps?) Vladimir Putin.

## Successful Populists?

Populists have generally made the deepest inroads in Eastern and East Central Europe in a region that has been only minimally affected by multicultural, antifascist ideology. It is also a region that does not have large populations of racial minorities or Muslim immigrants. Curiously, the inroads that populists have made in Eastern and East Central Europe—excluding Germanophone Austria, given its supposedly ominous German character—have not attracted the critical attention conferred on Germany and even France as hotbeds of fascism and neo-Nazism. This is noteworthy in view of the warnings from Western policy experts and political journalists about the imminent resurgence of right-wing authoritarianism in Eastern Europe after the collapse of the Soviet Empire. Flora Lewis at the *New York Times* and the political scientist Charles Gati were conspicuous among those who conjured up doppelgängers of Admiral Miklos Horthy in Hungary and General Josef Pilsudski in Poland who would seize power after the Soviet armies went home.[52] Back then, the Western media and policy experts seemed less concerned about the fascist temptation for Germans than about the specter of right-wing nationalism in the former Soviet Empire. That was true in the 1990s even though nationalist parties well to the right of the AfD were then winning votes in Germany. Perhaps today's Germanophobia among Germany's ruling class and the Western media and the greater cultural distance of certain European countries from Western journalists have caused even minimal evidence of German nationalism to arouse more antifascist panic than the rise of nationalist parties in East Central Europe.

There are certain exceptions that should be noted. The persona of Viktor Orban in Hungary has annoyed Western progressives because of Orban's clear dislike for his critics and his Trump-like delight in antagonizing them. Polish nationalism has also received unfavorable coverage in Western media mostly because its ruling Law and Justice Party ran afoul of the demands for reparations by certain Jewish organizations. But when Poland's extreme right-wing nationalist Confederation Party won seats in the Sejm (Polish parliament), this elicited nothing like the strong response to the vote totals gained by the far more centrist AfD.[53] The specter of Germany, as the source of Nazism, turning to the Right clearly seems far scarier than watching the antifascist Left yield ground in Eastern Europe.

There is, however, little reason to think that populist successes in Hungary, Poland, and Slovakia can be duplicated in Western Europe or Canada. It would also be a mistake to read too much into Donald Trump's 2016 electoral victory in the United States. Although Trump appealed to the forgotten worker and to opponents of mass immigration, once in office he did not carry out a notably nativist agenda. His most controversial stands—trying to keep illegal immigrants from entering the United States and restricting travel from countries with terrorist problems—recycled positions that the Democrats took in preceding decades. This includes the building of a border wall with Mexico, which in 2013 was a signature position of congressional Democrats.[54]

Trump, however, distinguished himself from more timid Republican heads of state by duking it out with media opponents and by working up his base at rallies, hurling insults at "the fake media." This has helped consolidate a constituency that shares Trump's anti-elitism and resonates with his mention of patriotic symbols. He also managed to improve job prospects for racial minorities and college-educated women, before the response to COVID-19 wrought havoc on the US economy.[55] But Trump's party's defeat in congressional and other electoral races in 2018 reflected the natural limitations of his populist style.[56] A mainstream website, *Business Insider,* stated this opinion on August 20, 2017: "For the first time in our history a Nazi sympathizer occupies the White House."[57] This judgment was supposedly based on Trump's statements made in response to the Charlottesville demonstration on August 11, 2017, an imbroglio that did feature, among others, neo-Nazis. Although there is no indication that Trump speaking at his press conference on August 15 praised Nazi demonstrators,[58] it is significant that the media could make it sound as if he did.

It is now clear that Trump failed in his bid for re-election and pending further evidence, failed to rally a majority of the electorate. Without minimizing the significance of the 74 million or so voters that Trump did attract, we might ask whether this support represented a great populist wave or whether it showed something of a mixed character. Most of Trump's voters were traditional Republicans, who were joined by a white working class that favored Trump's economic policies and which was probably well-disposed toward his defense of gun rights and religious liberties. Despite the claim Trump's movement was multiracial, the former president in his bid for re-election increased his share of the black vote by only 4 percent and his share of the Hispanic vote by only 4 to 5 percent. If the current Democratic administration encourages massive immigration while giving a path to citizenship to illegal residents, it may have enough votes to crush definitively a populist challenge from the Right. This may be the case even if Joel Kotkin is correct that Trump "has challenged in ways not seen for a generation the comfortable establishment politics." Trump accomplished this, according to Kotkin, by reintroducing along with Bernie Sanders "the relevance of class into American politics." Pace Kotkin, if Trump's white working-class base starts to shrink in a "diverse" America, that may end the populist dream of Trump and his followers.[59]

We might reflect on such possibilities as we consider whether the populists are gaining ground in Western countries. Antifascist activist Géraldine Schwarz complains that "far-right parties want to downplay Nazi crimes as a first step towards reawakening ideas from that era," and the notion has become prevalent in the West that "hierarchy can be drawn among humans according to their race or their religion."[60] Ms. Schwarz is clearly looking at a very different political landscape from the one that some of us see. The liberal democratic establishment shows remarkable durability, even when it takes controversial social and cultural stands. And this establishment's stability results from its proven power to mold opinion through its control of vital institutions.

Matteo Salvini's Lega Nord,[61] which at the time of this writing claims 32 percent of the Italian electorate, and the emerging Partido Vox in Spain provide examples of national populism that have gained solid footholds in Mediterranean countries. These fits of populist fervor may in fact be peculiar to Latin countries, areas with unstable economic conditions and traditionally masculine cultures. Not surprisingly, that ultimate establishmentarian Macron has worked to isolate Salvini as a "far rightist,"[62] and the Spanish media have labeled Vox as unprecedentedly "far right."[63]

The same political tendencies are not as strong in countries that reveal more fiscal stability and well-established public administration. Populism has a limited possibility for growth in countries like England and France, which feature a behaviorally predictable political majority, winner-take-all electoral rules, and an entrenched two-party system or one with alternating coalitions. Sizable numbers of minorities and the presence of Third World immigrant populations further limit the growth potential of populist movements, as soon as these new settlers gain electoral power. Such minorities as have come to England, France, Germany and other Western countries typically vote for the multiculturally-oriented Left, against any party associated with the nationalist Right. Although Third World immigrants, including disproportionately large numbers of young, sometimes unruly, and often uneducated males, have spurred as reactions populist movements, the same minorities also form a voting bloc on the pro-immigration Left. This bloc will likely expand significantly, given the higher birth rate of Third World immigrants relative to that of indigenous European populations.

The once successful populist leader, Salvini, was perhaps predictably ousted from his premiership by leftist coalition partners. This shake-up occurred after continuous media attacks against the contaminating populist, or fascist, presence in Italy. Both the French and German governments helped topple the government that Salvini led and promised his successor large loans, in return for taking in African refugees and Muslim migrants from the Middle East. In August 2019 the Vatican spoke out emphatically against Salvini and against those who vote for "*souvérainisme*" (sovereignty) in Italy and elsewhere in the West, as enemies of Catholic compassion and social justice. The idea that Catholic nationalists and populists could depend on an alliance with the Catholic Church (French, Italian, Polish, and Brazilian populists had identified with it strongly) has now been laid to rest, pending new, unexpected developments.[64]

Not surprisingly charges of wishing to return Italy to a latter-day equivalent of Mussolini's fascist government have bedeviled Salvini's political career, particularly since this young politician became a key player in Italian government. A rally that Salvini held in Rome on October 19, 2019, was likened by Europe's establishment press to Mussolini's March on Rome in October 1922. His political opponents maintain that "he struts around with the air of Mussolini."[65] To all such charges, Salvini responds by pointing out that, although he is "proud to be called a populist," he is most definitely not a fascist. Terms like "fascist, Communist, Left and Right and particularly how the media have chosen to throw them about," observes Salvini, "belong to a different era and have been dead for years."[66] Salvini may be right, but he is not likely to convince critics who have a deep emotional and professional investment in keeping alive associations that he rejects as obsolete.

In addition to being called fascists, would-be populist politicians will meet another obstacle in countries that lack strong ethnic roots and that are characterized by a pluralistic, fluid population. Attempts to build populist politics in the United States around human rights propositions or a cult of democracy, as some well-financed Americans hope to do, may be an exercise in futility.[67] One needs far better glue for holding together a populist movement. Beliefs that all people "are created equal" and that everyone in the United States should speak English may not be enough to sustain such a force. "The mystical chords of memory" to which Abraham Lincoln appealed as a source of American togetherness may now be as frayed as they were on the eve of the US Civil War.

Those in power will not necessarily remain there indefinitely. They will likely face challenges, and indeed some of their troubles could arise from their recent successes. The continued influx of uneducated, low-skilled immigrants from the Third World, the increasing costs of social programs, the tensions created by multicultural politics, and the seething dissatisfaction of what the

French call "peripheral populations" all spell long-term difficulties for the ruling classes.[68] But there is no reason to believe the establishment is collapsing before a populist adversary. Contrary to the hope of French populists grouped around "Les Identitaires," the populist phenomenon that has arisen in France and in other Western countries may be only a current, not the "tidal wave (*raz de marée*)" being conjured up.[69] One may come to doubt whether antifascist polemicists are addressing a real crisis when they rush to defend those still in control.

Chapter 6


# The Uses and Abuses of "Conservative" Antifascism


Antifascist polemics have played a critical role in conservative discourse by typically recycling the other side's arguments to make them fit the needs of establishment conservatives and the Republican Party. According to this account, the Democratic Party swarms with fascists, while the Republican Party is fighting for equality and human rights. Widely acclaimed conservative antifascists include journalist Jonah Goldberg, radio talk show host and author Dennis Prager, and author, filmmaker, and commentator Dinesh D'Souza. Although none of these celebrities has more than a nodding acquaintance with their subject, they do provide their base with a steady supply of sound bites.

Exemplifying media conservative antifascism is Jonah Goldberg's 2007 best-seller *Liberal Fascism*, which claims that the other national party has been historically linked to fascism. Goldberg, a nationally syndicated Republican columnist, focuses on the putative parallels between the rhetoric of Mussolini and Hitler and the proposals of 2016 Democratic presidential hopeful Hillary Clinton. Because Hillary Clinton favored extensive social programs that resembled those advocated by interwar fascists, her platform supposedly revealed a connection between fascism and the Democratic Party. Hillary's references to a new "village" under government auspices was really just a throwback to Hitler's Volksgemeinschaft, and the Democratic Party's endorsement of affirmative action programs for minorities and women is supposedly the modern equivalent of Hitler's exclusion of Jews from German public life under the Nuremberg Laws of 1935.[1] The reproduction at the end of his book of the 1920 Nazi Party Platform in translation is intended to point out that the Democratic Party, even before Barack Obama arrived on the national scene, was on its way to replicating the politics of the Third Reich.

Goldberg offers this antifascist principle that government should follow: "The role of the state should be limited, and its meddling should be seen as an exception."[2] Although there is nothing wrong with this maxim in theory, the devil, of course, is in the details. How exactly do we decide what is meddling and what is a proper form of state intervention? In Goldberg's case this question is a no-brainer. Every social and anti-discriminatory program passed before 2007 (when his book was published) was fine, providing both parties signed off on it. Accordingly, Goldberg disapproved of presidential candidate Rand Paul questioning the existence of a Department of Education or the public accommodations provision of the Civil Rights Act of 1964. Yet Goldberg also has a problem with far more moderate steps undertaken by Democrats Woodrow Wilson and FDR to erect a modern welfare state.[3]

Goldberg's work seems to have served as a blueprint for other Republicans who make it their business to address the fascist problem. Republican talk show host Dennis Prager has produced commentaries on the fascist peril for his Prager University, which his website describes as "the world's leading conservative nonprofit that is focused on changing minds through the creative use of digital media." Based on his sketch of the thinking of the neo-Hegelian Italian philosopher Giovanni Gentile (1875–1944), Prager's frequent guest Dinesh D'Souza opines that "fascists are socialists with a national identity." He notes, "The Left has vastly expanded state control over the private sector," and concludes that "fascism bears a deep kinship to the ideology of today's Left."[4] The logic is that any thinker, regime, or movement that has advocated an expansion of the state exemplifies both fascism and "today's Left."

The scholarly consensus, however, is that Gentile quite consciously rejected Marxism and Marxist socialism in favor of a philosophy of will that later merged with fascist theory.[5] Gentile's understanding of the fascist, organic state has nothing to do with D'Souza's and Prager's "Left." Rather it is a hierarchical structure that emanates from the will of the leader acting on behalf of a unified nation. Although an antifascist like Timothy Snyder who goes after Trump as the new Hitler or Mussolini may be sullying his scholarly reputation, Republican antifascists usually have no such reputation to compromise. They are political operatives trying to solicit votes for their party.

Even more illustrative of these partisan antifascist efforts are the books, films, and commentaries of D'Souza, which attempt to prove the fascist history of the Democratic Party. Toward this end, in 2017 D'Souza pieced together an entire book, *The Big Lie: Exposing the Nazi Roots of the Left*, to demonstrate that the Democratic Party, which incorporates the Left, exudes fascist and Nazi tendencies.[6] In an interview posted on the Breitbart website, D'Souza explains that the Left since the election of President Obama has been driven by "the glimpse of being able to establish exactly what the fascists always wanted: a complete centralized state." He also sounds this warning: "Remember, for example, that with the NSA today there are surveillance technologies that were completely unavailable to Mussolini in the '20s or Hitler in the '30s. So, in a sense, true fascism, full-scale fascism, is more possible today than it was in the twentieth century."[7] Again one has to ask this question: Does any progress toward centralized state power necessarily represent a movement in the direction of fascism? The consolidation of state power has been going on for a long time in many places; it seems unlikely that all such developments betray the influence of a unitary fascist ideology.

A libertarian author David Ramsay Steele, who usually constructs arguments with meticulous care, takes a position in his article "The Mystery of Fascism" that mirrors the perspective of Republicans like D'Souza.[8] According to Steele, "most of the world's people in the second half of the twentieth century were ruled by governments which were closer in practice to Fascism than they were either to liberalism or to Marxist-Leninism." Yet, the fact that governments are neither liberal (in whatever sense Steele is employing that term) nor explicitly Marxist hardly proves they are "Fascist"—it just means they are neither "liberal" nor Marxist.[9] Nor does the fact that welfare state governments exist internationally mean they have the same aims as the fascist internationalism that some fascist theorists like Asvero Gravelli tried to launch in the early 1930s.

Welfare state or social democratic governments have developed around the world in response to a variety of factors. These include the growth of modern administrative states, the universal franchise, popular demand for social programs, and the simultaneous breakdown of older communal and familial arrangements, a trend that has been accelerated by the reach and socializing functions of modern welfare states. But there is nothing peculiarly fascistic about these developments, even if fascists, like other governing elites, tried to provide for social needs within a centralized administrative state. Because interwar Italy, England, the United States, and the Soviets all practiced some form of economic collectivism does not prove they were all politically the same or, even less plausibly, "fascist." An equally questionable attribution of fascism to one's enemies on the Left can be found in Dennis Prager's blanket statement: "if there is a real fascist threat to America, it comes from the left whose appetite for state power is essentially unlimited."[10] Were fascists the only past political actors who craved "state power"? If this were the case, all political leaders who displayed an appetite for unlimited power throughout history would have to be classified as fascists.

Equally questionable is the notion that governments become fascist when they reach a certain tipping point in their acquisition of power or in their appropriation of GNP from the private sector. Although we may agree that giving the state unlimited power is detrimental to freedom, this is not the same as saying that to do so is to become fascist. The postwar Labour government in England nationalized industries on a scale that went beyond anything that was tried in fascist Italy between 1922 and 1943. Between 1945 and 1951 the Labour government of Clement Attlee nationalized one-fifth of the British economy, yet this did not mean that England by 1951 had become more of a fascist state than Italy was in 1930.[11] In England, the growth of state power proceeded from leftist, egalitarian, and at least implicitly internationalist premises; in Fascist Italy, the state appealed to hierarchy and revolutionary nationalist principles as it claimed to speak for all Italians. Noting that difference entails not a value judgment but an attempt to draw distinctions between unlike entities.

One further example of the antifascism of the current conservative establishment is the anti-Putin editorializing of James Kirchick. This conservative controversialist, who has been featured in *The Washington Examiner,* *National Review*, and *The Weekly Standard,* has published numerous commentaries linking Vladimir Putin and his government to the Far Right.

One example that he cites is Putin's inflexible heteronormative bias, which prevents him from accommodating Russia's growing and now vocal LGBTQ community.[12] Despite Kirchick's stated concern about the unbounded growth of the Right in Europe, he denies Nazism is making a comeback in the United States, because Trump's election was due "at least partly to white racial resentment." He finds no evidence that Trump is a Nazi and assures us that "there is no mass fascist political movement in America."[13]

Kirchick does, however, acknowledge that Trump's style of rule has engendered an antifascist movement and angry reactions from his opponents. American intellectuals, he tells us, "rightly see Trump as a blight on the American polity." Yet Kirchick artfully evades this question: What would prevent the same forces that are now blasting the "Nazi" Trump from doing the same to other politicians who displeased them? To his credit, Kirchick does not pretend that fascism is a leftist disease. He is quite happy in his political commentary to locate it on the Right.

Current conservative journalists dealing with this subject typically associate fascism with the interwar European Right, even if they opportunistically claim to be finding it in the Democratic Party as well. By contrast, the small-government interwar American Right was not particularly sensitized to a fascist danger. This was the case even if we exclude from consideration the interwar Catholic Right in the United States, which like the interwar American Left was attracted, however selectively, to Mussolini's regime. Most of the establishment Right in the interwar period dismissed fascist ideas as European nonsense that we should simply stay away from. Fascism was not so much denounced as a contagious moral evil as regarded as a European New Deal on steroids. At most European fascism and even German Nazism furnished a warning of what the United States could become if the New Deal were to be expanded. Interwar opponents of the welfare state, such as J. T. Flynn, Alfred J. Nock, and Garet Garrett, viewed European fascists as the pathbreakers of what they dreaded as the coming American socialism. They hazarded the opinion that FDR's labor legislation looked like a US imitation of Mussolini's Carta del Lavoro of 1927.[14]

This analysis, although not very deep, was not entirely false. The interwar Right was describing the modern administrative state that came to increasingly control the economy and civic life in Western countries from the Progressive Era onward. But this political development proceeded in some places less dramatically than in others and occurred in different places under diverse auspices. An egalitarian, universalist version of the welfare state would differ significantly from a revolutionary nationalist one. It is these ideological and cultural distinctions that the interwar American Right (which in many ways embodied a classical liberal tradition) neglected to analyze sufficiently.

The older Right was driven both by a desire to hold onto a more traditional America and a revulsion for the half-truths or outright lies that were being spread to push the country into the "War to End All Wars." Albert J. Nock acquired fame as a controversialist in exposing how the United States was drawn into war against Imperial Germany. His *Myth of a Guilty Nation*, which was published in book form in 1922, had been published earlier as a series of articles in the magazine *The Freeman*.[15] These essays excoriated the government of Woodrow Wilson for embroiling the United States in a needless military adventure. Nock's articles also warned against taking sides in the postwar quarrels that resulted from the Treaty of Versailles. Clearly, fascism was not a burning issue for Nock who, when Mussolini took the island of Corfu in 1923, insisted that it was not really America's business who owned that island. By having helped bring about an unconditional victory for the Allied side, he also observed, the US government opened the door to all kinds of mischief. It had enabled French president Poincaré to carry out his geopolitical ambitions by "looting the Ruhr and setting up his Napoleonic scheme of military hegemony in Europe."[16] The war also "fortified a universal faith in violence." The proper response for the US government to what it had helped unloose would be, according to Nock, a "disinterested response," rather than new military entanglements.[17]

Nock, Flynn, and others who deplored US foreign adventures associated fascism with what displeased them about changes taking place in American society, particularly the vast expansion of state power and the waging of foreign wars. In contrast, the current conservative establishment has generally accepted the former and vigorously promoted the latter. It also has extended the f-word to "isolationists" and to those who try to cut back public administration beyond what GOP advisers find acceptable or expedient. The conservative movement may even exceed the Left in the recklessness of its antifascist condemnations; for example, when William Bennett attacked Pat Buchanan in 1995 for his immigration stand as someone who was "flirting with fascism."[18] In 2011, the neoconservative culture magazine *New Criterion*, moreover, went after the evil of "microfascism," applying it to women who claimed "the right to triumph over the natural consequences of their sexual behavior by removing the natural burden of their unwanted children."[19]

Unlike the PC Left, today's antifascist conservatives are not even able to situate fascism consistently on the political spectrum, because they have reduced fascism to an all-purpose insult. The term "fascist" does, however, assume a more specific historical meaning for the conservative movement's Zionist sponsors: for them it signifies a policy that is not viewed as being in Israel's interest. In this case "fascist" may be treated as synonymous with "anti-Semitic." The longtime crusade waged by media conservatives against "Islamofascism" makes sense as an attempt to accommodate Jewish patrons of the conservative media who are concerned with the anti-Israeli positions of Muslim and anti-Zionist journalists and militants. Conservative activist David Horowitz has combated fascism in its allegedly Islamic form by setting aside special weeks on college campuses to protest this recrudescence of an interwar evil.[20] Horowitz and others at his Freedom Center have linked Islamic anti-Zionism to Muslim units that served in the Waffen SS and equally to the Grand Mufti of Jerusalem, who during World War II was a guest of Hitler's in Berlin.

Unlike media conservatism, which unceremoniously manipulates the f-word, the conservatism that took shape after World War II often ignored fascism as a powerful historical force. George Nash's voluminous study, *The American Intellectual Conservative Movement since 1945* (which in its second edition reaches into the 1990s), includes no references to fascism and only three fleeting ones to Nazism in the course of describing political conversions during the period of the Nazi-Soviet Pact.[21] By contrast, much of his book is taken up with the subject of conservative anti-Communism and for good reason. Fighting Communism was as much a fixation for the American Right throughout the Cold War as exposing anti-Semitism is for Jewish civic organizations. Another reason for this apparent lack of interest in prewar fascism was the care that the conservative movement took in the 1950s and 1960s to distance itself from any fascist association. This became an urgent necessity during the presidential campaign of Barry Goldwater in 1964, when a strongly anti-Communist Republican candidate was routinely identified in the media and by celebrities like Martin Luther King as a Nazi. Although this was a totally unfounded charge, it did elicit among self-described

conservatives a fear of any contact with fascism, perhaps to the point of refusing to talk about an unpleasant subject.

The postwar conservative movement thus assumed a critique of fascism
but did not articulate it, at least not in isolation from its view of larger ideological currents. Its paradigm for understanding adversary forces is found
in *Origins of Totalitarianism,* a widely read work published after World War II
by the German émigré scholar Hannah Arendt (1906–1975). Like Arendt,
American conservatives assumed that the grimmest political and spiritual
problem in the modern West was totalitarianism, which was manifested in
both German Nazism and Soviet Communism, particularly in its Stalinist
phase. According to Arendt, certain peculiarly modern circumstances gave
rise to bullying, aggressive regimes that systematically degraded their subjects and featured a cult of the leader surrounded by "the party."[22] Arendt
examined this new terrifying regime from a secular historical perspective,
looking at such developments as the more and more sophisticated means for
controlling subjects available to modern centralized states, the dehumaniz-
ing effects of nineteenth-century colonialism, the carnage of World War I,
anti-Semitism as a unifying ideology, and an impersonal mass society.

Conservative intellectuals during the Cold War fused their analysis of a
totalitarian danger with detailed discussions of a spiritual crisis. An entire
field of metaphysical speculation flourished around the reasons why twentieth-century societies succumbed to totalitarian ideologies. Concepts like the
"second reality," "immanentizing the Eschaton," and the recurrent "gnostic
heresy" became subjects for detailed treatment in *National Review, Modern
Age,* and other conservative publications of the period. Perhaps most fundamental for elucidating the appeal of totalitarian movements, particularly
Communism, was the historical theorizing of Eric Voegelin (1901–1985), who
treated modern ideologies as a religious heresy rooted in the dualistic end-
times beliefs of the ancient Gnostics.

Although himself hardly a man of the Far Right and someone who seemed
far more traumatized by Nazism than Communism, Voegelin became perhaps the most revered historical thinker for the anti-Communist Right by
the 1960s. It may not have hurt Voegelin's reputation that, although far from
being an orthodox Christian and an explicit Neooplatonist, he was both sympathetic to the Catholic Church and openly hostile to Protestantism and the
Protestant Reformation.[23] His religious sympathies harmonized with a view

that was then prevalent on the American Right that the Catholic Church was a bulwark against Marxism. Voegelin's speculative work was particularly compelling for former Communist Frank Meyer, who later became a staunch anti-Communist. Like other recovered Communists of his age, Meyer took a step that Voegelin never did by joining the Catholic Church.[24]

### Why There Are Few Conservative Critiques of Fascism

Today's conservative celebrities go along with the Left's identification of fascism with prejudice and discrimination even if they also apply the branding iron to the Democratic Party. Two explanations may be considered for this shared perspective. One, the conservative establishment is too beleaguered or outgunned by media opposition to try to apply the fascist label in a truer historical sense. As in Rilke's aphorism, they may be signaling to us, "Wer spricht von Siegen? Überstehn ist alles!" (Who speaks of victories? Enduring is everything!). Two, established conservatives who enjoy a media presence may actually believe many of the same things about fascism as those on the Left: little separates the Left's and the conservatives' perceptions of fascism. Fascists as seen through the lenses of both conservative media and their more leftist media associates—are white racists, anti-Semites, and others who should exist outside of acceptable political discourse. Establishment conservatives have worked to exclude these undesirables from polite conversation, although some media conservatives—for example, Ben Shapiro—have held back from calling for "de-platforming" them. In the face of Antifa demonstrations, American conservatives have evidenced little will to resist. Indeed, the Federalist Society's New York correspondent David Marcus has charged his fellow conservatives with abetting the statue-smashing, vandalizing Left by rushing to accommodate its demands. Marcus's thoughts are up front in the title of his 2020 newspaper opinion piece, "Conservative Cowards Are to Blame for Falling Statues."[25]

In any case, one searches in vain among current American conservative celebrities for a systematic understanding of how fascism develops other than as a malign force that is attributed to prejudice or else, more opportunistically, to one's Democratic opponents. This superficiality stands in contrast to how interwar Marxists examined fascism in a socioeconomic context. It is also markedly different from how historians like Ernst Nolte and Stanley

Payne situate fascist movements within the framework of interwar European struggles or distinguish between fascism and other movements of the Right. A far-ranging literature on fascism by serious scholars already exists, but its impact on our political class and journalists has yet to be seen. A conclusion to which we are therefore drawn is that American conservatism, even in its earlier and more cerebral stage, has never considered fascism very deeply. It has either seized on that term as a cudgel with which to beat its opposition or else absorbed whatever definition was then prevalent on the center Left. The rise of media conservatism has just added vulgarity and opportunism to this problem of neglect.

Can we speak, however, of a distinctively "conservative antifascism"? We can do so if we limit our examples to two cases: libertarian critics of fascist statism and European traditionalists. Neither group is simply imitating the Left's conception of fascism and throwing it back at the other side. Both consider fascism to be an essentially leftist movement and build arguments around that contention. One noteworthy illustration is the Irish libertarian philosopher Gerald Casey, who authored a thousand-page work *Freedom's Progress? A History of Political Thought*.[26] Casey emphatically rejects the argument that fascism was a movement of the Right, by which is meant the interwar revolutionary Right. He maintains that some historians pay too much attention to fascism's exaltation of hierarchy and particularity to the neglect of its war against liberty. Casey emphasizes fascism's call for a collectivized economy, which he associates with the socialist Left. Everything else about Italian fascism was subordinate to its statism and economic collectivism, which were evidence of its origin on the Left.

Much of this critical discussion of fascism from a free-market liberal perspective is not entirely new and reprises arguments developed by the Austrian economist Ludwig von Mises in the 1930s. What may distinguish recent criticism of fascism from a European liberal (or old liberal) position of the type represented by Mises is the treatment of fascism as distinctly leftist by virtue of its collectivist character. Whereas Mises and others of his generation treated the conflict between themselves and collectivist ideologies as one between liberalism and illiberalism, more recent criticisms from a libertarian or small-government perspective treat fascism as a movement of the Left, similar in nature to socialism and Communism. Casey and others who criticize fascism as a leftist movement from a libertarian perspective are standing in this newer interpretive tradition.

The European traditionalist and monarchist, Erik von Kuehnelt-Leddhin (1909–1990), famously places the Nazis in a line of descent issuing from the French Revolution. An Austrian aristocrat who was profoundly critical of late modernity, Kuehnelt-Leddhin presents both Hitler and the Communists as the offspring of Robespierre and the French Jacobins.[27] He documents his contention with a wealth of evidence, starting from the premise that, since the early twentieth century, most changes in regimes, particularly revolutionary ones, have come from the Left. This is not a perspective that will likely resonate in our late-modern society. Kuehnelt-Leddhin's critique is less about fascism than about political change that occurred outside of what the writer considered the gold age that prevailed before World War I. A Hapsburg loyalist, he felt little sympathy for the politics of the century in which he happened to live.

Another example of an antifascism that we might locate loosely on the Right came from predominantly Catholic critics of German Nazism. This group included Jewish converts Hermann Broch, Alfred Döblin, and Waldemar Gurian, as well as a former Nazi sympathizer Heimito von Doderer.[28] The novelist Franz Werfel never formally converted but was strongly attracted to the Catholic Church, and he too may be grouped together with the Germanophone, mostly Austrian Catholic anti-Nazis who lived during Hitler's coming to power. Common to this group, which consisted mostly of distinguished Austro-German literary figures (Gurian who was a Russian Jewish émigré and a political theorist may be regarded as an exception), was the view of the Catholic Church as a counterforce to a dangerous neopagan age. A similar resistance to Nazi ideas from professing Christians took form among Protestants, although their resistance depended more heavily on individual conscience than on any ecclesiastical institution as a bulwark against Nazi ideology.

Despite the great courage of these anti-Nazi Christians, whose resistance sometimes cost them their lives, it is hard to speak here of a well-developed theoretical critique of fascism. Rather we are referring to noble resistance to a particularly vicious modern form of tyranny and about the aid and comfort that these figures found in traditional Catholic or Protestant Christianity. Their critical ideas about modernity were very much evident among later exponents of conservative anti-Communism. Warnings against neopagan and ideologically crazed Nazi totalitarianism were later typically adapted to the struggle against atheistic Communism. The Left also benefited, in a strange way, from the Christian anti-Nazism of an earlier period. Some of the Protestant opponents of the Nazi "state religion," like Karl Barth and Ernst Niekisch, passionately defended Communist regimes in Eastern Europe as an antidote to anti-Christian fascism.

None of these stances, however, represents a methodical assessment of a fascist enemy, in the same way that Karl Kautsky or Ludwig von Mises analyzed the Nazi dictatorship. Broch and von Doderer placed Nazism within a very wide historical and cultural framework, which for them was late modernity. They focused on the Nazi era as exemplifying spiritual problems they believed would continue to plague modern Western societies after the Nazis had vanished. Their views about Nazism led Boissbeyond the tyranny they examined. It is therefore problematic to treat their observations about the Nazis as being at the heart of their critical work.

Interestingly, Heimito von Doderer's epic novel *Die Dämonen*, which is set in Vienna in 1926 and 1927, is often seen as throwing light on how Nazism seduced the socially and morally confused Viennese. Von Doderer's subjects are depicted as inhabiting "a second reality and dreaming of "changing the general situation because of their personal position." But one should not read too much into this gargantuan novel about the specific temptations of Nazism. Von Doderer (1896–1966) began writing *Die Dämonen* in 1931, continued writing it while he served as a Nazi Party member and later as a devout Catholic, and finally finished it in the 1950s.[29] It was later quoted to illustrate how modern people were drawn into totalitarian movements, especially by Eric Voegelin and his disciple Gerhart Niemeyer.[30] Finally, the anti-Nazi Catholics and Protestants to whom reference has been made tell us little about the contemporary Right's treatment of fascism. There is little or no linkage between the two.

## Discussing the Dearth of Critical Thinking about Fascism One Last Time

We might pose then one last time the speculative question that has wound its way through this chapter: Why has there been so little systematic critical thought from the Right about fascism as an historical problem? Let us engage this question by summarizing this chapter's findings. The interwar American Right was mostly concerned with keeping the United States out of foreign wars and limiting the growth of a centralized state. Its representatives had less interest in foreign political movements than they did in events closer to home. They lamented in European fascism what they thought was an advanced form of the growing "warfare-welfare state" that they were combating at home.

The post–World War II American conservative movement focused more on containing Soviet and world Communism than it did on a fascist danger in the past. Yet, with due respect to its leftist critics, this movement was never profascist or even soft on fascism. Rather its adherents were less eager to fight what they regarded as an interwar peril than they were in resisting Communist expansion. If this movement offered any critical response to fascism or Nazism, it came mostly through studies of totalitarianism like Hannah Arendt's analysis and Eric Voegelin's examination of modernity. The conservative movement that came along later and that is now mostly a media phenomenon had a strong leftist imprint. It stemmed from the moderate Left of the 1980s, when the neoconservatives ascended to a position of dominance in the establishment Right. When the present conservative movement speaks about fascism, it does so in phrases that originated on the antifascist Left. What renders this "conservative" antifascism different from its leftist model, however, is the use that it makes of charges of fascism. It turns an essentially leftist antifascism against the Democratic Party, while occasionally linking fascism to a more advanced form of the welfare state than the one the Republicans defend.

The more authentic Right—that in contemporary Europe—has not constructed a systematic critique of fascism for other reasons. The contemporary European Right is populist and views itself as having arisen in a postfascist epoch. One might be tempted to dismiss this stated lack of interest in critically examining fascism as a cover-up for the practice of taking fascist-like positions. According to their enemies, European right-wingers are trying to conceal the telltale origin of their politics, which is mired in the fascist past. What better way to do this than by pretending that fascism is now gone? One might strengthen this indictment by noting that the New Right in France, Italy, Spain, and elsewhere in Europe devoted magazine issues in the past to exonerating those associated with fascism and accused Nazi collaborators. It would therefore be inaccurate to state that there is absolutely no connection between any European postwar Right and earlier fascist associations.[31]

The contemporary populist Right, however, only reveals such antecedents in a very limited way. The view propounded by Salvini when he announced that "il fascismo è un idea morta" (fascism is a dead idea) is an eminently defensible position.[32] It may indeed be the case that the political reference points that marked interwar Europe are no longer relevant. The "post-fascist" party that followed the MSI as the Alleanza Nazionale in 1995 turned eventually into a run-of-the-mill center-right party,[33] when Fini became president of the Italian Chamber of Deputies in 2008. Giorgio Almirante did organize a neofascist party, the Movimento Sociale Italiano (MSI), in 1946, but by the time this protean party morphed into Gianfranco Fini's Futuro e Libertà per l'Italia in 2010, there was little left of its original substance. Those who keep looking for the fascist elements in Salvini's style, as French commentator Élisabeth Lévy has observed, are often "the orphans of Marxism in search of a substitute faith contributing significantly to the victory of globalist neoliberalism."[34] It may also be the case that antifascist polemicists have vested interests in selectively adapting memories, because they have built careers around charging their opponents with being fascists.

In any case, what authorizes the antifascist Left to decide at what point fascism as a movement or mentality should come to an end? Are we supposed to believe that what Ernst Nolte called "the European civil war" of the 1930s goes on forever or at least until that moment when the antifascist Left decides to throw away the f-word? In a review of the movie *Dunkirk* for the *New York Times*, Manohla Dargas reminds us that "the fight against fascism continues."[35]

Populists in France and Italy also insist in a more questionable way that "Right and Left no longer exist," just like "fascism and Communism." In other words, Right and Left as they operated as reference points in the 1930s are no longer relevant.[36] The confrontation between contending sides has changed, and the insurgents on the Right now present themselves as still identifiably cohesive nations battling a globalist capitalist class that has occupied vital institutions. A key point for European populists is that nations are not just "populations" but possess a "qualitative and not only quantitative character that took sometimes thousands of years to acquire."[37] Those engaged in this struggle to preserve historical identities belong to the Right, inasmuch as they appeal to a national past, organic relations, and a principle of identity beyond the self-determining individual. But these populists have roots equally on the traditional Left. They invoke working-class solidarity and oppose global corporate capitalism. They also cultivate a blue-collar identity, even if that image does not always correspond to demographic reality.

Although Latin fascists and Nazis also attempted to attract a working-class base, today's populists depend on that base much more heavily and, unlike the fascists, are not fighting interwar Marxism. Their enemies are corporate capitalism, Third World immigration, intersectional politics, and, at least in Europe, globalization as represented by US political and cultural control. Most continental European populist movements have absorbed leftist elements, including occasionally Marxist rhetoric. Although fascism once incorporated some of the same elements, the resulting mixture looked quite different. Fascist or fascistoid movements in Central and Eastern Europe often expressed such unpleasant traits as ferocious anti-Semitism and bellicosity, both of which seem to be absent from contemporary populism. The populists are therefore justified in wishing to turn the page while treating both fascism and Communism as movements of the past. It is not they but the other side that has a deep investment, and not always for high-minded reasons, in structuring public discourse around the f-word. Those on the populist Right, who wish to treat both fascism and Communism as movements of the past, may be urging the more sensible and better-grounded course.

A preoccupation with antifascism characterizes the political Left far more than it does the political Right. Although it may be possible to find genuine conservatives and religious traditionalists critically analyzing fascism, this activity has been far more common on the Left than the Right. Moreover, most of the conservative critics of fascism were more disturbed by Nazism than generic fascism, viewing the latter as a passing disruption. A typical response of the European Right to Mussolini's authoritarian regime in the interwar period was to regard it as a means of controlling leftist violence or else as a temporary interruption in the process of governing certain countries. Nazism, by contrast, aroused stronger opposition from traditional European liberals and conservatives. The view expressed by the conservative Lutheran and disillusioned former Nazi sympathizer, Hermann Rauschning (1887–1982), that the Nazis were carrying out a "revolution of nihilism" was widespread among self-described conservatives during and after Hitler's rise to power.[38]

The American Right, or what has been conventionally designated as such, has reacted differently to fascism at different times. In the interwar period, the fascist movement did not arouse sustained interest among US critics of the New Deal, who wanted to stay out of foreign war. Fascists in power provided mostly a cautionary tale for the isolationist, anti-New Deal Right about where government overreach in the United States might lead. The best way to fight fascism at home, it was contended, was to convince Americans to rein in their own corporate state and command economy. For these opponents of expanding government, fascism was just one among other forms of "statism" whose leaders happened to speak Italian or German.

In the post–World War II period, the discussion of a threatened freedom by those on the American Right produced critiques of totalitarianism rather than fascism. Both Nazism and Communism posed threats to liberty and Western civilization, but after the defeat of the Third Reich, the remaining totalitarian danger was thought to issue from the Soviet Empire and the spread of Communist ideology. For today's conservative fraternity, antifascism works as an attack strategy for countering the opposing party, and it functions by reprising mostly leftist descriptions of fascism. One should not read too much into what has become predictable, ritualized partisanship. Among the European populist Right a distancing from fascism has become essential for survival. The populists have been targeted throughout Western Europe as the successors of interwar fascists, and it is natural they should be working to dissociate themselves from this charge. They therefore insist that they are not ignoring fascism but are treating it as an "object of study" that has reference to an earlier period. This obvious division between antifascists and populists may be the most critical one for studying current ideological polarities. All other political struggles in the Western world have become secondary.

Chapter 7

# THE ANTIFASCIST STATE

We begin this chapter by tracing how the antifascist regime evolved and what distinguishes it from other forms of government. Although antifascist regimes rarely describe themselves as such, the post–World War II German government came close to taking this step when it defined itself in its Basic Law as a "militant democracy" (*Streitbare Demokratie*).[1] When the term "antifascist" is applied to a regime, what is being designated is a political society that consciously acts in relation to a transformative design. Aristotle famously argued in the first book of the *Politics* that the polis was the model toward which the Greeks tend to move as a people because of their ethnic and cultural characteristics. Supposedly only the Greeks were able to achieve this ideal of governing themselves as citizens.[2] Aristotle was indicating a path the Greeks would likely have taken without social planners forcing them to act against their nature (*para phusin*).

The English political theorist Michael Oakeshott contrasted governments that operate according to legal procedure to their pernicious, goal-driven opposite. The antithesis of nomocracy, according to Oakeshott, is "telocracy," which treats government as a means toward realizing a collective visionary end. Oakeshott also describes telocratic collectivists as "rationalists," because they believe that human beings can be shaped according to their designs, without regard for personal freedom. According to his exponent Timothy Fuller, Oakeshott aims his criticism at those who "insist on ideologies or technocratic schemes of social engineering to guide the decisions of political life, overriding the practical sense of affairs to be found in experienced politicians."[3]

Although it would be difficult to imagine this distinction fully operating outside of Oakeshott's classical liberal frame of reference, and although one might wonder who these experienced politicians are who are immune to social engineers, it should be apparent that some states are more deeply motivated by ideology than other ones. The modern liberal democratic form of government has an aim at least partly determined by what it does not want to be. Just as the Greeks, according to Aristotle, sought to avoid the snares of Persian despotism and just as the Hebrews were told by the God of the Old Testament not to be like the Egyptians, so too are liberal democratic citizens exhorted not to be fascists. Modern democracies are to be constantly on guard against fascism, and their perhaps unnamed telos is to combat this danger, partly by seeking to act and think in a way that clearly distinguishes democracy from what it opposes. Although the average citizen may not always grasp this telos, social engineers in and outside the media do.

The exercise of state power as a means of combating a presumed fascist danger goes back to the 1930s United States. Fighting against an external fascist and Nazi threat required an expanded use of governmental power. Internally, means were taken at that time to suppress domestic forces that were viewed as allied to foreign fascist enemies; politically promoted indoctrination occurred, especially in the Anglo-American world, to protect the antifascist side mentally and morally against contamination by its adversary. A harbinger of things to come in the United States was provided by a widely read essay by Columbia University professor Karl Loewenstein in 1937, "Militant Democracy and Fundamental Rights, II." Here Loewenstein calls for a government that dedicates itself with total commitment to fighting democracy's greatest enemy: "In order definitely to overcome the danger of Europe's going wholly fascist, it would be necessary to remove the causes, that is, to change the mental structure of this age of the masses and of rationalized emotion. . . . Emotional government in one form or another must have its way until mastered by new psycho-technical methods which regularize the fluctuations between rationalism and mysticism."[4]

One can easily locate in Loewenstein's writing the blueprint that others would follow in mounting crusades against fascist sentiments. This crusade would include and be inspired by educator-philosopher John Dewey and his followers and then, in an even more significant way, by the fathers of the Frankfurt School, particularly those theorists who moved to the United States, leaving their disciples behind. These figures, as well as social psychologists and public administrators who were influenced by them, helped create here and in countries that followed in our footsteps a form of democratic government characterized by extensive social engineering. Although fascism has not been the only evil that therapeutic government has battled against, implicit in the war against prejudice and discrimination has been a continuing concern with its resurgence. During the Cold War, attention was called to a "red fascist" danger, which combined Soviet features with stereotypes that date back to the struggle against Nazism. American leftists complained with some justification that the government and anti-Communist politicians and journalists could not bring up the Soviets without comparing their government to the Third Reich. This may have been due not so much to anti-Communist hysteria as it was to the image of fascism or Hitler as the ever-present, ultimate evil. As soon as the Soviet Union collapsed, American culture and educational elites went back to older preoccupations with a fascist peril. By the early 1990s antifascism had become an ideological pillar of the Western-style democratic administrative regime. With fascism designated as the ultimate foe, Western governments continued to implement social and educational measures to combat what Jason Stanley calls "performative fascism."[5]

A certain time perspective may be useful for understanding this history. Democratic administrative regimes did not come into existence to fight fascism, particularly those formed before the twentieth century. Older forms of governments were not concerned with fighting discrimination and least of all with ensuring equality of esteem among subjects or citizens. Constitutional republics and monarchies in the past treated moral attitudes and family relations in civil society as lying outside their purview—that is, unless those arrangements threatened the state's authority.

The fact that we are speaking here about the modern state as a welfare state tells us little about what kind of welfare state now prevails in the Western world, because past welfare state regimes served a wide range of ideologies:

nationalist, fascist, Christian, and so on. The modern welfare state, to the extent it has a distinctive character, speaks for humankind and engages in an ongoing struggle against national particularity and traditional forms of social discrimination. It follows this course at least partly to avoid being "fascist." Although the political model under consideration is a subgenus of the Left, it is not directly derived from Marxism or Communism. It is leftist because of its egalitarian, globalist vision and because, especially in Europe, it targets fascism as a rightist enemy. Although this kind of regime seeks to expand its economic control, it is also working steadily toward cultural and social transformation. In their concern with psychic reconditioning, those who shape our political culture resemble Frankfurt School intellectuals. Although critical theorists were economic Marxists, they saw fascism as the source of the prejudices they identified and were primarily concerned with fighting it.

Not all antifascists are dedicated to socialism or Marxism. Today's progressives have formed alliances with large corporations, and antifascists have readily participated in building a global economy based on interlocking capitalist enterprises.[6] There is, of course, an anti-globalist wing of the antifascist Left, found in the Occupy Wall Street demonstrations and in European anti-globalization protests have been going on among antifascists for decades. But this manifestation of anti-globalism is mostly limited to the economic sphere.

Jason Stanley reminds us that nationalism (read Western nationalism) is "at the core of fascism." Fascist ideology stresses "group identity," which "can be variously based—on skin color, on religion, on tradition, on ethnic origin." That hardly leaves much space for the survival of particularities, at least not in Western countries.[7]

An interesting attempt to combine anti-globalist socialism with the total globalization of the West can be found in *Empire*, a best-selling work by Italian Marxist (and co-organizer of the Red Brigade), Antonio Negri, and Duke University English professor Michael Hardt. The authors of this work foresee a happy future in which Third World populations swallow up a capitalist, imperialist West and manage to repopulate it. Once this happens, Third World socialists will be given the opportunity to reorganize Western economies for the benefit of the formerly exploited.[8] They will also be able to enrich the West with their own values and habits.

In August 2019 the French and German centrist governments of Macron and Merkel pulled out all the stops to unseat Salvini's anti-immigration coalition.[9] The French and German heads of state then tried to induce by means of generous loans the successor government to Salvini to accept African migrants. Although these efforts had definite economic implications, they were not intended to advance Marxist socialism or abolish corporate capitalism. (And corporate capitalists have stood behind these immigration policies from which they profit.) The French and German leaders undertook these actions, because among other reasons, the elites themselves are dedicated to a transformational social vision. When former British prime minister Tony Blair stated that he exaggerated the economic benefits of his immigration policy because he was a cosmopolitan idealist, the Western media and his former colleagues were not at all troubled by this revelation.[10]

Whether antifascists are corporate capitalists or socialist protesters, they have a closely related cultural agenda for the transformation of Western countries. Their common denominator is less socialism than the cultural reconstruction of Western societies for the purpose of fighting fascism. This is very different from the efforts of earlier leftists to restrict immigration to protect indigenous workforces and, when expedient, to appeal to national particularities.

## The Fascist State: A Study in Contrasts

Given that those with antifascist politics fear that a new fascist state will arise, we should speculate about what antifascists would have found particularly terrible about actual self-described fascist governments. The generic fascist state as represented by the interwar Italian regime and by those outside of Italy who tried to adapt its ideas glorified the state as a living organism. The German Jewish philosopher Ernst Cassirer applied the term "statolatry" to characterize regimes that teach veneration of the state; he certainly had in mind Italian fascism when he coined that usage.[11] Further, his term would have applied to Italian fascism far more than to the German Nazi regime. The latter was too violent and murderous to fit easily into the revolutionary nationalist model of fascism constructed by such scholars as Stanley Payne and Renzo De Felice. Carl Schmitt was undoubtedly right when in 1934 he pointed out that, in contrast to the Italian fascist glorification of the state, the Nazi regime prioritized the "Volk" in its new order.[12] But given the nature of the Nazi dictatorship, even the "Volk," or whatever the Nazis defined as such, would become cannon fodder in Hitler's wars of conquest and domestic bloodbaths.

Renzo De Felice in his last work on Italian fascism, which was published posthumously, focuses on Mussolini's "fascistization of the state (*fascistizzazione dello stato*), which was undertaken between 1925 and 1929.[13] *Il Duce* reduced the party to a position of "secondary importance" and finally hollowed it out, viewing it as a collection of squabbling factions that had to be sacrificed on the altar of a fascist state. A hierarchical, revolutionary nationalist instrument of rule would become his work, and it would be maintained by functionaries who were loyal to their political head. A "myth of the leader" would be fashioned and propagated to allow Mussolini to operate in a" free zone" while delegating specific tasks to prefects who would carry out his will, if necessary, against the Party.[14] This subordination of the "one party" in what became by stages a one-party state to the revolutionary regime clearly distinguished fascist Italy from Nazi Germany or Soviet Russia.

A lucid and learned discussion of the fascist conception of the state can be found in the entry on fascism in the 1931 edition of the *Encyclopedia of the Social Sciences* by the German scholar Erwin von Beckerath. Four years earlier Beckerath had published a longer treatment of the same subject in *Das Wesen und Werden des faschistischen Staates* (Nature and Becoming of the Fascist State), which has been periodically reissued and which still stands as a model of dispassionate scholarship on a controversial subject.[15] Beckerath spent considerable time in fascist Italy and knew many of its political leaders, although he was an old-fashioned European liberal, who became a close friend of the post–World War II German chancellor Ludwig Erhard. In his encyclopedia entry, Beckerath describes fascism as follows:

> The idea of the sovereignty of the state is the very kernel of Fascist political and social theory. The contrast with the French Revolution as well as with the pluralistic conception of the state is apparent here. . . . Although group associations between the state and the individual are recognized in the order created by the fascist national revolution, they are to be strictly subordinated to the interests of the state. This conception leaves no room for the notion or practice of class struggle, even if fascism was less emphatic in its insistence on the solidarity of capital and labor in the production process over and above their antagonism in the division of the social product.[16]

Beckerath dwells on the way in which the Fascist Party transformed the Italian state "by cutting through the horizontal layers of society, which with the aid of the arbitrary state government holds it together like a clamp." He considers the elaborately developed structure of state authority created by the architects of the fascist order. "Concentrations of authority and hierarchy of membership imply that all the reins of party activity come together eventually in the hands of Mussolini. All nominations are traceable directly or indirectly to him and throughout the varied ramifications of the party machine, the will of the leaders as a general rule prevails over the component organs."[17] In addition to providing command positions for party leaders, the revolutionary order enacted by Mussolini and his cohorts was hierarchical and corporative. National confederations and federations were created that reached through ascending levels of control all the way up to *Il Duce*. These corporate bodies also drew up lists of candidates for the Chamber of Deputies, which disseminated party teachings and directives. At the top of the legislative hierarchy and directly under Mussolini loomed the Fascist Grand Council, which advised him and drafted legislation, such as the Work Charter (Carta del Lavoro), which set up the Italian corporatist economy in 1926.[18]

Despite its elitist, anti-individualist character, the fascist state nonetheless had links to the French Revolution and the Italian Risorgimento.[19] It drew on the Latin nationalist aspects of both but emphasized the statist precondition for the achievement of Italian national unity and national expansion and pushed this emphasis in an explicitly authoritarian direction. Giovanni Gentile, the most distinguished theorist of the fascist movement, highlighted its revolutionary and nationalist origin. Gentile looked back to the democratic advocates of Italian unification in the nineteenth century, Giuseppe Maria Garibaldi (1807–1882) and Giuseppe Mazzini (1805–1872), in finding progenitors for his movement.

Even earlier, it was the French Revolution that helped produce a modern French administrative state that other national movements would come to incorporate. In later fascist efforts at building a party state, one might recognize an updating of the *état postiche*, the concept of double governance that originated with the French Revolution. The revolutionary reorganization of France's administration attempted to impose a new, artificial state on top of an older one. In France, this move was prefigured by the centralizing initiatives that came from pre-revolutionary monarchs. In the order established by the Revolution the ancient provinces were divided into *départements*, which were placed under the authority of *préfets* subject to the central government in Paris. In any case, the party state devised by the Italian fascists bore a noticeable resemblance to the French revolutionary model, even if party functionaries were substituted in the newer form for revolutionary administrators. Thus, although Beckerath emphasized the elitist and neo-medieval elements in Italian fascism, which were certainly present in its genealogy, it is nonetheless possible to trace fascism's development from earlier forms of European nationalism.

Essential to nineteenth-century nationalist movements was the quest for an independent state, which would become the protector of national identity. In the interwar period, Zev Jabotinsky, the Revisionist Zionist who wished to create a Jewish state on both sides of the Jordan, insisted that a powerful state (*memlachti*) was foundational for the resurrection of the Jewish people.[20] An Eastern European, Jabotinsky was expressing the sentiment of other nationalists in his region, like Josef Pilsudski and Roman Dmowski in Poland.[21] Not surprisingly Jabotinsky and other nonsocialist Zionists venerated Mussolini and regarded Italian fascism as a model for his own nationalist enterprise—until *Il Duce*'s defection to Nazi Germany and his partial accommodation of Hitler's anti-Semitic policies.

Nationalism and statism have often marched together, but as Beckerath observes, it was the centrality ascribed to the state in Latin fascism that set it apart from earlier attempts to fuse political power with national identity. We might also ask whether Italian fascism included a wholesale rejection of the "liberal nationalism" of the nineteenth century. More likely, fascism incorporated, without appropriate acknowledgment, some aspects of an older bourgeois nationalism while ostentatiously throwing out others. The fascist movement and later the fascist state stressed nationalist and irredentist themes while relying on broad support from the Italian middle class.[22] This does not mean that Italian nationalism was predestined to move in a fascist direction, but it does suggest that the contention that fascism was the opposite of liberal nationalism is not entirely true.

Fascism also exhibited traits that are also found in antifascist politics. Both have been post-liberal and have abandoned such nineteenth-century bourgeois values and attitudes as strict adherence to constitutional principles, academic and intellectual freedom, and a separation between political administration and the institutions of civil society. Both fascists and antifascists have displayed an ambiguous, not entirely consistent attitude toward a collectivist economy and vacillate between support for corporate capitalist interests and calls for state control of the economy. Both have likewise maintained a cynical and often hostile relationship to long-standing Christian institutions. Each has drawn on a Christian legacy, when necessary, to justify their positions, but has otherwise sought to marginalize what each has regarded as a cumbersome remnant of the past. The antifascist Left has scorned traditional Christian institutions, while the Italian fascist government, even after the Lateran Accords were concluded in 1929, remained on a collision course with the Catholic Church. The bullying of Catholic youth and other organizations by the fascist authorities in the early 1930s indicated the unwillingness of Mussolini's government to allow the Catholic clergy to form a "state within a state."

More significant than these intersecting points, however, are the critical differences between the fascists and antifascists. Whereas the fascists built their base on a bourgeois foundation, however misleadingly they denounced liberal institutions, the present antifascism has a post-bourgeois and post-liberal character. It offers a counter-morality to traditional bourgeois Christian ethics and advocates for feminism, Third World immigration, and LGBTQ causes. The issue here is not whether these intersectional positions are defensible, but the wide gulf between them and what the Western bourgeoisie believed about the social good up until recently.

One should be careful not to exaggerate the similarities between those financial interests that rallied to fascism and those that now align with self-described antifascist groups. Although in both cases, large corporate interests are financing movements calling for change, the political-cultural attitudes motivating the two groups are clearly not the same. The General Confederation of Italian Industries (*Confindustria*), which in the interwar years cooperated with the Italian fascist regime, was not exactly an ingathering of cultural radicals. It was anti-Communist and explicitly Italian nationalist, and it held the traditional social views of the age. Whatever might be said of the executive boards of Citibank, Coca Cola, and other large American corporations, it is foolish to equate groups from different eras that seem similar in terms of relative wealth and degrees of economic dominance without considering the critical cultural differences between them.

Perhaps a more significant criterion for distinguishing between fascist and antifascist political projects is where their advocates have stood on the ideological spectrum. Whereas the intersectional, pro-immigration antifascists belong to the Left, interwar fascists revealed what were unmistakably right-wing characteristics. Generic fascism epitomized and in fact came to define a *revolutionary* Right. It was proudly elitist, mocked the aspiration toward universal equality, and exalted the particularistic, which it identified with its own nation.[23] When the Italian fascist government took sides in the Spanish Civil War in 1936, it sent troops to fight with the Nationalists, not the Left. This does not mean that the fascists, in their Italian or Spanish Falange manifestation, did not have a socialist wing or did not call periodically for making capitalists serve the interests of the nation. But such positions were hardly incompatible with the interwar Right, which was generally critical of both capitalism and individualism.

It may be helpful to look at fascism situationally to understand what made it a movement of the Right. Perhaps most significantly it opposed those principles that are inherent in the Left, and as a more traditional Right began to lose importance with the decline of an aristocratic society, fascism became an improvised replacement. We should further consider the historical situation in which fascists found themselves and to which they were responding. Fascism prospered as a movement in what were economically Second World countries. Most of Italy's industrial growth occurred after World War II, not on Mussolini's watch.[24] *Il Duce*'s base of support was drawn largely from the traditional bourgeoisie, which rallied to organic nationalism as an alternative to leftist revolutionary threats. The fascist movement also provided a sense of cultural cohesion and a positive view of the Italian past, linked to a public appreciation of the glories of the Roman Empire. Its derivation from a Latin Catholic culture also played a role in its appeal. The theory of a corporate economy that the fascists featured had its roots in neo-medieval and even older scholastic sources.

Fascism's incompatibility with the Anglo-American neoliberal conception of the Right tells us little about where it belongs ideologically. As an instantiation of the essentialist Right, fascism does not have to fit into an electoral spectrum that pertains to a later time and place.[25] One might even argue that given the social changes that have occurred in Western societies in the last fifty years, our present "center Right" seems peculiar to late-modern politics. Its practitioners and advocates generally accept most of what the social Left has accomplished since the 1960s while being eager to defend corporate capitalism and what they interpret as "human rights." The present center Right is also committed to military intervention against "antidemocratic" countries and occasionally interferes in Western countries that are thought to have moved too far away from our liberal democratic template. It is hard to see how the conservatism that developed in the post-World War II-Anglosphere corresponds to what was considered the Right in interwar Europe.

The only perspective that may reveal shared interests is a Marxist one that treats both the continental European and Anglo-American "Rights" within the context of an advanced capitalist economy. The coming together of Right and Left predicted by Christopher Lasch and other scholars decades ago may indeed have occurred, although consumer capitalism may not be the main glue, as Lasch contended, that holds this front together.[26] Although today's antifascists are not unambiguously Marxist, in other ways they remain leftists. They are waging a war for equality against particularity, in any traditional Western sense. The coercion and suppression that will be required in the meantime to reach this goal may be compared to the dictatorship of the vanguard of the proletariat that was supposedly needed to achieve Marx's socialist vision.[27]

In certain respects, the intersectional Left and its antifascism are far more radical than any Marxist Left that preceded it. Unlike a merely socialist Left, which seeks to change the dominant form of production and to redistribute earnings under a powerful state, the newer Left is bent on revolution. It can never allow the crusade against fascist prejudice to come to a halt, lest this stasis permit a Hitler, Mussolini, or Donald Trump to reverse earlier reforms. It is also immoral and equally an invitation to fascism from this standpoint to treat any present moment as fixed and no longer subject to progressive transformation. Trump in the United States and the AfD in Germany were considered evil not because they wished to take us back to some distant past but because they refused to carry the cultural revolution forward. Both were stuck in the Western world as it existed twenty or thirty years ago, Trump somewhere at the beginning of the present century when the Democrats still favored large border walls and sending back illegal immigrants, and Alexander Gauland, Nicholas Fest, and other former CDU pillars who have resisted the movement of their party toward the multicultural Left.

Although interwar fascism is no longer a real adversary for the antifascist Left, it nonetheless stands for what antifascists are seeking to transform. Antifascists insist they are resisting fascism in the name of "human rights" when they oppose the populist Right. This war for "tolerance" and humanity has also attracted considerable support from would-be moderates and upholders of the political status quo in Western countries. Recently deceased former French president Jacques Chirac worked energetically to separate his right-center Rassemblement pour la République (RPR) party from the National Front.[28] During Chirac's presidential race in 2012, he loudly proclaimed his support for the culturally and socially leftist establishmentarian candidate Francois Hollande against the Front's candidate, Marine Le Pen. In Germany, the enemy on the "Far Right" remains the only major political enemy. Germany's centrist Christian Democrats would be ready to form a coalition with any party on the Left but condemns the AfD, which is now the country's only significant right-of-center party, as fascistic. In both cases the ruling center has accepted the rules provided by antifascist activists about acceptable political associates and discourse.

## The Moralization of the Political

A key distinction between the fascist and antifascist concepts of the state is their differing ethical goals. No evidence justifies the belief that the Left is morally relativistic. (Being hateful toward the unconverted is another matter.) The antifascist Left is as morally driven as any past revolutionary cause dedicated to reconstructing humankind. The fact that its morality often contradicts traditional morality hardly proves that antifascists lack moral convictions. The aim of bringing down what is seen as a fascist order replete with gross inequalities is profoundly moral in its intent. It may be the case that Antifa engages in nihilistic violence, but what lies behind the rioting is moral anger and not the belief that all cultures are equal.

This view clashes with a core belief held by American conservatives in the middle of the twentieth century that "relativism" was an essential characteristic of the Left. The political theorist and former Yale professor Willmoore Kendall (1909–1967), who taught William F. Buckley, was the best-known exponent of this position. According to an admirer Tom Woodlief writing in *The American Conservative*, this "outcast Yale professor predicted 2020 better than his erstwhile colleagues." Kendall had warned against "the suicidal pact with relativism," which is allegedly what is now driving the antifascist Left. "Not speech that calls for dismantling the society's institutional foundations or moral presuppositions, nor even speech that calls for spilling blood in the streets. No, the doyens of the suicidal society will instead feel an irresistible compulsion to silence the voices insisting that there is truth, even Truth, and that therefore many other beliefs are in error."[29]

Antifascist activists may recognize the need for some people to speak "their truth," as long as that does not include expressing opinions they deem to be fascist. This is a moral stand, hardly a relativistic one; it is also a political-existential one, in the sense in which Carl Schmitt understood "the Concept of the Political" as the most intensely antagonistic of human relationships.[30] It is impossible to imagine that what has become the more activist side in a culture war is not actuated by moral fervor, which expresses itself in righteous rage. In *The Madness of Crowds* Douglas Murray asks, "Are reciprocity and tolerance principles or fig-leaves? Do those who have been censored go on to censor others when the ability is in their own hands?"[31]

One may or may not be astonished when a popular journalist, Ezra Klein, justifies the statements made on Twitter by former *New York Times* writer Sarah Jeong, whose "jokes" included the phrase "#CancelWhitePeople." According to Klein, Jeong's tweets were not what they seemed to be. Supposedly Ms. Jeong was offering comments about the "dominant power structure and culture."[32] Still it would be hard to read deep thought into Jeong's expression of antifascism when in 2015 she announced on Twitter, "I was equating Trump to Hitler before it was cool."[33]

Interwar fascism rejected outright any politics of white male disparagement. Its advocates glorified virility and martial prowess and, as in the French Revolution, consigned women mostly to a distaff role. Mussolini's *Dottrina del Fascismo*, published in 1931 and prepared with the assistance of Giovanni Gentile, stresses the virtues of masculinity and the spiritual unity of the historic nation. Without getting into the ambiguities of Ernst Nolte's use of this phrase, we may describe fascism as an attempted "escape from transcendence." Fascists were rejecting any effort to rise above what they understood as man's essential nature; namely, being organically tied to an ancestral community and living as a creature of instinct and as someone who viewed life as a struggle against an ancient collective enemy. Instead of trying to remake humanity, in accordance with a plan for universal pacification and altruism, fascists called for allowing human nature to reassert itself.

This commitment was not exclusively rooted in the crude, murderous biologism of the Third Reich but took a less murderous form in Latin fascism and its focus on Roman neo-paganism and the cult of the warrior. But in either case, according to Nolte, fascism rejected the project of refashioning people by extinguishing their authentic nature. This, however, leaves open the question of whether humans by their very nature fit the model ascribed to them by fascism. Certainly, the examples of transcendence that Nolte provides, from Christianity through a succession of humanitarian projects, suggest that human nature may be more complex than the fascists assumed. Nolte is correct nonetheless to argue that fascists attempted to release energies and impulses that older Christian standards of behavior and later reformist social models tried to suppress or root out.

Another difference between the concepts of the state held by fascists and antifascists is their divergent sources of authority. Direction and rule in the Italian fascist state came from *Il Duce*. The hierarchy of fascist doctrine pointed upward toward the fascist leader, who gave direction to the regime and who, in Carl Schmitt's phrase, "decided the challenge of the exception." The essence of fascism," a keen German observer, Oswald Spengler, noted in the early 1930s, was "not its party but rather the shape given to it by its creator. Mussolini was not a party leader but the head of his land. In all probability, his model, Lenin, would have filled the same role if he had lived long enough. Mussolini rules alone."[34] What Spengler calls a "perfected Caesarism," one in which "power is vested in a person not a party,"[35] was a distinguishing mark of Italian fascism and eventually of all interwar fascist movements. Whether we are speaking about the Spanish Falange, the British Union of Fascists, the Romanian Iron Guard, the French Parti Populaire Francais, or Julius Gombos's Party of National Unity in Hungary, all fascist movements favored a cult of the leader. The German Nazis likewise adopted this fascist hallmark, however much they mixed their fascism with other more sinister ingredients.

The antifascist state stands in contrast to the fascist one in the understanding of governance. It involves a sprawling administration, along with efforts to de-masculinize and de-ethnicize "populations," a term favored by the German government officials of our time who do not want to be associated any longer with a "nation" or "Volk." The antifascist regime operates with forces dedicated to fighting "hate," mass media, and public education.

In contrast to the fascist state, which held plebiscitary events to affirm what the regime planned to do, the antifascist state holds elections between mostly indistinguishable candidates and parties. Leaders of the antifascist state can mold public opinion without having to resort to overly transparent manipulation, because they can avail themselves of an international body of support consisting of multinational corporations, the mainstream media, and almost all public institutions in the West. Next to the sophisticated resources available to the antifascist state, the sight of Mussolini delivering a speech from Rome's Palazzo Venezia seems bizarre and ancient.

Should a country elect a leader that the antifascist state disavows, there are multiple ways of letting the citizens know of the state's disapproval. The fact that the antifascist Left of 2020 supported violence to hurry along its consolidation of power is not at all incompatible with the older system of control. Peaceful methods for shaping social conscience and behavior were pursued when other possibilities were not present. That situation has changed, and the managerial path to power has been replaced by a more direct and more riotous one.

## Antifascist Consistencies

Where the fascist view sees identities as fixed, the antifascist perspective regards identities as variable options open to individual choice. Cases in the United States dealing with the right to determine one's gender have gone as far as the Supreme Court.[36] Campaigns for gender-neutral bathrooms and related legislation have proceeded apace.[37] Corporate capitalists like Goldman Sachs are now "defining pronouns" for their employees: "Pronouns are words that an individual would like others to use when talking to or about them . . . Pronouns should not be assumed by someone's name or gender expression."[38] This is fully consistent with how the antifascist Left understands human nature. It may be a sign of the time that critics of LGBTQ individuals, no less than supporters, have reached for the f-word in describing the other side.[39] Given the present focus of antifascism, it is also reasonable that *The Guardian* should scold Hungarian premier Orban for promoting a law that requires registering newborns according to their birth genders.[40]

The popular idea that a critical attitude toward the feminist movement is by itself evidence of fascist sentiments has spread among US educators and journalists. In *How Fascism Works*, Jason Stanley tells us quite bluntly: "Fascist opposition to gender studies in particular flows from its patriarchal ideology. National Socialism targeted women's movements and feminism generally; for the Nazis feminism was a Jewish conspiracy to destroy fertility among Aryan women."[41] Stanley also quotes feminist Kate Manne, who confirms his view about the threatening misogyny that "faces women who are blamed when patriarchal expectations are left unfulfilled. The logic of fascist politics has a vivid model in Manne's logic of misogyny."[42] According to Stanley, the complaint issuing from unhappy men that quotas for women are harming their professional advancement betrays definite patriarchal and fascist prejudices.[43] In a less fascistically inclined society, men would welcome these efforts to overcome sexism. There is no evidence, however, that Stanley has vacated his endowed chair at Yale in favor of a woman.

The British Feminist Antifascist Assembly, which held a mass rally in London in November 2018 on International Women's Day, may have gone beyond Stanley in seeing fascist patriarchs everywhere. From the perspective of this group, the fascist, antifeminist evil has become so widespread and pervasive, even as women continue to be ground down, that only the overthrow of the socioeconomic system can end the oppression: "We don't want more women in the boardrooms; we don't want to smash the glass ceiling. We want to destroy the boardroom and burn down the building."[44]

Although it is possible to discern here traces of the Frankfurt School's critical study of patriarchy going back to the 1930s, certain differences are equally apparent. The detailed examination of patriarchy in *Studien über Autorität und Familie* (1936), for example, criticizes the "unnatural" mentality of "self-subordination" among those who are lower in the family chain of command than the patriarch. Critical theorists also attribute some of the psychic harm caused by this subordination to the effects of late capitalism and to the form of domination produced by this economy.[45] Yet nowhere do Adorno, Horkheimer, and other first-generation critical theorists demand the obliteration of gender distinctions, which like others of their generation they assumed were real and valid, as opposed to a social construct. Although antifascist feminists are right when they claim to be drawing on older radical traditions, the first -generation critical theorists hoped to establish parity between the sexes within the family structure, however much they believed in social engineering and a socialist economy.

The present degree of antifascist radicalization goes well beyond earlier efforts. On the cultural front, today's antifascists are radical in a way that begs for historical precedent.

# EXCURSUS

## *Antifascism and the Nature of Hobbesian Authority*

The free association that is now characteristic of the use of the f-word re-calls the examination of language undertaken by the philosopher Thomas Hobbes (1587–1679). In *Leviathan* (1651) and in his earlier work, *The Elements of Law Natural and Politic* (1641), Hobbes draws on a nominalist theory of knowledge and reality that arose first in the late Middle Ages and reflected the reaction against Catholic and Anglican Aristotelianism. Unlike medieval Catholic philosophers, Hobbes denies the universal character of terms like man, woman, state, and church. He holds that these terms do not correspond to and derive from universal ideals that are inherent in the human mind but instead arise from generalizations derived from observing individual objects and organisms. Hobbes therefore insists, "There being nothing in the world universal but names; for the thing named are all individual and singular."[1] He further states, "One universal name is imposed on many things, for the similitude in some quality or other accident: And whereas a proper name bringeth to mind one thing only, universals recall any one of many things."[2]

The universal character that we conventionally confer on an entity called "man," for example, is nothing more than what we infer from encountering particular people. As Hobbes famously concludes in *The Elements of Law*, "no universal things, but only universal names."[3]

This theory for Hobbes has obvious ramifications for anyone who seeks to ascertain specific meanings, and to engage in interpersonal communications For instance, can two people ever mean the same thing when they use the same word to denote an object? This question perhaps can never elicit an affirmative answer because "the truth consisteth in the right ordering of names in our affirmations"[4] and this "right ordering" is no easy matter. Perhaps when one person refers to a book, the one listening may think that he is designating a vase or banana. Hobbes raises the possibility that human beings share only vague images of the way things exist.

These imagistic associations may also be so diffuse that they do not prevent confusion about what a speaker has in mind when he calls things by what he thinks are their proper names.

At least in mathematics, particularly in geometry, some consensus about meaning is possible. Mathematics deals with differences in quantities and fits in with Hobbes's materialist understanding of the perceived world. "Only in geometry, which is the only Science that it hath pleased God to bestow on mankind," says Hobbes, "men begin at settling the significations of their words, which is a settling of significations they call definitions."[5] Not surprisingly, Hobbes applies what look like geometric theorems when he explicates the rules of sound politics.[6]

Still there is no way out of this semantic fog for those who are trying to communicate with others—hence the need for someone who can fix for us the correspondence between words and what they refer to. This quandary is truly acute, explains Hobbes, because "what one man calleth wisdom, another calleth fear, and one cruelty what another justice." When no agreement is possible about "definitions," we may have to call on an arbitrator or judge who can convince both sides in a dispute what the words really "signify."[7] This is the path by which Hobbes in *Leviathan* arrives at his defense of sovereignty. A sovereign ruler should exercise undivided political authority to prevent the "war of all against all." An authority figure may also be required to settle the matter of what words mean. Strife will likely result unless someone can definitively relate words to specific meanings for the benefit of the populace.

This brings us to the problem of political semantics where we are again confronted with the need for fixed meanings. For many decades, political-ideological designations have floated around in a nominalist universe. What was considered to one generation fascistic or liberal ceased to signify that at a later time. Indeed, the same actions and thinking that passed for liberal for one generation could easily bring the accusation of being fascistic for another generation. In the nineteenth century, liberals typically favored restricting the franchise to property owners and accepted the legal recognition of gender differences. Opposing immigration and urging one's country to stay out of foreign wars were not the signature positions of interwar fascists. Political designations migrate over the long term toward what is viewed as the side of progress. This shift may be inevitable given the institutional and social changes that are taking place. But certain questions remain.

Who decides what terms mean and who assigns these labels to whom? This brings us back in a peculiarly contemporary way to Hobbes's maxim as enunciated in chapter 26 of *Leviathan*, titled *"Auctoritas non veritas facit legem."* Laws are valid not because of their intrinsic truth but owing to the authority from whence they derive.

Some traditionalists want to distinguish between authority and publicity, insisting that the two should not be confused. Whereas the former refers to long-accepted sources of leadership, the latter is about access. Those who assign political labels are heeded because they belong to a class that diffuses "information" and provides "public education." This identification is now so well established in people's minds that it may be hard to discuss political labeling without considering those who provide socially acceptable opinions. We might therefore substitute for Hobbes's maxim about authority determining law this variation in defining fascism: "Fieri mori facit veritatem" (Being in fashion determines truth).

# Afterthoughts

This book has an obvious and intended relationship to my 2016 volume, *Fascism: Career of a Concept.*[1] Both deal with changing understandings of fascism over different time periods: both emphasize the transition from traditional Marxist, conservative, and classical liberal critiques of fascism to the antifascism of the post-Marxist Left. Ever since the antifascist Left gained influence throughout the Western world, it has provided the lens through which both fascism and antifascism are interpreted. Fascism is no longer considered something firmly anchored in time and place but as a ubiquitous, continuing danger to democratic societies. Fascism and antifascism belong to a rhetorical arsenal wielded by the powerful, and the operative terms are applied in such a way as to silence pesky dissenters. All fascism is linked ultimately to Nazi atrocities; therefore, anyone to whom the term is attached must bear the stigma of the Third Reich.

Fascism has become eel-like, slipping from the grasp of whoever tries to seize it conceptually, politically, or culturally. Part of this elusiveness is traceable to the subjective way in which the fascist danger is presented and processed. Some of those who are reacting to it are experiencing a reaction that is profoundly personal. For example, those descended from European Jews who perished in the Holocaust may genuinely believe that any retreat from a continued political war against discrimination endangers them as a minority. They may also think that Christianity has been foundational for anti-Semitism, and so any effort to restore it to a place of honor in Western society endangers Jews. What is relevant here is not whether this perception or anxiety is justified, nor is it a question of whether someone may be exploiting it for personal gain. Many who support an antifascist ideology feel genuinely threatened by what they are vocally opposing.

For these people, such emotions do not have to spring from an analytic approach to political dangers. They view antifascism as the necessary response to a real fascist or Nazi threat, and these antifascists understandably feel at risk. If some Antifa demonstrators are paid for their activities, others are demonstrating for idealistic or deeply personal reasons. We may regard in a similar way German university students who oppose total academic freedom because they consider it a rightist tactic for poisoning public discourse. Although German students may want to suppress traditional liberal freedoms for other reasons, they may also feel guilt for Nazi crimes. Antifascist socializing forces have been at work on them almost from the time they became sentient. If one has heard repeatedly that one's nation has been wicked throughout its history and has a special duty to fight "right-wing extremism," then getting rid of freedom is a small price to pay for spiritual healing and for keeping the rest of the world safe.[2]

None of this should be interpreted as a defense of how antifascists understand "freedom" and "tolerance." It may be helpful to note an observation made by A. James Gregor about how Italian fascists processed such notions as freedom and justice.[3] (These comments could be applied just as easily to believing Communists.) According to Gregor, fascists did not categorically reject those principles that their opponents valued. Rather they interpreted them differently, to conform to their worldview as revolutionary nationalists.[4] Antifascist activists also reconstruct meanings when they proclaim themselves to be the defenders of freedom, not its enemies. Their call to shut down all possible opposition to their plans is made to protect a free society against a return to the horrors of the Third Reich or against a Christian theocracy. With the same goal, tens of millions of American voters on the multicultural Left may think that extraordinary antifascist measures are needed to protect us against fellow citizens.

Another shared attitude of the present Left and the fascists and Communists is viewing themselves as living at a critical hour, when their movement is struggling to survive. This view is defensible in the case of the genuinely marginalized, such as the Old Right in the United States or advocates of a Bourbon restoration in France. More puzzling, however, is the alarm bell sounded by those in power who claim to be defenseless objects of fascist attack. Clearly entire careers have been built or extended based on ominous warnings about a fascist threat. Mark Bray and Jason Stanley in the United States, Bernard-Henri Lévy in France, and multiple writers for *Tageszeitung*, *The Guardian*, *Le Monde*, and the *New York Times*, among other publications, have all capitalized on the prevalent alarm about fascism.

Moreover, what Norman Finkelstein characterizes as "the Holocaust industry" has sprung up in every Western country and dragged commemorations of the catastrophe it claims to be memorializing into contemporary political battles. Finkelstein, whose parents survived internment in a Nazi extermination camp, writes with understandable indignation about the "exploitation of Jewish suffering," and he provides multiple examples of how and why this exploitation has taken place.[5] He is correct that Zionists have exploited the Nazi persecution of European Jewry to justify controversial actions by the Israeli government and silence critics of Israel's relationship with the Palestinians.

Those who stress the continued relevance of the Holocaust often seek to affect culture in other, more ambitious ways. Some of these promoters of selective historical memory have tried to lay all-purpose guilt trips on American Christians who had nothing to do with Nazi atrocities, except in some cases to liberate Nazi victims from concentration camps. The failure to back what is presented as the latest phase in a crusade against fascism may be characterized (and often is) as forgetting the lessons of Auschwitz.[6] Promoters of Holocaust studies have also waged a campaign against "Holocaust deniers" and "Holocaust trivializers," whose number and influence, Finkelstein argues, have often been exaggerated. "Holocaust trivialization" has been instrumentalized to shut off debate about subjects that are only distantly related to the fate of European Jewry under the Nazis.

Finkelstein justifiably underlines how memories of the Holocaust and often arbitrary ascriptions of guilt have been weaponized against those holding unpopular opinions. How this operates can be seen in the career of German Holocaust publicist Horst Selbiger, who has worked for decades to bring together children of Holocaust survivors to discuss their life experiences.[7] The eighty-eight-year-old Berliner is half-Jewish and spent the closing year of World War II in a forced labor battalion. Although neither of his parents perished in the Holocaust, many of Selbiger's father's relatives did. Selbiger says he was so traumatized by his experience under the Nazis that he moved to East Germany and worked for its Communist regime. Eventually he grew tired of his dreary life under socialism and managed to sneak back into West Germany. Once he arrived there, Selbiger became an antifascist activist and is now warning against surging fascism among his fellow Germans and throughout the Western world. He is particularly sought in German leftist circles to explain to the descendants of Nazi victims why the AfD imperils their lives.[8] No decent person would deny that Selbiger's extended family suffered grievously under the Third Reich. What should concern us is how he uses that trauma in the service of his leftist politics.

Victims of Nazism are honored in a way that Communist victims are not. By the time the US Holocaust Memorial Museum was established in Washington, DC, in 1993, Holocaust centers already existed throughout the country. And yet, although the number of people who perished under Communist rule may have been as high as 100 million, it was difficult to raise funds even for a memorial to Communist victims in the capital; one was not built until 2007.[9] This may exemplify the fate of being politically less favored victims. Even though I agree with those who regard the crazed mass killings of the Nazis as being uniquely evil, what nonetheless raises questions is the brushing away of Communist mass murders, particularly by those who wish to treat Communist tyrants as precursors of their own multicultural experiments.

The enemy in our current political culture is the anti-globalist Right (or what is perceived as such), and therefore focusing on Auschwitz and Nazi genocide helps fuel and reinforce the dominant political ideology. As a result, particular mass killings will receive more notice from the media and educators than other ones, in accordance with already established ideological guidelines. This is reflected not only in the emphasis placed on the Holocaust as the ultimate crime committed by a quintessential fascist Right. Equally relevant, as Peter Novick documents in *The Holocaust in American Life*, is the changing way in which Nazi enormities have been depicted.[10]

Since the 1960s, according to Novick, the blame for Nazi crimes has shifted from German neo-pagans to Western Christian societies. This has the effect of strengthening an antifascist narrative that emphasizes the culpability of what is peculiarly Western and Christian.[11] Obviously anti-Communism would not fulfill the same needs for antifascists, who are intent on implicating the Western past in their indictment of fascism. Equally relevant, Communism is seen as belonging to the antifascist Left, and therefore its victims may count only as collateral damage in bringing about a needed transformation.

An illustration of this last point can be seen in the brouhaha that erupted among German historians in the 1980s and early 1990s over the views of Ernst Nolte, who insisted that Nazi genocide was not a "singular" evil but a reaction to Soviet crimes under Stalin. The occasion for the ensuing fireworks was the publication of a commentary in the *Frankfurter Allgemeine Zeitung* (FAZ) on June 6, 1986, in which Nolte stated, "Even if we concede the singularity of Hitler's annihilation of European Jewry that does not change the situation that it was a reaction or distorted imitation of the original."[12] This led to a series of angry responses from the German antifascist, antinational professoriate, led by Jürgen Habermas. According to Habermas, Nolte's argument allowed Germans to disregard what they should be doing as a people, which is meditating on their troubling past. Nolte also supposedly denied the singularity of German crimes by "minimizing" them, refusing to treat Hitler's deeds in a pedagogically sound fashion as the most monstrous evil of all times.[13]

A prominent Hitler biographer and FAZ editor, Joachim Fest, commented that Habermas seemed not to have noticed that Nolte indeed recognized the uniqueness of Hitler's crimes. That was explicitly stated in his newspaper commentary before he segued into Stalin's crimes as a precedent for Nazi horrors. Habermas was also behaving hypocritically, according to Fest, when he charged Nolte with "minimizing" an unprecedented evil. This self-appointed moral authority would not even recognize something as obvious as Stalin's inflicting a famine on the Ukraine. Habermas would only refer to the "expulsion of Kulaks" when he discussed this mass killing through famine.

According to Fest's colleague at the FAZ, Johann Georg Reissmüller, Habermas had difficulty even conceding that the fifteen million Germans who had been expelled from Eastern Europe at the end of World War II, together with the victims of Stalin's crimes, had "an equal claim to recognition" along with Nazi victims. Although these atrocities may not have been as gruesome as the Holocaust, they were real enough evils. Despite Habermas's highly selective moral indignation, his judgments make perfectly good sense within the framework of his antifascist worldview.[14] Former editor of the FAZ, Frank Schirrmacher, points out that the claim by Habermas and his antifascist followers to be defending pluralism and open discussion diverts attention from what they actually want: "a standardized historical picture" and a "monstrous Habermasian project of modernity" that will erase any real differences in political and historical views.[15]

Power claims, according to the Greek-German intellectual historian, Panajotis Kondylis, are fundamental to how human beings act in a social context. Theoretical, economic, and political forms of decision making typically involve asserting one's will in relation to others, and so conflict may be inescapable even in adversarial relationships that do not flow from political differences.[16] But this clash of positions looks more ominous when those who already enjoy political and journalistic advantage seek to humiliate others. This action exemplifies what is called "virtue signaling" in which the custodians of correctness seek to shame and ostracize designated bigots.[17] In Germany respected academics and political leaders have declared war against the term "ethnic German," especially after that description passed the lips of an official of the AfD.[18] Despite this ban it is still permissible to refer to the autochthonous German population as "bio-Germans," although this too may change if those who control permissible discourse decide to shame their opposition as racists. It is also possible that those with influence could decide to change course and allow their fellow citizens to speak of "ethnic Germans" but not "biological" ones. Hannah Arendt properly noted that a feature of modern totalitarian rule is the tendency of those wielding power to alter or reverse meanings.[19]

This practice of semantic manipulation has gained ground in higher education and in the media, and it has encouraged branding those identified with the Right often quite indiscriminately as fascists. In the United States and Western Europe, those who are the objects of these righteous attacks may increasingly suffer socially and professionally.[20] Despite the self-image cultivated by the American conservative establishment as defenders of freedom, it too frequently bends to the antifascist Left. Influential conservatives have purged their own ranks as soon as they are accused of harboring right-wing extremists.[21] Bullying does not exist in a vacuum; it succeeds whenever the timid run for cover.

A cultural lag can be observed in some rural areas or in what the French describe as "peripheral" areas. Nonetheless, those who go through the now-dominant socializing process come out with predictable opinions. The political party preferred by the college-educated young in Western Europe are the Greens, and Green partisans advocate a peculiar mix of positions: ecological discipline, deindustrialization, the opening of Western countries to Third World immigration, advanced feminism, and guaranteed LGBTQ rights. It makes no difference to their proponents whether these positions are internally inconsistent.

We observe on the Left and in a more diffuse fashion elsewhere on our political spectrum not a coherent configuration of ideas or a consistent worldview but a collection of sentiments and attitudes.[22] Those who espouse them and who often describe themselves as antifascist are making a statement against the Western past, and they mobilize in order to show their displeasure. Calling someone a fascist identifies one's enemy, and the invocation of a shared enemy helps brings together all members of the Left, past and present. It matters little whether this name-calling reflects an accurate understanding of the historical situation. (For example, Communists like Fidel Castro and Che Guevara, who declaimed against homosexuals as decadent bourgeoisie and who called for imprisoning and torturing them, continue to be celebrated on the Left.[23])

Further, the appeal to a revived Popular Front in the tracts of Mark Bray and other antifascists overlooks the inconvenient fact that in the 1930s the Communists murdered a lot more people than those against whom they and their allies were then organized. Evidence of homophobia also marked the Frankfurt School, which has enjoyed iconic status on the Left. In 1960, two premier critical theorists, Theodor Adorno, and Max Horkheimer, worked to prevent Golo Mann, the son of the literary giant and himself a learned, widely published historian, from obtaining a professorship at the University of Frankfurt. In his snide comments to associates Adorno accused Mann of anti-Semitism while mocking his homosexuality.[24] The first attribution was invented; the second happened to be true. Bray and his antifascist comrades-in-arms may be aware of the long history of leftist homophobia, but may find it necessary to suppress this fact for the sake of the myth of an invariable Left locked in combat with an equally eternal Right.[25]

Antifascism has fared well as a militant stance because it reflects how the United States and other Western countries now understand the nature of the "moral." Our modern conception of democracy privileges pluralism and equality while rejecting social hierarchy and ethnic homogeneity. This is also the standard of judgment when our "conservatives" judge traditional societies that have not yet reached our present stage of modernization. Any questioning of the principle of equality, as that principle is currently understood, would put the speaker beyond the parameters of polite discussion. The authorized Left and the authorized Right now fight over which side believes more deeply and more consistently in egalitarian ideals. In the heat of battle, each side may charge the other with betraying a shared moral patrimony.

What Max Weber considered the great struggle of the modern era over "ultimate values"[26] has ended with a consensus about which values should be given pride of place. Although freedom as individual autonomy has an honored place in this ranking, it is inseparably linked in modern democracy to both pluralism and equality. Individuals, we are led to believe by educators, the media, and politicians, can only justly exercise their freedom if they work to make it accessible to every human person across the globe. Accordingly, the celebration of freedom should in no way lessen human equality but should help advance groups that until now have been disadvantaged or have not been given the chance to live in a Western country. If freedom, according to this teaching, is at all defensible, then it should lead to greater equality, in the name of social justice.[27]

One cannot find a more perfect illustration of what Western leaders believe about morality than a speech given by French president Nicolas Sarkozy on December 17, 2008. Sarkozy's speech included this memorable passage: "What is our aim? That aim is the mingling of races. The mingling of the races of various nations is the challenge of the twenty-first century. It is not a choice but an obligation. . . . We shall all change at the same time—commercial enterprises, governments, political parties, and we shall dedicate ourselves to this aim. If peoples do not agree to this voluntarily, then states will have to impose this change by force."[28] The transformational enthusiasm evinced by the former French president seems to be entirely in line with the antifascist call for change.

Another Frenchman, Edouard Berth (1875–1930), an anarcho-syndicalist and spokesman for an older Left, presented social views antithetical to those of Macron. Berth viewed both corporate capitalism and "intellectualists" as enemies of settled communities and as vehicles for submerging the entire human race into an undifferentiated mass of interchangeable parts. According to Berth, the "social dogmatists" who accept such a vision "cannot tolerate the inevitable variety of human beings and of things. They seek to absorb everything into the One. Why then should we have motherlands? Why different languages? Why classes? Why sexes? Why not a single humanity, a single language, a single sex, a unique association without war, without antagonisms, in the happy peace of an eternal idyll. Everything could then become interchangeable, races, countries, classes and sexes."[29] Today Berth's anti-globalist position might bring down the wrath of the entire antifascist Left.

The collapse of the Soviet Empire and the transformation of Western Communist parties that had been under Soviet control opened the door to the present antifascist Left and its intersectional agenda. The Soviets and their proxies maintained a standard of doctrinal and moral orthodoxy for decades in Russia, and wherever Communist Parties sprang up in the West, efforts were made to uphold those Soviet-approved behavioral standards. What was viewed as "bourgeois decadence" was forbidden for party members, and for decades the Soviet government treated the Frankfurt School and critical theory as a corruption of Marxist-Leninism. Communist authorities not only condemned homosexual behavior but railed also against artistic modernism in the forms of Abstract Expressionism and twelve-tone music.[30]

In the West in the 1950s and 1960s, the Right urged a crusade against "godless Communism," while the Left was mostly concerned with criticizing what it considered the exaggeratedly anti-Communist character of the Cold War and calling for friendlier relations with Communist and postcolonial governments. This is not to say that the Left throughout the period of the Cold War of more than forty years had no other interest but defending Communist powers or trying to explain their transgressions. But it is to note that mitigating Communist actions, rather than other positions—such as attacking racial prejudice, calling for the prosecution of alleged Nazi war criminals, or deploring colonialism—was the continuing focus of leftist political energies. The end of the struggle between Communist and non-Communist countries, in which the United States and Russia, and then the United States and Russia and China, became the dominant powers, allowed the present antifascist Left to grow in influence.[31] Perhaps not surprisingly, those countries in Eastern Europe that had been under the Soviet aegis were least affected by a leftist current that succeeded Marxist-Leninist ideology. Although former Communist countries have kept features of the socialist or pre-socialist economic past, they have not undergone the fundamental social transformation that has affected Western Europe and Anglophone countries. Americanization has not proceeded as fully in Eastern Europe as it has elsewhere.

Some final observations may be in order about the Antifa riots that have erupted in US cities since the election of Donald Trump. In Seattle, Portland, Minneapolis, Philadelphia, Chicago, Washington, DC, and New York City, leftist protests have resulted in considerable property loss, injury, and death. These well-organized events were signaled in universities and colleges, particularly when critics of intersectional ideology were invited as speakers. The presence on campuses of dissenting celebrities, who are usually sponsored by Republican organizations, have caused students, faculty, and administrators to stand with the protestors. In some places the police have backed off when Antifa demonstrators unleashed violence against the suspected fascists.

The reason the police backed off is not far to seek. In cities such as Portland and Seattle, local governments sympathize with the antifascist activists. A member of the House Armed Services Committee, New Mexico Democratic congresswoman Deb Haaland, praised the "peaceful protesters" after a violent demonstration broke out in Portland in August 2019 in which Antifa militants clashed with the right-wing Proud Boys.[32] Just a few weeks earlier, Antifa demonstrators in Portland had inflicted near-lethal blows on hapless observers in the downtown area.[33] By June 2020 Antifa activists played a role in setting up its own ministate in Seattle—the Capitol Hill Autonomous Zone—in conjunction with BLM activists. This zone operated with the indulgent sympathy of local and state government officials, while the federal authorities decided to let this political seizure play out.[34]

It would be a mistake to view such disruptions as the work of isolated "extremist" groups. Antifa has been mostly immune from criticism by Democratic presidential candidates and most members of Congress.[35] Unlike contemporary right-wing parties in the United States and Western Europe, the antifascist Left is not a weak minority persuasion but a growing political and cultural force. It engages in a cleansing process driven by the fear of an ever-present contamination that must be fought night and day. R. R. Reno in *Return of the Strong Gods* associates the "open-culture side of the postwar consensus" with an "open-economy" and a demand for absolute power. The leadership class in this arrangement bases its rule on both a globalist vision and carefully sustained fear. "Without their leadership, the 'takers' who just want 'free stuff' will destroy our vibrant economy and the racists, xenophobes and fascists will force women back into subservience and reestablish white supremacy."[36]

It might be asked whether leftist activists are really calling for total regime change. Except for the diehard socialists in their ranks, the antifascist Left is only pushing the political establishment at least partly in the direction in which it is already moving; that is, toward transforming Western countries into multicultural societies, erasing the remnants of a reactionary historical past, and assuring popular acceptance of nontraditional lifestyles. In other cases, as noted, the disrupters seem motivated by a nihilistic urge to destroy the civilization that preceded them. The term used by conservative media to describe this behavior as "cancel culture" may be entirely appropriate.[37] This is the case, even if conservative critics embrace a more moderate form of the "cancel culture" for those aspects of the past that do not fit their own progressive agenda.

In *Three Faces of Fascism*, Ernst Nolte observes that fascists viewed themselves as being in a crusade against "transcendence"; that is, they battled against the drive toward a global society based on the overcoming of national and biological identities. Today's antifascists are still combating the fascist attempt to "escape from transcendence," long after Nolte's subjects are gone. If fascism, according to Nolte, was an attempt to affirm the biological and familial in a sometimes brutal manner, today's antifascism promotes frenetically the very project that according to Nolte the fascists had resisted. Achieving this aim of "transcendence" has become a preoccupation among political, economic, and cultural leaders,[38] who are hoping to integrate Western societies into their conception of a world community. Although non-Western societies will be permitted, at least for the time being, to go on practicing their traditional cultures, Westerners will be required to plunge theirs into a sea of change. Western countries will be expected to sacrifice themselves, ethnically and culturally, so they can assume a more fluid global identity. Only then will they be able to transcend the burden of their fascist past.

While this transformational work is in progress, those held to be fascists will continue to be ostracized. Increasing media focus will be placed on right-wing deviationist regimes in the Western world, such as Victor Orban's rule in Hungary, which is described in *Der Spiegel* as a dangerous expansionist nationalist government of the interwar fascist variety. An already well-established practice is depicting the antifascist multicultural order as perpetually in danger and requiring extreme measures, like the suppression of what remains of liberal freedoms, to check an ostensible fascist threat to our survival. In this respect antifascists will reveal their links to what they claim to be opposing—namely a movement of the revolutionary Right—which, like the antifascists, depicts itself as surrounded by enemies, even once in power. In a like manner, Communist governments portrayed themselves as beleaguered by counterrevolutionaries, and therefore they were impelled to take extreme measures to avoid being marginalized.

A telling illustration of the doubtful reasoning to which antifascist writers have resorted is an article in the *New Statesman* on April 10, 2019, by frequent *Atlantic* contributor Samuel Earle. Earle expresses his uneasiness that people are once again reading the German political theorist Carl Schmitt, who joined the Nazi Party in 1933. According to Earle, Brexiteers "hankering nostalgia for Britain's past" are following Schmitt's "friend/enemy antithesis" in opting for war against the existential enemy. "War creates a cohesive identity. As the enemy comes clearly into view, so do we."[39]

Earle finds Schmitt's thought to be equally at work in "the popularity of Jordan Peterson and Joe Rogan, pseudo-intellectuals who see the same fraught world in which man must fight for himself, to the current trend of 'Nemesis Twitter,' where social media users vaunt their unnamed foes, affirming a strong identity through reference to opponents." This too is somehow an extension of Schmitt's worldview and of "what, in his anti-Semitism, he succumbed to," which was "the attraction of enmity." In Earle's view, "this politics plagues every nation and is why Brexit . . . finds such support abroad, whether in Salvini, Trump, or the Alternative für Deutschland." He writes that "all nationalists speak the same language. Schmitt may as well have written their script."

Earle's argument is based on questionable assumptions. The revival of interest in Schmitt's work was already well underway in the 1980s and attracted both rightist and leftist participants, depending on what exactly Schmitt's devotees were looking for in a prolific, long-lived theorist. (For full disclosure, I was an active participant in this revival and have written extensively on Schmitt's oeuvre.) The first edition of *Begriff des Politischen* (Concept of the Political) was published not when Schmitt was a "budding Nazi" but in 1927, when he was a legal adviser to the Catholic Center Party.[40] The second edition of his germinal work, which appeared in 1932, famously contains an appended commentary by Schmitt's Jewish admirer Leo Strauss. It is doubtful that in 1932 Strauss could have dreamt that his intellectual hero would opportunistically defect to the Nazi Party in May 1933.

But even if one accepts Earle's simplistic interpretation of what may be one of the great political classics of all times, there would be no reason to assume that Brexit advocates like Nigel Farage embrace Schmitt's concept of the existential enemy. It is also not clear why we should believe these "nationalists" read Schmitt or feel any special affection for his political theories. Is there no other reason that one might read Schmitt (assuming one does) other than an intensified friend–enemy relationship that, according to Earle, culminated in the Nazi movement? Where, moreover, is the evidence that those whom Earle attacks (perhaps as existential enemies?) are building a cohesive community by demonizing the Other? And why, finally, are European nations obliged to accept their transformation under the guidance of enlightened elites to prove that they are not aping the Third Reich? Earle raises undemonstrated accusations on the way to reaching unfounded conclusions.

A particularly ludicrous example of this leaping to conclusions comes in Earle's opening sentence when he informs us that "on the anniversary of Benito Mussolini's birth, Italy's far-right interior minister Matteo Salvini posted on Twitter "tanti nemici, tanto onore" (So many enemies, so much honour)—a variation on the fascist dictator's notorious motto." In fact, the saying tweeted by the "Far Right" interior minister (there are, it seems, "Far Right" ministers but never "Far Left" ones) preceded Mussolini's birth by several hundred years and can be found in multiple European languages. It goes at least as far back as the Battle of Creazzo in 1513, when a mercenary commander of Emperor Charles V, Georg von Frundsberg, put the now-famous aphorism into its German form as "viel Feinde, viel Ehre." By the twentieth century Frundsberg's early sixteenth-century statement of bravado had become a common saying throughout Europe. It is possible that Matteo Salvini, who is no longer Italian premier, quoted those words on Twitter not in celebration of *Il Duce* but as an expression of defiance toward his own enemies.

# Notes

### Introduction

1. Paul Gottfried, *Fascism: Career of a Concept* (De Kalb: Northern Illinois University Press, 2016).

2. Paul Gottfried, *The Strange Death of Marxism: The European Left in the New Millennium* (Columbia: University of Missouri Press, 2005).

3. Gottfried, *Fascism: Career of a Concept*, 59–82; H. B. Bradford, "The Abuse of 'Fascism,'" https://humanevents.com/2020/06/11/the-abuse-of-fascism/.

4. Peter Beinart, "What Trump Gets Wrong about Antifa," August 16, 2017, http://peterbeinart.net/trump-gets-wrong-antifa/.

5. George Orwell, "As I Please," *Tribune*, March 24, 1944; Paul Gottfried, "The Uses and Misuses of Fascism," *Society* 54 (Spring 2017): 315–19; and Michael Ledeen, "Nobody Knows Anything about Fascism," *Forbes*, May 19, 2016, https://www.forbes.com/sites/michaelledeen/2016/05/19/nobody-knows-anything-about-fascism/#42f322af658e.

6. *Meet the Press*, Chuck Todd interviews Mark Bray, August 20, 2017, https://www.nbcnews.com/meet-the-press/meet-press-august-20-2017-n794321.

7. Mark Bray, *Antifa: The Anti-Fascist Handbook* (Brooklyn: Melville House, 2017); and Melville House's advertisement for Bray's book, https://www.mhpbooks.com/books/antifa/.

8. https://www.vox.com/2017/8/25/16189064/antifa-charlottesville-dc-unite-the-right-mark-bray," June 1, 2020, https://www.vox.com/2017/8/25/16189064/antifa-charlottesville-dc-unite-the-right-mark-bray; also Paul Gottfried, "The Myth Making of Antifa Intellectuals," *The American Conservative*, October 18, 2018, https://www.theamericanconservative.com/articles/the-myth-making-of-antifa-intellectuals/.

9. Stanley G. Payne, *Fascism, Comparison and Definition*, repr. (Madison: University of Wisconsin Press, 1983), and *A History of Fascism, 1914–1945* (Madison: University of Wisconsin Press, 1995).

10. Ernst Nolte, *Die Krise des liberalen Systems und die faschistischen Bewegungen* (Munich: Piper, 1968), 35–69.

11. See, for example, Paul Gottfried, *After Liberalism: Mass Democracy in the Managerial State* (Princeton, NJ: Princeton University Press, 1999).

12. Peter Beinart, "What Trump Gets Wrong About Antifa," blog, August 16, 2017, http://peterbeinart.net/trump-gets-wrong-antifa/; Maggie Tennis, "Madeleine Albright on Fascism, Democracy, and Deplomacy," Brookings Institution, September 11, 2018, https://www.brookings.edu/blog/order-from-chaos/2018/09/11/madeleine-albright-on-fascism-democracy-and-diplomacy/.

13. Madeleine Albright, *Fascism: A Warning* (New York: Harper Collins, 2018).

14. See Peter Furth, "Epigonaler Antifaschismus," *Tumult* 1 (Spring 2016): 30–32. A work that influenced Furth and me regarding the relation between what is now called "virtue signaling" and the quest for power is a short book, *Machtfragen* (Darmstadt: Wissenschaftliche Buchgesellschaft, 1998), 28–129, by the Greek Germanophone political theorist Panajotis Kondylis (1943–1998).

15. Timothy Snyder, "The Test of Nazism That Trump Failed," *New York Times*, August 18, 2017, https://www.nytimes.com/2017/08/18/opinion/the-test-of-nazism-that-trump-failed.html.; two books by Timothy Snyder, *On Tyranny: Twenty Lessons from the Twentieth Century* (New York: Crown, 2017) and *The Road to Unfreedom* (New York: Crown, 2018), reprise his now-familiar theme that Trump's presidency and the appearance of right-of-center parties and governments in Europe portend a return to fascism.

16. Christopher R. Browning, "The Suffocation of Democracy," *The New York Review*, October 25, 2018, https://www.nybooks.com/articles/2018/10/25/suffocation-of-democracy/.

17. Gottfried, *The Strange Death of Marxism*, especially 12–31, 104–15.

18. Allan Bloom, *The Closing of the American Mind,* rev. ed. (New York: Simon & Schuster, 2012), 141–56, 217–28.

19. Raphael Ahren, "At Yad Vashem, German President Says Germans Haven't Learned Lesson of Holocaust, *The Times of Israel*, January 23, 2020, https://www.timesofisrael.com/at-yad-vashem-german-president-says-germans-havent-learned-lesson-of-holocaust/.

20. Benjamin Fearnow, "Alexandria Ocasio Cortez Says US "Not an Advanced Society," *Newsweek*, December 24, 2019, https://www.newsweek.com/alexandria-ocasio-cortez-america-not-advanced-society-us-fascism-wealth-inequality-1479027.

21. Joshua Kaplan, "Bernie Campaigner Kyle Jurek Arrested Days Before Project Veritas Exposé," Breitbart, January 16, 2020, https://www.breitbart.com/2020-election/2020/01/16/bernie-campaigner-kyle-jurek-arrested-days-before-project-veritas-expose/.

22. Heavy, "Project Veritas Video of Bernie Sanders Staffer Kyle Jurak," January 14, 2020, video, https://heavy.com/news/2020/01/watch-project-veritas-video-bernie-sanders-kyle-jurak/.

23. A remarkably similar explanation for the success of the antifascists to the one herein offered can be found in the Spanish interview of today's leading historian of fascism Stanley Payne: https://www.ahorainformacion.es/wp-content/themes/AhoraInfo/images/logoAI_hor_sub.png.

24. Rolf Wiggershaus, in *Die Frankfurter Schule* (Munich: C. Hanser Verlag, 1987), 432, quotes the long letter sent to Theodor Adorno in February 1947 by Herbert Marcuse affirming the unswervingly socialist mission of the Frankfurt School. This letter was occasioned by Adorno's plan to reopen the Institute in Frankfurt. See also Gottfried, *Fascism: Career of a Concept*, 61–64.

25. See Georg Lukacs, *Die Zerstörung der Vernunft* (Munich: Luchterhand, 1960). An illuminating essay on Lukacs as a forerunner of modern antifascism has come from German literature scholar Till Kinzel, "Dem Denken die Bahn vorgeben," in *Festschrift für Karlheinz Weissmann*, ed Dieter Stein (Berlin: Edition JF, 2019), 141–48. See also the characterization of Lukacs in Ernst Nolte's *Der kausale Nexus: Über Revisionen und Revisionismen in der Geschichtswissenschaft* (Munich: Herbig, 2002), 57.

26. Kampf gegen Rechts, October 25, 2018, "Parliament Demands Ban on Neo-Fascist and Neo-Nazi Parties in the EU," https://www.hessen-depesche.de/politik/schon-116-millionen-im-jahr-kosten-f%C3%BCr-%E2%80%9Ekampf-gegen-rechts%E2%80%9C-explodieren.html.

27. Kampf gegen Rechts, October 25, 2018, "Parliament Demands Ban on Neo-Fascist and Neo-Nazi Parties in the EU."

28. This is the major theme of Mircea Eliade's classic, *The Sacred and Profane: The Nature of Religion*, trans. Willard R. Trask (New York: Harcourt, Brace and Jovanovich, 1987). For a study of the reliance of the multicultural Left on romantic and primitive mythology, see Jérome Blanchet-Gravel, *La face cachée du multiculturalisme* (Paris: Cerf, 2018).

## 1. Antifa and the Mainstreaming of Antifascism

1. Alex Kasprak, "Is This Minnesota AG Keith Ellison with 'Antifa Handbook'?," Snopes, June 5, 2020, https://www.snopes.com/fact-check/ellison-antifa-book/.

2. Brian Bierschbach, "Congressman Accused of Domestic Abuse by Former Girlfriend," NPR, August 13, 2018, https://www.npr.org/2018/08/13/638199556/congressman-accused-of-domestic-abuse-by-former-girlfriend.

3. Justin Caruso, "Alexandria Ocasio-Cortez Silent on Fundraising for Antifa-Associated Protesters," Daily Caller, September 4, 2019, https://dailycaller.com/2019/09/04/alexandria-ocasio-cortez-silent-on-antifa/.

4. Katherine Lam, "Dartmouth Faculty Supports Comments Justifying Antifa Violence," Fox News, September 25, 2017, https://www.foxnews.com/us/dartmouth-faculty-supports-professors-comments-justifying-antifa-violence.

5. Ishaan Tharoor, "Is It Time to Call Trump the F-Word?" *Washington Post*, June 3, 2020, https://www.washingtonpost.com/world/2020/06/03/trump-protests-fascism/.

6. Nicholas Kristof, "When Antifa Hysteria Sweeps America," *New York Times*, June 17, 2020, https://www.nytimes.com/2020/06/17/opinion/antifa-protests.html.

7. Frieda Powers, Leo Terrell Is Furious at Fellow Dems over Riots," Mary 30, 2020, https://www.bizpacreview.com/2020/05/30/leo-terrell-is-furious-at-fellow-dems-over-riots-im-a-black-voter-and-you-have-lost-me-if-you-dont-stand-up-to-these-criminals-927841.

8. Todd Huston, "Joe Biden Allows Staffers to Donate Bail Money to Antifa," *Washington Sentinel*, June 1, 2020, https://thewashingtonsentinel.com/joe-biden-allows-staffers-to-donate-bail-money-to-antifa-rioters/.

9. Project Veritas is an undercover investigating agency that targets the Left. https://www.youtube.com/watch?v=VLR76_e_koE&feature=youtu.be.

10. "Fiery Clash Erupts between Police and Protesters over George Floyd's Death, *New York Times*, May 30, 2020, www.nytimes.com/2020/05/31/us/george-floyd-protests-white-supremacists-antifa.html.

11. Mark Bray, "Antifa Isn't the Problem," *Washington Post*, June 1, 2020, https://www.washingtonpost.com/outlook/2020/06/01/trump-antifa-terrorist-organization/.

12. On the rise and decline of the alt-right, see George Hawley, *Making Sense of the Altright* (New York: Columbia University Press, 2017).

13. Antifa's "rise to prominence" in the wake of its clash in Charlottesville can be found in a story in *Newsweek* (August 26, 2018) by Jason Lemon, "Antifa in Charlottesville, Ahead of Unite the Right Rally, to 'Keep the Community Safe' Activist Says," https://www.newsweek.com/antifa-charlottesville-keep-community-safe-activist-says-1069878. The most thorough and balanced report about this clash came from the federal prosecutor Timothy Heaphy in the form of a 220-page report. See Hunton and Williams, Final Report: Independent Review of the 2017 Protests in Charlottesville, Virginia, November 24, 2017, https://www.policefoundation.org/wp-content/uploads/2017/12/Charlottesville-Critical-Incident-Review-2017.pdf.

14. See Mary Grabar's critical examination of "Mark Bray's Lies about Antifa," *American Spectator*, June 3, 2020, https://spectator.org/mark-brays-lies-about-antifa/.

15. Megan Fox, New Undercover Video Blows Lid Off Antifa Domestic Terrorists," PJ Media, June 4, 2020, https://pjmedia.com/news-and-politics/megan-fox/2020/06/04/new-undercover-video-blows-lid-off-antifa-domestic-terrorists-n491956.

16. John Crump, "Piles of Bricks Stage at Protest Sites across the Country, Ammoland, June 1, 2020, https://www.ammoland.com/2020/06/piles-of-bricks-staged-up-at-protest-sites-across-the-country-video/#axzz6R8tQkyVw.

17. *Elizabethtown Advocate*, June 11, 2020, pp. A1 and A5.

18. See Alexander Reid-Ross, *Against the Fascist Creep* (Stirling, UK: AK Press, 2017).

19. Keith Preston, "Attack the System, Against the Antifascist Creeps," Attack the System, February 22, 2017, https://attackthesystem.com/2017/02/22/against-the-anti-fascist-creeps/

20. Alexander Reid-Ross, *Against the Fascist Creep*, 2017.

21. Eric Mann, "Growing Activism," UC San Diego, April 30, 2007, https://www.uctv.tv/shows/Growing-Activism-Labor-Community-Strategy-Center-12261.

22. Dan MacGuill, " Did a 'Convicted Terrorist' Sit on the Board of a BLM Funding Body?" Snopes, July 14, 2020 https://www.snopes.com/fact-check/blm-terrorist-rosenberg/.

23. Eric Mann, "Growing Activism," April 30, 2007.

24. Harnk Berrien, "Antifa Gone Wild," Daily Wire, August 28, 2017, https://www.dailywire.com/news/antifa-gone-wild-no-trump-no-wall-no-usa-all-hank-berrien.

25. Penny Starr, "Protesters Take Over City Blocks in Seattle, Blokade Streets, Call for Armed Guards," June 9, 2020, https://www.breitbart.com/politics/2020/06/09/protesters-take-over-city-blocks-in-seattle-blockade-streets-call-for-armed-guards/.

26. Associated Press, "Seattle Mayor Orders 'Occupied' Area Cleared, Police Arrive," July 1, 2020, https://www.politico.com/news/2020/07/01/seattle-mayor-orders-occupied-area-cleared-346800.

27. Soeren Kern, "A Brief History of Antifa: Part Two," Gatestone Institute, June 23, 2020, https://www.gatestoneinstitute.org/16149/antifa-history-part-2 According to online critics, the Gatestone Institute is a "Far Right" institute, a description that supposedly discredits its findings. Although the data published by this institute may require further study, charging it with being "far right" does not refute its evidence.

28. "Antifa," Influence Watch, https://www.influencewatch.org/movement/antifa/.

29. "Black Lives Matter," Influence Watch, https://www.influencewatch.org/non-profit/black-lives-matter-foundation/.

30. Pippa Stevens, "Companies Are Making Bold Promises about Greater Diversity but There's a Long Way to Go," CNBC, June 11, 2020, https://www.cnbc.com/2020/06/11/companies-are-making-bold-promises-about-greater-diversity-theres-a-long-way-to-go.html.

31. Daniel Cox and Robert P. Jones, "The Religion Vote 2016," PPRI, October 27, 2016, https://www.prri.org/spotlight/religion-vote-2016/.

32. Rasmussen Reports, "49% Say 'Antifa' Is a Terrorist Organization," June 3, 2020, https://www.rasmussenreports.com/public_content/politics/current_events/social_issues/49_say_antifa_is_a_terrorist_organization.

33. Jennifer Agiesta, CNN Poll: Trump Losing Ground to Bien Amid Chaotic Week," CNN, June 8, 2020, https://www.cnn.com/2020/06/08/politics/cnn-poll-trump-biden-chaotic-week/index.html.

34. For the definitive study of the CPUSA, see Theodore Draper's *The Roots of American Communism* (New York: Ivan R. Dee, 1988).

35. The Vigilant Citizen, "Netflix Is Losing Subscribers in the US: The Untold Reason," July 18, 2019, https://vigilantcitizen.com/latestnews/netflix-is-losing-subscribers-in-the-us-the-untold-reason/.

36. See Heinrich Brüning, *Memoiren, 1918–1945* (Stuttgart: Deutsche Verlagsanstalt, 1970), 607–86; Richard J. Evans, *The Coming of the Third Reich* (New York: Penguin 2003), 232–66.

37. Samuel Fitoussi, "Black Lives Matter: Un conformisme comme un autre?" June 2, 2020, https://www.causeur.fr/blacks-lives-matter-big-business-reseaux-sociaux-179339.

38. Jim Hoft, "Far Left Companies and Brands—Pepsi, HP, Doritos, Paypay, Adobe, BMW—Pull Ads from Facebook until They Ban Conservative Voices and President Trump's Posts," The Gateway Pundit, June 2020, https://www.thegatewaypundit.com/2020/06/far-left-companies-pepsi-hp-doritos-paypal-adobe-bmw-pull-ads-facebook-ban-conservative-voices-president-trumps-posts/.

39. Roland Baader, *Totgedacht:Warum Intellektuelle unsere Welt zerstören*, 2nd ed. (Lichtschlag Medien und Webung, 2020), especially 87–93 and 233–61. The 2020 edition was published by Lichtschlag Verlag, Grevenbroich, Germany.

40. Paul Gottfried, *Multiculturalism and the Politics of Guilt: Toward a Secular Theocracy* (Columbia: University of Missouri Press, 2002); and John Binder, "Only 1-in-6 Protesters Are Black; 46% Are White," Breitbart, June 24, 2020, https://www.breitbart.com/politics/2020/06/24/pew-research-only-1-in-6-protesters-are-black-46-percent-are -white/.

## 2. Origins of Antifascism

1. For the most detailed treatment of Mussolini's early life and the formation of the fascist party, see Renzo De Felice, *Mussolini il Rivoluzionario 1883–1920* (Milan: Einaudi, 1965).

2. For the definitive organization of the labor corporations and the Gran Consiglio, see Appendix II, "L'organizzazione dello Stato fascista," in Renzo De Felice's *Mussolini il fascista* (Turin: Giulio Einaudi, 1968), 542–53.

3. For the upshot of an illuminating interview with De Felice and his reasons for doing research on the fascist period, see Michael E. Ledeen, "Renzo De Felice and the Controversy over Italian Fascism," *Journal of Contemporary History* 11, no. 4 (October 1976): 269–83.

4. Fabio Filippi, *Una Vita Pagana: Enrico Corradini dal Superromismo Dannunziano a una Politica di Massa* (Florence: Vallecchi Editore, 1989)

5. Ernst Nolte, *Der kausale Nexus: Über Revisionen und Revisionismen in der Geschichtswissenschaft* (Munich: Herbig, 2002), 45–46.

6. John P. Diggins, *Mussolini and Fascism: The View from America* (Princeton, NJ: Princeton University Press, 1972).

7. Wolfgang Schivelbusch, *Entfernte Verwandtschaften: Faschismus, Nationalsozialismus, New Deal 1933–1939* (Munich: Carl Hanser Verlag, 2005), 25–36, 136–42.

8. A. James Gregor, *Giovanni Gentile: Philosopher of Fascism* (New Brunswick, NJ: Transaction Publishers, 2001); for a far more comprehensive English-language biography of Gentile, see H. S. Harris, *The Social Philosophy of Giovanni Gentile* (Urbana: University of Illinois Press, 1960).

9. See Renzo De Felice, *The Jews in Fascist Italy* (Oxford: Enigma Books, 2001) and Michele Sarfatti, *The Jews in Mussolini's Italy: From Equality to Persecution*, trans. John Tedeschi and Anne C. Tedeschi (Madison: University of Wisconsin Press, 2006).

10. Renzo De Felice, *Mussolini: Il Duce: Lo Stato Totalitario* (Turin: Luigi Einaudi, 1981).

11. A surprisingly detailed discussion of Mussolini's patronage of the arts and architecture can be found in Werner Brauninger's *Dux: Mussolini oder der Wille zur Macht* (Graz: Ares Verlag, 2018), 122–70. Like Nicholas Farrell's massive biography, *Mussolini: A New Life* (Burlington, VT: Phoenix Books, 2005), Brauninger's work has been dismissed for whitewashing an oppressive dictator. But both Farrell and Brauninger ad-

dress a question that goes begging in most account of Mussolini's rule, which is why an earlier generation across the political spectrum idolized *Il Duce*. See also my commentary, Paul Gottfried, "Exonerating Mussolini?," American Thinker, April 3, 2018, https://www.americanthinker.com/articles/2018/04/exonerating_mussolini_comments.html For an unrelievedly critical biography of Mussolini by the dean of English historians of Italy, see Denis Mack Smith, *Mussolini: A Biography* (New York: Knopf, 1982). Smith's longtime dispute with De Felice, whom he accused of "rehabilitating Mussolini," is discussed in the sketch of his life in "Morto lo storico Denis Mack Smith:.L'Italia vista da un liberal inglese," *Corriere dell Sera*, July 12, 2017, https://www.corriere.it/cultura/17_luglio_12/denis-mack-smith-morto-storia-italia-inghilterra-cavour-garibaldi-mussolini-2113c918-6726-11e7-9cb7-9d56a32dcee8.shtml.

12. De Felice, *Mussolini il fascista*, 81–93.

13. De Felice, *Mussolini il fascista*, 101–13.

14. Don Luigi Sturzo, Attualità nella Politica Moderna, series of website articles, https://digitalis-dsp.uc.pt/bitstream/10316.2/39534/1/Don%20Luigi%20Sturzo%20a%20man.pdf.

15. From 1947 until his death in 1959, Sturzo, a passionate decentralist and enemy of Italy's postfascist restored *partitocrazia*, raged against the Christian Democratic government. For a collection of these critical commentaries, see Luigi Sturzo, *Servir non servirsi: La prima regola del buon politico* (Soveria Mannelli, Italy: Rubettino, 2015).

16. For a treatment of this Catholic antifascist position and its post–World War II ramifications, see my book. *Fascism: Career of a Concept* (DeKalb: Northern Illinois University Press, 2016), especially 43–47, 137–44.

17. For a comprehensive biography of Ludwig von Mises by a disciple, see Jörg Guido Hülsmann, *Mises: The Last Knight of Liberalism* (Auburn, AL: Mises Institute, 2007).

18. Ludwig von Mises, *Liberalismus*, new printing (Santkt Augustin: Akademia Verlag, 1993), 50–51. This reprint has an introduction by Hans-Hermann Hoppe. The original was published in 1927.

19. Mises, *Liberalismus*, 45.

20. Mises, *Liberalismus*, 45–46; the reader is also referred to the English edition of this work, *Liberalism,* trans. Ralph Raico, preface by Bettina Bien Greaves (Irvington-on-Hudson, NY: Liberty Fund, 1985), 47–51, and to Karlheinz Weissmann's essay, "Faschismus -liberal," in *Sezession*, March 9, 2007), https://sezession.de/2383/faschismus-liberal.

21. See Paul Gottfried, *After Liberalism: Mass Democracy in the Administrative State* (Princeton, NJ: Princeton University Press, 1999), especially 135–44.

22. An indispensable study on the "golden age" of Marxist theory is Leszek Kolakowski, *Main Currents of Marxism* (New York: Norton, 2008)

23. Franz Neumann, *Behemoth: The Structure and Practice of National Socialism 1933–1944*, 2nd rev. ed. (Chicago: Ivan R. Dee, 1944). See also this posthumously published collection of Neumann's essays, Alfred Söllner, ed., *Wirtschaft, Staat, Demokratie, 1930–1954* (Frankfurt: Suhrkamp, 1978) and Duncan Kelly's essay, "Rethinking Franz Neumann's Route to 'Behemoth,'" *History of Political Thought* 23, no. 3 (Autumn 2002): 458–86.

24. See Friedrich Pollock's essays in Helmut Dubiel, ed., *Studien des Kapitalismus* (Munich: Beck Verlag, 1975) and Rolf Wiggershaus, *Die Frankfurter Schule: Geschichte,*

*Theoretische Entwicklung, Politische Bedeutung*, 6th ed. (Munich: Deutscher Taschenbuchverlag, 2001), 301–27, 401–28.

25. James Burnham, *The Managerial Revolution: What Is Happening in the World* (Bloomington: University of Indiana Press, 1962); Bruno Rizzi, *The Bureaucratization of the World*, trans. Adam Westoby (New York: Free Press, 1985). For an informative assessment of Rizzi's place as a social theorist, see Ernest E. Haberkern, "Review of *The Bureaucratization of the World*," *Telos* (66), 162–67.

26. Quoted in Wiggerhaus, *Die Frankfurter Schule*, 320–21.

27. For a comprehensive treatment of Kautsky's formulation of Marxism, see Jukka Gronow, *On the Formation of Karl Kautsky's Theory of Capitalism, the Marxism of the Second International, and Karl Marx's Critique of Political Economy* (Leiden: Brill, 2016), especially 190–208 for Kautsky's dispute with Lenin.

28. Karl Kautsky, *Terrorismus und Kommunismus: Ein Beitrag zur Naturgeschichte der Revolution*, reprint (Altenmünster: Jazzybee Verlag, 2019), 40, 152. Lenin's righthand man Leon Trotsky famously replied to Kautsky's brief in 1920 in his *Kommunismus und Terrorismus: Antikautsky* (Hamburg, 1920).

29. Particularly relevant here are the introduction to Rudolf Hilferding's "Das historische Problem," *Archiv für Politik* (1953), 295–303, written by Benedict Kautsky, Karl Kautsky's son; Franz Borkenau, *The Totalitarian Enemy* (London: Faber and Faber, 1940); and Hannah Arendt, *Origins of Totalitarianism* (New York: Harcourt Brace Jovanovich, 1973), especially 301–90.

30. In *Mussolini il fascista*, 480–84, De Felice tells us that Mussolini's democratic and socialist opposition saved the honor of the antifascist side, because it refused to accept his offer of collaboration. It is quite possible the opposition did not believe Mussolini would keep his word if they returned to Italy.

31. Reproduced in De Felice, *Mussolini il fascista*, II, 563–67.

32. See "Il Corriere degli Italiani: La Parabola di un quotidiana antifascista in Francia," *L'Ecole Francaise de Rome* 94 (1986): 285–321.

33. Ernst Fraenkel, *The Dual State: A Contribution to the Theory of Dictatorship*, trans. E. Shils and introduction by Jens Meierhenrich (Oxford: Oxford University Press, 2017).

34. Max Weber, *Gesammelte Aufsätze zur Wissenschaftslehre*, ed. Johannes Winckelmann (Tübingen: J. C. B. Mohr, 1988), 118–45.

35. Wiggershaus, *Die Frankfurter Schule*, 429–31.

36. See Mircea Eliade, *Mythes, rêve, et mystères* (Paris: Gallimard, 1972); Eric Voegelin, *The New Science of Politics* (Chicago: University of Chicago Press, 1952) and *Wissenschaft, Politik und Gnosis* (Munich: Kosel und Pustet, 1959); Hermann Rauschning, *The Revolution of Nihilism: Warning to the West* (Whitefish, MT: Kessering Press, 2005); and Hans Jonas, *The Message of the Alien God and the Beginnings of Christianity* (Boston: Beacon Press, 2001).

37. This observation, from Pasolini's *Scritti Corsari*, is reproduced on an Italian libertarian website, https://secolo-trentino.com/politica/pasolini-quella-profezia-sugli-antifascisti/.

### 3. Post–World War II Antifascism

1. Susan Neiman, *Learning from the Germans: Race and the Meaning of Evil* (New York: Farrar, Straus, and Giroux, 2019); Chauncey Devega, "Philosopher Susan Neiman Says Trump Is Evil—and She Literally Wrote the Book," Salon, September 24, 2019, https://www.salon.com/2019/09/24/philosopher-susan-neiman-says-trump-is-evil-and -she-literally-wrote-the-book/.

2. Alex Clark, "Interview: Nazism, Slavery, Empire," Guardian, September 13, 2019, https://www.theguardian.com/books/2019/sep/13/susan-neiman-interview-learning -from-the-germans.

3. See James Bacque, *An Investigation into the Mass Deaths of German Prisoners at the Hands of the French and Americans after World War Two* (Toronto: Stoddart, 1989) and, by the same author, *Crimes and Mercies: The Fate of German Civilians under the Allied Occupation 1944 to 1950,* repr. (Vancouver: Talon Books, 2007); and Giles MacDonogh, *After the Reich: The Brutal History of the Allied Occupation,* repr. (New York: Basic Books, 2009). Books like these are controversial, although perhaps less so for their facts than for what they investigate.

4. Two useful studies on the collapse of Germany are Adam Tooze, *Wages of Destruction: The Making and Breaking of the Nazi Economy* (New York: Viking, 2008); and Ian Kershaw, *The Defense and Destruction of Nazi Germany, 1944–1945* (New York: Viking, 2012).

5. See Alfred Maurice de Zayas, *Revenge: The Ethnic Cleansing of the East European Germans,* expanded ed. (New York: St. Martin's, 2006 and R. M. Douglas, *Orderly and Humane: The Expulsion of the Germans after the Second World War* (New Haven: Yale University Press, 2013).

6. A carefully weighed critique of the trials came from Eugene Davidson, longtime editor of the *Yale Review,* in his *The Nuremberg Fallacy* (Columbia: University of Missouri Press, 1998).

7. Mark Duell, "Churchill 'opposed Nuremberg and Wanted Nazi Leaders Executed or Jailed without Trial,' Extraordinary MI5 Wartime Diaries Reveal," Daily Mail, October 26, 2012, https://www.dailymail.co.uk/news/article-2223383/Churchill-opposed -Nuremberg-wanted-Nazi-leaders-executed-jailed-trial.html.

8. A useful overview of the events leading into the Cold War is in A. J. Levine, *The Soviet Union, the Communist Movement, and the World Prelude to the Cold War* (New York: Praeger, 1992) and René Rémond, *Le XXe siècle de 1914 à nos jours,* rev. ed. (Paris: Seuil, 2002), 158–88.

9. Two relevant recent studies of Soviet behavior at the end of World War II and at the beginning of the Cold War are Norman M. Naimark, *The Russians in Germany: A History of the Russian Zone, 1945–1946* (Cambridge, MA: Harvard University Press, 1997) and Robert Gellately, *Stalin's Curse: Battling for Communism in World War and Cold War* (New York: Viking, 2012). Perhaps the definitive English-language study of this subject is Hugh Seton-Watson, *Neither War nor Peace: The Struggle for Power in the Postwar World* (London: Kessinger, 2010).

10. For the observations of a famous writer exposed to this process, see Ernst von Salomon, *Der Fragebogen* (Berlin: Rowohlt, 1961).

11. A gold mine of information about the changing treatment of Germany at the hands of the occupying powers and the phased-in reeducation of the defeated enemy is available in Caspar von Schrenk-Notzing, *Charakterwäsche: Die Politik der amerikanischen Umerziehung in Deutschland* (Munich: Kristall bei Langen-Müller, 1981).

12. Harvard professor of philosophy W. E. Hocking, in *Experiment in Education: What We Can Learn from Educating Germans* (Palala Books, 2018), produced an early critical study of German reeducation.

13. Daniel Jonah Goldhagen, *Hitler's Willing Executioners: Ordinary Germans and the Holocaust* (New York: Viking, 1997); and the minutely detailed refutation of this work by Norman Finkelstein and Ruth Bettina, *A Nation on Trial: The Goldhagen Thesis and Historical Truth* (New York: Holt, 1998).

14. Gefährlich und Unzulässig, "Politiker und Medien straiten, ob ein Appell von rechts erlaubt ist," Focus Magazin, November 16, 1995, https://www.focus.de/politik /deutschland/8-mai-1945-gefaehrlich-und-unzulaessig_aid_151504.html.

15. See, for example, Hans Mommsen's comments in *Frankfurter Rundschau*, July 14, 1994.

16. See Rainer Zitelmann, "Vom antitotalitären zum antifaschistischen Geschichts-bild," in *Von der Wiederkehr des Sozialismus, ed. Christian Striefler and Wolfgang Templin* (Berlin: Ulstein, 1996), 230–55. For a restatement of most of the same arguments by a recently deceased scholar, see Jost Bauch, *Abschied von Deutschland: Eine politische Grab-schrift* (Rothenburg: Kopp, 2018).

17. Zitelmann, "Vom antitotalitären zum antifaschistischen Geschichtsbild," 254.

18. See the expressions of antinational sentiment in *Jungle World,* a website publica-tion that is ideologically associated with the German Greens and the Party of Demo-cratic Socialists, October 29, 2009, http://jungle-world.com/artikel/2009/44/39686.html; and the Kampf gegen Rechts site, http://www.kampf-gegen-rechts.de/.

19. A work that explores Merkel's upbringing and early career in East Germany with remarkable thoroughness is Ralf Georg Reuth and Günter Lachmann, *Das Erste Leben der Angla Merkel* (Munich: Piper Verlag, 2013).

20. Antonio Gramsci, *Quaderni del Carcere* (Turin: Einaudi, 1977), especially 36–40. Gramsci was concerned that his country's "intellectuals" might separate themselves from the revolutionary working class or exhibit a Jacobin temperament that had no serious political content" (54). He also affirmed the need to create an "organic relation" between the intelligentsia and the class that it hoped to guide.

21. For a comprehensive treatment of the evolution of the Frankfurt School in the United States, see Martin Jay, *Permanent Exiles: Essays on the Intellectual Migration from Germany to America* (New York: Columbia University Press, 1985).

22. Critical theory continued to thrive in the United States, despite the decline of in-terest in Freudian psychotherapy, a practice that Fromm, Harney, and other "Freudian Marxists" pursued after World War II. On the vicissitudes of American Freudianism, see J. Burnham, *After Freud Left: A Century of Psychoanalysis in America* (Chicago: Uni-versity of Chicago Press, 2012); for a fascinating study of postwar countercurrents, see Paul M. Dennis, "Bishop Fulton Sheen: America's Public Critic of Psychoanalysis," *Jour-nal of the History of Behavioral Sciences* (2019): 1–15.

23. See Theodor Adorno et al., *The Authoritarian Personality* (New York: Harper, 1950) and Rolf Wiggershaus, *Theodor W. Adorno* (Munich: Beck'sche Verlagsbuchhandl ung, 1987), 71–79.

24. Quoted in Rolf Wiggershaus, *Die Frankfurter Schule*, 6th ed. (Munich: Deutscher Taschenbuchverlag, 2001), 432.

25. See Wiggerhaus, *Die Frankfurter Schule*, 430–38.

26. The definitive, exhaustive biography of this flamboyant figure is T. Harry Williams, *Huey Long* (New York: Viking Books, 1981)

27. See Sheldon Marcus, *Father Coughlin: The Tumultuous Life of the Priest of the Little Flower* (Boston: Little Brown and Co., 1973) for an admirably balanced account of the life of this controversial radio priest. Especially after 1940, when Coughlin was forced by his clerical superiors to give up his radio program, his published writings became increasingly bland. To the surprise of some, he ended up as a JFK Democrat.

28. See T. Lothrop Stoddard, *The Rising Tide of Color: Against White World Supremacy* (Honolulu: University of Hawaii Press, 2003) and Pat Shipman, *The Evolution of Racism* (New York: Simon & Schuster, 1994).

29. See Sinclair Lewis, *It Can't Happen Here* (New York: NAL Trade, 2003).

30. Nancy Cott, "A Good Journalist Understands That Fascism Can Happen Anywhere, Anytime," Literary Hub, April 20, 2020, https://lithub.com/a-good-journalist -understands-that-fascism-can-happen-anywhere-anytime/.

31. Bertram Myron Gross, *Friendly Fascism: The New Face of Power in America* (Boston: South End Press, 1980)

32. Bertram Myron Gross, *The Managing of Organizations: The Administrative Struggle*, 2 vols., (New York: Free Press, 1964)..

33. Adorno et al., *The Authoritarian Personality,* 891–960.

34. Christopher Lasch, *The True and Only Heaven* (New York: Norton, 1991), 457–61.

35. For an attempt to fit F-scale testing into a broader American cultural context, see Angelo M. Codevilla, "America's Ruling Class and the Perils of Revolution," *American Spectator* (August 2010).

36. See Bob Altemeyer, *Right-Wing Authoritarianism* (Winnipeg: University of Winnipeg Press, 1981) and *The Authoritarian Specter* (Cambridge, MA: Harvard University Press, 1996).

37. Two relevant critiques of the *TAP* and its influence on American culture and political practices are in William F. Buckley's *Up from Liberalism*, (New York: McDowell and Obolensky, 1959), 59–62. and the excellent anthology, Richard Christie and Marie Jahoda, eds., *Studies in the Scope and Method of the Authoritarian Personality* (Glencoe, IL: Free Press, 1954).

38. See Lipset's observations about "Working Class Authoritarianism," *American Sociological Review* 24 (1959): 482–501.

39. Lasch, *The True and Only Heaven*, 460–61.

40. Philip Jenkins, *Hoods and Shirts: The Extreme Right in Pennsylvania 1925–1950* (Chapel Hill: University of North Carolina Press, 1997).

41. Jenkins, *Hoods and Shirts*, 606–28.

42. See Hermann-Josef Grosse Kracht, "Fritz Fischer und der deutsche Protestant-ismus," *Zeitschrift für Neuere Theologie-Geschichte*, 10, no. 2 (2003): 196–223.

43. See the most recent English edition of this work: *War of Illusions: German Poli-cies from 1911 to 1914*, trans. Marian Jackson (New York: Norton, 1973).

44. Fritz Fischer, *Hitler war kein Betriebsunfall* (Munich: C. H. Beck, 1998).

45. See Georges Henri Soutou, *La grande illusion: Comment la France a perdu la paix 1914–1920* (Paris: Tallandier, 2015); Stephane Audoin-Rouzeau, "Von den Kriegsursa-chen zur Kriegskultur: Neuere Forschungstendenzen zum erstenWeltkrieg in Frank-reich," *Neue Politische Literatur* (1994): 201–04; and Paul Gottfried, review of *Georges-Henri Soutou La grande illusion: Comment la France a perdu la paix 1914–1920, Independent Re-view* 23, no. 2 (Fall 2018), http://www.independent.org/publications/tir/article.asp?id =1332.

46. On Franco-Russian complicity, see, for example, Friedrich Stieve, *Iswolski und der Weltkrieg* (Berlin: Verlagsgesellschaft für Politik und Geschichte, 1924) and Sean McKeekin, *The Russian Origins of the First World War* (Cambridge, MA: Harvard Uni-versity Press, 2013).

47. For a remarkably cogent and thorough summation of all the major criticisms of the Fischer thesis, see Gunter Spraul, *Der Fischer Komplex* (Halle: Cornelius, 2011), 254–388.

48. See Gerhard Ritter's three-volume work, which particularly in the final volume offers an alternative to the Fischer thesis about Germany's road to war in 1914: *The Sword and the Scepter* (Miami: University of Miami Press, 1972); and Ritter's early critical re-sponse to Fischer's work in "Eine neue Kriegsschuldthese," *Historische Zeitschrift* 194 (1962): 657–68. Less viscerally expressed responses to Fischer's key points are found in Egmont Zechlin's anthology, *Krieg und Kriegsrisiko: zur deutschen Politik im Ersten Welt-krieg* (Düsseldorf: Droste Verlag, 1979); Konrad Jarausch, "Revisiting German History: Bethmann-Hollweg Revisited," *Central European History* 21, no. 3 (September 1988): 224–43; and Edwin Hölzle, "Das Experiment des Friedens im Ersten Weltkrieg, 1914–1917," *Geschichte in Wissenschaft und Unterricht,* 8 (1962): 514.

49. German historian Egmont Zechlin first advanced this counterargument in "Juli 1914: Antwort auf eine Streitschrift," *Geschichte in Wissenchaft und Unterricht* 4 (1983): 244–46; see Dietrich Erdmann, "Zur Beurteilung Bethmann Hollwegs," *Geschichte in Wissenchaft und Unterricht* 15 (1964): 525–40.

50. See Spraul, *Der Fischer Komplex*, 148–82. The German historian Thomas Nip-perdey in *Nachdenken über die deutsche Geschichte*, second ed. (Munich: C.H. Beck, 1991), 208–48, raises numerous critical points about the Fischer-Geiss interpretation of the Ger-man Second Empire and the direction in which it supposedly inevitably went. Accord-ing to Nipperdey, that German government viewed in the context of its time, could have moved in multiple directions, including toward a more a liberal constitutional regime. Germany in the late nineteenth century showed numerous signs of modernization and admirable legal and academic institutions, even while retaining certain outdated author-itarian features.

51. See Hajo Holborn's introduction to *Germany's Aims in the First World War* (New York: W. W. Norton, 1968) and Fritz Stern, *The Politics of Illiberalism: Essays on the Po-litical Culture of Modern Germany* (New York: Columbia University Press, 1992).

52. For Wolfgang Mommsen's praise of Fischer for stressing the responsibility of all German social classes for the aggressive nationalism that led to war in 1914, see *Die deutsche Kriegszielpolitik: Zum Stand der Diskussion* (Munich: Nymphenburg Verlagshandlung, 1970), 61–100.

53. See *Der Spiegel*, March 29, 2004, 134; and Günter Spraul, *Der Fischer Komplex*, 98–100. *der Diskussion* (Munich: Nymphenburgverlag, 1971), 60–101.

54. Quoted in Spraul, *Der Fischer Komplex*, 110–12. For the original source, see Immanuel Geiss, *Der polnische Grenzstreifen 1914–1918* (Dresden: Matthiesen, 1960), foreword.

55. Volker Ullrich, Griff nach der Wahrheit. Zum Tod des Hamburger Historikers Fritz Fischer, 55, 1999, https://www.zeit.de/1999/50/199950.f.fischer_.xml.

56. Helmut Lindemann, "Monument deutscher Maβlosigkeit," *Gewerkschafltiche Monatshefte* 5, no. 13 (1962).

57. On the efforts to make the Fischer thesis the standard view of Imperial Germany among school students, see Rüdiger Bergien, "Fritz Fischers Thesen in Schulbüchern," *Militärgeschichtliche Zeitschrift* 64 (2005): 133–45.

58. See Herbert Butterfield, *Origins of History* (New York: Basic Books, 1984); Kenneth McIntyre, *History, Providence, and Skeptical History* (Wilmington, DE: Intercollegiate Studies Institute Press, 2011); Geoffrey Elton, "Herbert Butterfield nd the Study of History," *Historical Journal* 23, no. 7 (September 1984): 729–43.

59. Hans-Georg Gadamer, *Wahrheit und Methode*, ed. Günter Figal (Berlin: Akademie Verlag, 2007), especially 1–8, 219–36.

60. Thomas C. Holt, "When the Cruel War Was Over," *Washington Post*, May 15, 1988, https://www.washingtonpost.com/archive/entertainment/books/1988/05/15/when-the-cruel-war-was-over/0730449c-f1f5-48bc-887b-8fc364a16888/?utm_term=.bc006 1039305.

61. William McFeely, "A Moment of Terrifying Promise," *New York Times*, May 5, 1988, https://www.nytimes.com/1988/05/22/books/a-moment-of-terrifying-promise. html.

62. Eric Foner, *Reconstruction in America: The Unfinished Revolution 1863–1877* (New York: Harper and Row, 1988), xxi–xxii.

63. Eric Foner, "The Making and Breaking of the Legend of Robert E. Lee," *New York Times*, August 29, 2017, https://www.nytimes.com/2017/08/28/books/review/eric-foner-robert-e-lee.html. A particularly bizarre restatement of Foner's depiction of Reconstruction ("Defending Reconstruction,") can be found in the establishment conservative publication, the *Claremont Review*, in an article by the historian Allen C. Guelzo, *Claremont Review* 17, no. 2 (Spring 2017): 74–81. Guelzo pours unqualified praise on Reconstruction, which "was a bourgeois revolution that was crushed by the resurgent political power of a bloodied but unbowed aristocracy" (80), and celebrates the humiliation of the white South in the Civil War as the removal of a malignant growth on a Northern democratic society.

64. *Dissent* 41 (Summer, 1994), 371–76, 386–88.

65. Mary Grabar, *Debunking Howard Zinn: Exposing the Fake History that Turned a Generation against America* (Washington, DC: Regnery History, 2019). Southern historian Brion McClanahan observes in his critical essay, "Reconstruction," in *Chronicles:*

*A Magazine of American Culture* 44, no. 2 (February 2020): 9–13. that what principally distinguishes Guelzo and Foner from Dunning is their emphasis on racial oppression. The focus of Reconstruction studies has shifted not toward the Marxist Left but rather toward intersectionality. For a similar point of view, see Robert L. Paquette, "The Unemancipated Country: Eugene Genovese's Discovery of the Old South," *Academic Questions* 27, no. 2 (2014): 204–12.

66. Mary Grabar, 31.

67. Eric Foner, "Majority Report," *New York Times*, March 2, 1980, p. BR3.

68. Howard Zinn, *A People's History of the United States*, reissue (New York: Harper Perennial, 2015), 9.

69. The Partido Vox in Spain has pushed back hard against all these tendencies. See for examples the remarks of José Contreras, the party's ideological leader, at https://www.actuall.com/criterio/democracia/hacia-una-fusion-de-vox-y-pp/. José Francisco Contreras, "Miseria del voto útil," Actuall, September 12, 2015.

70. See Stanley Payne, "Recent Historiography on the Spanish Republic and Civil War," *Journal of Modern History* 60, no. 3 (September 1988): 540–56 and Arnaud Imatz's interview with Moa, "L'historien de la Guerre d'Espagne qui fait scandale," *Nouvelle Revue Historique* 17 (March/April, 2005): 27–29.

71. See Serafin Fanjul, *Andalus contra Espāna: La forja del mito* (Madrid: Siglo XI, 2000) and *Andalus: Un imagen en la Historia* (Madid: Royal Academy of History, 2012).

72. See Fanjul, *Andalus contra Espāna* and *Andalus: Un imagen en la Historia*.

73. The author used the French edition of this book, which was the one that was available to him. See Serafin Fanjul, *Al-Andalus: L'invention d'un mythe*, trans. Nicholas Klein and Laura Martinez (Paris: L'Artilleur, 2017).

74. Fanjul, *Al-Andalus*, 463–512.

75. Fanjul, *Al-Andalus*, 32–33.

76. Stanley Payne's last monumental work on Spanish history, *Spain: A Unique History* (Madison: University of Wisconsin Press, 2011), addresses the question of what determines Spanish national identity and why Al Andalus is peripheral to shaping it.

77. Among Mack Smith's more noteworthy books are *Cavour and Garibaldi, 1860* (Cambridge: Cambridge University Press, 1954); *Mussolini* (New York: Knopf, 1982); *Modern Italy, A Political History*, rev. ed. (Ann Arbor: University of Michigan Press, 1997); and *Italy and its Monarchy* (New Haven: Yale University Press, 1989).

78. Guido Pescosolido, "Mack Smith e la storia d'Italia," Editoriale, http://www.storiamediterranea.it/public/md1_dir/r1490.pdf. Similar statements can be found in the work of an Italian Communist historian Paolo Altari, *Studi storici*, 2 (1959–60).

79. One may find broad hints of how far to the left Mack Smith moved from his early patron in his "Benedetto Croce: History and Politics," *Journal of Contemporary History* 8, no. 1 (January 1973): 41–61.

80. Steinberg's praise appeared in *The Guardian*'s obituary for Smith on July 24, 2017, The reference into Steinberg is a biographical Sketch on the UPenn website, https://www.theguardian.com/books/2017/jul/24/denis-mack-smith-obituary. A similar obituary, celebrating Mack Smith's courageous independence of mind, appeared in the *New York Times*, https://www.nytimes.com/2017/08/02/books/denis-mack-smith-dead-historian-of-italy.html.

81. See Rosario Romeo, *Cavour, il suo tempo*, 3 vols. (Bari: Laterza, 1990). Although it may seem to US reviewers that Mack Smith was more willing than Romeo to acknowledge regional economic disparities in the creation of the modern Italian state, it was Romeo, a Sicilian, who wrote the authoritative work on this problem, *Mezzogiorno e Sicilia nel Risorgimento* (Naples: ESI, 1963).

82. Mack Smith's legendary wars with Romeo and De Felice are recounted in the obituary for him that appeared in *Modern Italy* 22, no. 3 (2017): 231–32. For Mack Smith's more measured review of De Felice's massive work, see *Modern Italy* (2000) 5.2, 193–210.

83. Typical of this form of historical remembrance that dispenses with the paraphernalia of technical scholarship is the 1619 Project advanced by the *New York Times* in August 2019. This Project is a penitential exercise but not explicitly antifascist. https://www.nytimes.com/interactive/2019/08/14/magazine/1619-america-slavery.html.

## 4. Defining and Redefining Fascism

1. Patrick Bahners, "Die Lehrer Deutschlands," *Frankfurter Allgemeine Zeitung*, September 29, 2018, https://www.faz.net/aktuell/feuilleton/debatten/deutsche-historiker -stellen-sich-gegen-die-afd-15812149.html.

2. Frank Böckelmann, "Nazis Raus," *Tumult* (Winter 2018/19): 5.

3. Böckelmann, "Nazis Raus," 6.

4. Severin Weiland, " Rechts, deutsch, jüdisch," *Spiegel*, June 10, 2018, http://www .spiegel.de/politik/deutschland/juden-in-der-afd-warum-sich-eine-juedische-gruppe -in-der-afd-organisiert-a-1231676.html.

5. "Schulz: Gauland gehört auf den Misthaufen der Gechichte," *Berliner Morgenpost*, December 9, 2018, https://www.morgenpost.de/politik/article215309549/Haushaltsde batte-im-Bundestag-Schlagabtausch-erwartet.html.

6. Eckhart Lohse, "Merkels maximaler Druck," *Frankfurter Allegemeine Zeitung*, June 2, 2020, https://www.faz.net/aktuell/politik/inland/kemmerich-tritt-zurueck -merkels-maximaler-druck-16620549.html.

7. Katrin Bennhold and Melissa Eddy, "'Höcke or Hitler?' Germany's Far-Right Party Radicalizes," *New York Times*, October 26, 2019, https://www.nytimes.com/2019 /10/26/world/europe/afd-election-east-germany-hoecke.html.

8. Tomas Spahn, "Der ewige Landtag," *Tichys Einblick*, February 13, 2020, Einblick, February 2020, https://www.zeit.de/2020/05/uwe-tellkamp-schriftsteller-lesungen-dres den-afd-zensur.

9. August Modersohn, "Uwe Tellkamp: Tumult im Gesinnungskorridor," Die Zeit, January 27, 2020, https://www.zeit.de/2020/05/uwe-tellkamp-schriftsteller-lesungen -dresden-afd-zensur.

10. *Tagesspiegel*, June 10, 2019.

11. *Die Welt*, February 27, 2017.

12. Timothy Snyder, "Donald Trump Borrows from the Old Tricks of Fascism," *The Guardian*, October 30, 2018, https://www.theguardian.com/commentisfree/2018/oct/30/t rump-borrows-tricks-of-fascism-pittsburgh.

13. See David Beito's well-documented presentation of "FDR's War against the Press," *Reason* (May 2017), https://reason.com/archives/2017/04/05/roosevelts-war-against-the -press.

14. https://www.trumanlibrary.org/trivia/letter.htm.

15. Kenneth D. Williamson, "What Bernie Sanders Shares with Trump—and Mussolini," New York Post, February 21, 2019, https://nypost.com/2019/02/21/what-bernie -sanders-shares-with-trump-and-mussolini/.

16. Jason Stanley, *How Fascism Works: The Politics of Us and Them* (New York: Random House, 2018), xii-xiii; also 133–35.

17. See among other books on this subject Wayne Cole, *America First: The Battle Against Intervention, 1940–1941*, reprint (Read Books Limited, 2016); Justus D. Doenecke, *The Challenge to American Intervention* (Krieger Publisher: Anvil series, 1996) and *Storm on the Horizon: The Challenge to American Intervention, 1939–1941* (Lanham, MD.: Rowman and Littlefield, 2003).

18. https://cis.org/Report/American-Unionism-and-US-Immigration-Policy.

19. Ibid., 178–79.

20. Ibid., 153.

21. Ron Dreher, " F-K You, A-holes Argued the Yale Professor," *American Conservative*, September 28, 2016, https://www.theamericanconservative.com/dreher/swinburne -jason-stanley-homosexuality/.

22. Timothy Snyder, *On Tyranny: Twenty Lessons from the Twentieth Century* (New York City: Tim Dugan Books, 2017), 12.

23. Ibid, 19.

24. Mark Bray, *Translating Anarchy: The Anarchism of Occupy Wall Street* (New York: Zero Books, 2013).

25. Mark Bray, *Antifa: The Anti-Fascist Handbook* (Brooklyn and London: Melville House, 2017, 3–39.

26. Ibid., 82–83.

27. Ibid., 96–104.

28. See *La France Interdite*, 60–62; and Hugues Lagrange's two works on the effects of sub-Saharan immigration to France, *Le déni des cultures* (Paris: Seuil, 2010), and *En terre étrangère. Vies d' immigrés du Sahel en Île-de-France* (Paris: Seuil, 2013).

29. Ibid., 80.

30. Ibid., 125–26.

31. Ibid., 32–36.

32. Ibid., 134–35.

33. Mark Bray, *Antifa*, 149.

34. Ibid., 156.

35. Ibid., 158.

36. Amitai Etzione, "Is America on the Road to Becoming an Authoritarian State," *National Interest*, August 1, 2020, https://nationalinterest.org/feature/america-road-be coming-authoritarian-state-165990?fbclid=IwAR2VkKlLzOFVjCaE4xzRujObelJ8aI 6AKlY29XwJRNNMxtJGhV9TIZ82HYU.

37. Richard North Patterson, "Trump's Authoritarian Impulse," The Bulwark, June 5, 2020, https://thebulwark.com/trumps-authoritarian-impulse/.

38. See Jens R. Hentschke, *Vargas and Brazil: New Perspectives* (New York: Palgrave Macmillan, 2008)

39. Alejandro Horowicz in *Los cuatros peronismos* (Buenos Aires: Hysperamerica, 1987) treats Peron's periods of rule and the changing movement he left behind by examining their differences as well as overlaps.

40. See Juan L. Linz, *Totalitarian and Authoritarian Regimes* (Boulder, CO: Lynn Riennder Publishers, 2000); Stanley G. Payne, *Fascism: Comparison and Definition* (Madison: University of Wisconsin Press, 1980); Amos Perlmutter, *Modern Authoritarianism* (New Haven: Yale University Press, 1984). John E. Fagg's *Latin America: A General History* (New York: Macmillan,1963) makes this point about the perennial character of Latin American authoritarianism less judgmentally than Linz or Perlmutter.

41. Gabriele Nadlinger, "Wann spricht man von Rechtsextremismus, Rechtsradikalismus und Neonazismus?" Bundeszentrale für politsche Bildung, July 25, 2008, https:// www.bpb.de/politik/extremismus/rechtsextremismus/41891/streitbare-demokratie.

42. "Jair Bolsonaro Denies He Is a Fascist and Paints Himself as a Brazilian Churchill," Guardian, October 30, 2018, https://www.theguardian.com/world/2018/oct/30/jair-bol sonaro-denies-he-is-a-fascist-brazilian-churchill.

## 5. Antifascism versus Populism

1. Anelique Chrisafis, "Macron Warns of Rising Nationalism as World Leaders Mark the Armistice," *The Guardian*, November 11, 2018, https://www.theguardian.com /world/2018/nov/11/trump-joins-macron-and-world-leaders-at-armistice-ceremony,

2. "Le fascisme italien s'est régénéré sous la forme du populisme," March 23, 2019, https://www.europe1.fr/emissions/L-edito-international/edito-le-fascisme-italien-sest -regenere-sous-la-forme-du-populisme-3878930 L'Europe 1.

3. Alexander J. Motl, "Is Vladimir Putin a Fascist?" *Newsweek*, April 27, 2015, https:// www.newsweek.com/vladimir-putin-fascist-325534.

4. Alexander J. Motyl, "Is Putin's Russia Fascist?," *The National Interest*, December 3, 2007, https://nationalinterest.org/commentary/inside-track-is-putins-russia-fascist-1888.

5. George Will, " Putin's Fascist Revival Carries Echoes of Hitler," *Jewish World Review*, September 4, 2014, http://www.jewishworldreview.com/cols/will090414.php3.

6. See my article, Paul Gottfried, If Loving Putin Is 'Right,' I Want to be Wrong," *The American Conservative*, July 17, 2017, "https://www.theamericanconservative.com/ar ticles/if-loving-putin-is-right-i-want-to-be-wrong/.

7. See Paul Gottfried, *The Strange Death of Marxism: The European Left in the New Millennium* (Columbia: University of Missouri Press, 2005).

8. Eric Mann, "Growing Activism," Labor Community Strategy Center, UC San Diego, video, April 30, 2007, YouTube, https://www.uctv.tv/shows/Growing-Activism -Labor-Community-Strategy-Center-12261.

9. Thomas Haldenwang, "Mobilisierungsfähigkeit im politischen Extremismus," Bundesamt für Verfassungsschutz, May 13, 2019, https://www.verfassungsschutz.de/de /oeffentlichkeitsarbeit/vortraege/rede-p-haldenwang-20190513-bfv-symposium-2019; see also Günter Scholdt, "So geht totalitär," *Freilich* 105 (August 2019): 88–91. A work

that is written with deep patriotic concern and tries to make sense of the passivity of the German public in the face of their continuing self-degradation as a people is Thorsten Hinz, *Die Psychologie der deutschen Niederlage: Über die deutsche Mentalität* (Berlin: Antaios, 2016).

10. An academic who seems shocked by the recent intensification of the war against "pluralistic democracy in German universities, Andreas Rödder, express his concern in comments in the *Neue Zürcher Zeitung*, November 4, 2019. What makes these comments particularly striking is the author's obvious sympathy for the Rainbow Coalition before it turned in his view "repressive."

11. "Verfassungsschutz macht AfD zum Prüffall: Partei will sich juristisch wehren," YouTube, January 15, 2019, https://www.tagesschau.de/multimedia/video/video-496129 .html.

12. A particularly egregious example of the efforts to marginalize the AfD was the dismissal of an official associated with the Ministry of Culture in Hesse for eating with an AfD member. The Green feminist Minister of Culture was outraged by this happening. "Chef der Filmförderung gefeuert wegen Mittagessens mit dem AfD Vorsitzenden," Tichyseinblick, September 24, 2019, https://www.tichyseinblick.de/daili -es-sentials/chef-der-filmfoerderung-gefeuert-wegen-mittagessens-mit-dem-afd-vorsit zenden/.

13. Alice Weidel, *Widerworte: Gedanken über Deutschland* (Kulmbach: Börsen Verlag, 2019).

14. "BHL assimile les Gilets-jaunes au nazisme et appelle à soutenir Macron," Sputnik, December 12, 2018, https://fr.sputniknews.com/france/201812071039207383-france -bhl-gilets-jaunes-levy-macron/.

15. "Majority of French People Say Immigration Is Harmful to the Nation," Ipsos Polls, December 2018, https://www.ipsos.com/sites/default/files/ct/news/documents/2018 -08/french_fractures_2018.pdf.

16. "Why Nationalism Is Rising Globally," YouTube, February 12, 2019, https://www .youtube.com/watch?v=P2mO42uvlMg.

17. "The Number That Tells the Story of Immigration in France," Local, October 8, 2019, https://www.thelocal.fr/20160823/immigration-negative-for-france-majority-says.

18. Roger Eatwell and Matthew Goodwin, *National Populism and the Revolt against Liberal Democracy* (London: Penguin, 2018), 3–39.

19. Eatwell and Goodwin, *National Populism*, 43–48, 57–63.

20. "Tory MP Criticized for Using Antisemitic Term 'Cultural Marxism,'" *The Guardian*, March 26, 2019, https://www.theguardian.com/news/2019/mar/26/tory-mp-criti cised-for-using-antisemitic-term-cultural-marxism.

21. For a defense of this term in a very mainstream Republican website, see Dominic Green's article, mostly in praise of Jordan Peterson, in *American Spectator*, "What's Wrong with. Cultural Marxism," *Spectator*, March 28, 2019, https://spectator.us/whats-wrong -cultural-marxism/. Peterson, William Lind, and, at one time, I favored the use of the term "cultural Marxist," but already in *The Strange Death of Marxism* and even more explicitly in *Fascism: Career of a Concept* (DeKalb: Northern Illinois University Press, 2016) I began to avoid a phrase that I considered misleading. The reason was certainly not the one offered by the Board of Deputies of British Jews. It just seemed confusing to

refer to positions that are clearly not classical Marxist ones as something they are not. An article in *Daily Kos* by David Neiwert presented my position tersely and accurately. Daily Kos, January 23, 2019, https://www.dailykos.com/stories/2019/1/23/1828527/-How -the-cultural-Marxism-hoax-began-and-why-it-s-spreading-into-the-mainstream. See also my attempt to dissociate myself from the term "cultural Marxist" in *American Thinker*, https://www.americanthinker.com/articles/2018/01/the_frankfurt_school_and _cultural_marxism.html.

22. The term "cultural Marxist" was first popularized in the United States by the self-described Marxist Troy Schroyer. See for example *The Critique of Domination: The Origin and Development of Critical Theory* (New York: Braziller, 1973).

23. Paul Bedard, "Cesar Chavez Elevated into an Anti-Illegal Immigration Hero," *Washington Examiner*, March 26, 2018, https://www.washingtonexaminer.com/washing ton-secrets/cesar-chavez-elevated-to-anti-illegal-immigration-hero.

24. Barbara Jordan, History, November 9, 2009, https://www.history.com/topics /black-history/barbara-c-jordan.

25. See Georges Marchais's editorial comment *in L'Humanité*, January 6, 1981.

26. Georges Cogniot, *Réalité de la nation, l'attrape-nigaud du cosmopolitisme* (Paris: Éditions Sociales, 1950).

27. See Ulla Plener's biography of the post–World War II chairman of the German Socialist Party Kurt Schumacher (1895–1952). A Socialist reformer who spent World War II in a Nazi concentration camp, Schumacher was also a passionate German patriot. To the consternation of the US occupying forces, he tried to negotiate with the Soviets to establish a neutral but unified Germany.

28. Eatwell and Goodwin, *National Populism*, xxi–xxv.

29. "Interview with Gyula Thürmer: With Kadar Gone, Soros Arrived," Visegrad-post, March 3, 2020, https://visegradpost.com/en/2020/02/03/gyula-thurmer-with-kadar -gone-soros-arrived/.

30. "Belföld-Thürmer Gyula," *Belföld*, August 12, 2019, https://index.hu/belfold /2019/05/19/thurmer_gyula_munkaspart_interju_ep-valasztas_2019/.

31. Eatwell and Goodwin, *National Populism*, 284–92; and Markus Wagner's "posi-tive Bilanz" of his party's achievements in 2018 given at the New Year's reception for the AfD in January 2019, "Das wird eine AfD-Regierung sofort ändern," YouTube, Novem-ber 27, 2019, https://www.youtube.com/watch?v=gpak1pHJxgE.

32. A variation on this view of reconciliation between warring ideological sides comes from the Göttingen sociologist Wolfgang Sofsky, who sees the growing size of the ad-ministrative state as an incentive to extreme parties to moderate their positions. Sofsky's aphorism is "Ämter überdauern Inhaber" (positions outlast their occupants), a situation that forces ideological partisans into "a liberal consensus" for professional advancement. See Wolfgang Sofsky, "Das Volk schaut nur zu," *Neue Zürcher Zeitung*, February 20, 2019, https://www.youtube.com/watch?v=gpak1pHJxgE.

33. Alain de Benoist, BoulevardVoltaire, "Il y aura un avant et un après gilets jaunes," April 1, 2019, https://www.bvoltaire.fr/alain-de-benoist-il-y-aura-un-avant-et-un-apres -gilets-jaunes/.

34. Thilo Sarrazin, *Deutschland schafft sich ab* (Berlin: Deutsche Verlagsanstalt, 2010) and *Feindliche Überrnahme: Wie der Islam den Fortschritt behindert und die Gesellschaft*

*bedroht* (Berlin: FinanzBuch, 2018); and Laurent Obertone, *La France Interdite* (Paris: Editions Ring, 2018), especially 51–77. For a revealing look at German crime figures since the arrival of the migrants, see Tichys Einblick, "Bundeskriminalität mit anderem Bild zur Zuwanderung als Bundesinnenminister," April 10, 2019, https://www.tichysein blick.de/daili-es-sentials/bundeskriminalamt-mit-anderem-bild-zur-zuwanderungskrim inalitaet-als-bundesinnenminister/.

35. Quoted in *Le Figaro*, June 13, 2018.

36. See Jérôme Fourquet, *L'Archipel francais: Naissance d'une nation multiple et divisée* (Paris: Seuil, 3019). Fourquet's book challenges the conventional populist wisdom as expressed by Patrick Buisson and Francois Bousquet, both advisers to the Le Pen family and to the Rassemblement National. For a commentary with a similar point of view, see my opinion-piece in *The American Conservative*, December 31, 2018, "The Populist Right is Less Popular Than You Think," https://www.theamericanconservative.com/articles /the-populist-right-is-less-popular-than-you-think/.

37. Eros Banaj and Jabeen Bhatti, "Germany's Anti-Immigrant Party Sees Election Surge Against Angela Merkel's Moderates," *The Washington Times*, September 1, 2019, https://www.washingtontimes.com/news/2019/sep/1/alternative-germany-election-surge -hits-angela-mer/.

38. Ellen Ehni, "Grüne erstmals vor Union," DEUTSCHLANDTREND, June 6, 2019, https://www.tagesschau.de/inland/deutschlandtrend-1671.html.

39. Matthias Wyssuwa, "Hamburg wählt sich selbst," Frankfurter Allgemeine Zeitung, February 23, 2020, https://www.faz.net/aktuell/politik/wahl-in-hamburg/wahl-in -hamburg-afd-und-wohl-auch-die-fdp-in-buergerschaft-16648163.html.

40. See Benedikt Kaiser, "Der Weg der AfD," *Neue Ordnung* 1, 20: 2020, 11–15.

41. See Alexander and Margerete Mitscherlich, *Die Unfähigkeit zu trauern* (Munich: Piper Verlag, 2009) and Géraldine Schwarz, *Les Amnésiaques* (Paris: Flammarion, 2019).

42. Stefan Locke, "Was tut man sich an?" Frankfurter Allgemeine Zeitung, March 9, 2018, https://www.faz.net/aktuell/feuilleton/buecher/themen/der-schriftsteller-uwe -tellkamp-ist-ein-afd-sympathisant-15485914.html.

43. Natalia Antonova, "From Britain to Ukraine the far right is thriving on shared emotion," *The Guardian*, March 5, 2018, https://www.theguardian.com/discussion /p/87zcd.

44. Zusammengestellt von Wilko Zicht and Matthias Cantow, "Wenn am nächsten Sonntag Bundestagswahl wäre," https://www.wahlrecht.de/umfragen/

45. Josef Schüsslburner's *Scheitert die AfD?* (Schnellroda: Institut für Staatspolitik, 2020).

46. https://www.diepresse.com/5698960/die-turbulente-geschichte-der-freiheitlichen -in-osterreich

47. Martin Fritzl, "Heinz-Christian Straches Abgang in die Polit-Pension," *Die Presse*, October 12, 2020, https://www.diepresse.com/5881247/heinz-christian-straches-abgang -in-die-polit-pension.

48. According to the pro-Conservative *Telegraph*, the best thing about Johnson's diversity is that he practices it without even having to acknowledge it. Rosa Prince, "The Best Thing about Boris Johnson's Diverse Cabinet Is That Its Diversity Is Irrelevant,"

*The Telegraph*, July 25, 2019, https://www.telegraph.co.uk/politics/2019/07/25/best-thing
-boris-johnsons-diverse-cabinet-diversity-irrelevant/.

49. On Johnson's effusive, widely announced support for gay marriage, see also Rowena
Mason, "Let Same Sex Couples Enjoy the 'Happy State' of Marriage," *The Telegraph*,
April 4, 2020, https://www.telegraph.co.uk/news/politics/london-mayor-election/9488094
/Boris-Johnson-let-same-sex-couples-enjoy-the-happy-state-of-marriage.html.

50. See for example this syndicated column by Frank Buckley, a prominent pro-Trump
commentator. F. H. Buckley, "Boris Johnson, Donald Trump's Secret to Success: Take
Best from Right, Left," *New York Post*, December 16, 2019, https://nypost.com/2019/12/16
/boris-johnson-donald-trumps-secret-to-success-take-best-from-right-left/.

51. See the examination of what is called "stripped-down populism" in my book, *After Liberalism: Mass Democracy in the Managerial State* (Princeton, NJ: Princeton University Press, 1999), 112–31.

52. Marion Smith, "Crusade against Hungary," *National Review*, March 5, 2012,
https://www.nationalreview.com/2012/03/crusade-against-hungary-marion-smith/;
Charles Gati, *Hungary and the Soviet Bloc* (Durham, NC: Duke University Press, 1986).

53. See Michael Krupa, "A New Right Arises in Poland," *Chronicles: A Magazine of American Culture* 44, no. 2 (February 2020): 42–44.

54. Alana Mastrangelo, "Flashback: 7 Democrats Who Once Endorsed Border Fence,
Tougher Security," Breitbart, January 8, 2019, https://www.breitbart.com/politics/2019
/01/08/flashback-7-democrats-who-once-endorsed-border-fence-tougher-border-security/.
This used to be more of a Democratic than Republican position. John Binder, "Yes, Democrats used to Support Walls on the Border" Breitbart, January 8, 2019.

55. Karl W. Smith, "Trump's Economy Is Working for Minorities, Bloomberg, January 6, 2019, https://www.bloomberg.com/opinion/articles/2019-11-06/trump-s-economy
-is-historically-good-for-minorities.

56. On Trump's continued lack of public acceptance and his poor showing in polls
against prospective Democratic rivals, see these figures from Real Clear Politics: https://
www.realclearpolitics.com/epolls/latest_polls/.

57. Reuben Brigety, "Trump is a Nazi sympathizer," *Business Insider*, August 20, 2017
https://www.businessinsider.com/donald-trump-is-a-nazi-sympathizer-2017-8.

58. Steve Cortes, "Trump Didn't Call Neo-Nazis 'Fine People.' Here's Proof!," Real
Clear Politics, March 21, 2019, https://www.realclearpolitics.com/articles/2019/03/21
/trump_didnt_call_neo-nazis_fine_people_heres_proof_139815.html; Hannah Bleau,
"Jake Tapper Admits Trump Did Not Call Neo-Nazis 'very fine people," Breitbat, August 8, 2019, https://www.breitbart.com/politics/2019/08/08/flashback-jake-tapper-admits
-trump-did-not-call-neo-nazis-very-fine-people/.

59. Joel Kotkin, "Why Trump's America Will Live on," Spiked, December 4, 2020,
https://www.spiked-online.com/2020/12/04/why-trumps-america-will-live-on/.

60. Géraldine Schwarz, "My family Has a Nazi Past," *The Guardian*, April 18, 2018,
https://www.theguardian.com/profile/geraldine-schwarz.

61. A work that shows Salvini's skills as a populist leader in tuning a regional party
into a national force within a few years is Marie d'Armagnac, *Matteo Salvini: Indiscipline*
(Paris: L'artilleur, 2019).

62. Tony Barber, "The Tide is Flowing Matteo Salvini's Way-for Now," *Financial Times*, February 10, 2019, https://www.ft.com/content/d4a20574-2af4-11e9-a5ab-ff8ef 2b976c7.

63. Martin Caparrós, "Vox and the Rise of the Extreme Right in Spain, *New York Times*, November 14, 2019, https://www.nytimes.com/2019/02/16/world/europe/spain -elections-vox-far-right.html. The Spanish website Magnet has described Vox as a party that in its xenophobia and racism has never before existed in Spain. Apparently the web-masters forgot about what Spain was like before the 1980s, and particularly under the Franco regime. Magnet also seem to believe that unlike rightist authoritarian regimes, for example those in the United States, "Spanish parties until now have operated entirely within the constitutional order." There is of course no evidence that Vox or the winners in the US presidential election in 2016 violated this order. Magnet, "Qué piensa y qué propone realmente el programa de voxx para Espana," November 8, 2019, https://mag net.xataka.com/en-diez-minutos/que-piensa-que-propone-realmente-programa-vox -para-espana.

64. Katholisches, "Die Allianz des Vatikums gegen Matteo Salvini," August 19, 2019, https://katholisches.info/2019/08/19/die-allianz-mit-dem-vatikan-gegen-matteo-sal vini/.

65. Ana Bonalume, October 19, 2019, " Ne pas laisser duper par Salvini," *Le Point International*, https://www.lepoint.fr/monde/ne-pas-se-laisser-duper-par-salvini-19-10 -2019-2342193_24.php.

66. Giorgia Baroncini," "Il fascismo è un'idea morta." *Il Giornale*, October 17, 2019, https://www.ilgiornale.it/news/politica/salvini-fascismo-unidea-morta-1770386.html.

67. Paul Gottfried, "American and European Populists are Talking Past Each Other," *The American Conservative*, August 27, 2018, https://www.theamericanconservative.com /articles/american-and-european-populists-are-talking-past-each-other/. A revealing symposium published in the pro-Trump website, *American Mind*, suggests reasons why populism may have no real future in the United States. The participants address the ques-tion of whether American nationalism is morally permissible given the country's history of racial injustice. The group concludes this appeal is defensible, providing those "mag-nificent phrases" in the Declaration of Independence about all men being created equal can be made into the basis for American identity. This universalist proposition is then held up as a counterpoint to the Left, which is condemned for practicing identitarian politics. " Populism and Identity Politics," American Mind podcast, December 21, 2018, https://americanmind.org/audio/populism-and-identity-politics/. Paul Gottfried, "The New Nationalism Won't Save the Right," *The American Conservative*, January 17, 2019.

68. In 2016 *The Atlantic* published a penetrating essay on the abandonment of the non-urban working class at the beginning of the century by the Democratic Party, as it pursued leftist identitarian politics, in alliance with large corporations: Matt Stoller," How Democrats Killed Their Populist Soul," *Atlantic*, October 24, 2016, https://www .theatlantic.com/politics/archive/2016/10/how-democrats-killed-their-populist -soul/504710/.

69. Jean-David Cattin, "Populisme: C'est une vague? Non, Sire, c'est un raz de marée," *Les Identitaires*, May 19, 2019, https://www.les-identitaires.com/2019/09/16/populisme -cest-une-vague-non-sire-cest-un-raz-de-maree/.

## 6. The Uses and Abuses of "Conservative" Antifascism

1. See Jonah Goldberg, *Liberal Fascism: The Secret History of the American Left, from Mussolini to the Politics of Meaning* (New York: Doubleday, 2007), 317–57.

2. Goldberg, *Liberal Fascism*, 404.

3. See my commentary on the takimag website detailing the inconsistencies in Goldberg's polemic, "Jonah Goldberg: A Comfortable Conservative in the Belly of the Beast," http:takimag.com/article/Jonah_goldberg_a_comfotable_conservative_in_the_belly _of_the_beast/print#axzz21XfT0j2W.

4. "PragerU and Dinesh d'Souza Unearth the Leftist Roots of Fascism," PragerU, December 5, 2017, https://www.prageru.com/press-release/prageru-and-dinesh-d'souza -unearth-the-leftist-roots-of-fascism/; Paul Gottfried, "Rightwing Celebrities Play Fast and Loose with History," *The American Conservative*, December 27, 2017, https://www .theamericanconservative.com/articles/right-wing-celebrities-play-fast-and-loose-with -history/; "Is Fascism Right or Left?" PragerU video, December 4, 2017, https://www .prageru.com/video/is-fascism-right-or-left/.

5. See A. James Gregor, *Giovanni Gentile: Philosopher of Fascism* (New Brunswick: Transaction Publishers, 2001), 101–4; Augusto del Noce, *Giovanni Gentile: Per una interpretazione filosofica della storio contemporanea* (Bologna: Il Mulino, 1990), 288–92; and H. S. Harris, *The Social Philosophy of Giovanni Gentile* (Urbana: University of Illinois Press, 1960), 290–334.

6. Dinesh D'Souza, *The Big Lie: Exposing the Nazi Roots of the American Left* (Washington, DC: Regnery, 2017).

7. Dinesh D'Souza, Breitbart News Daily, August 31, 2018, https://soundcloud.com /breitbart/breitbart-news-daily-dinesh-dsouza-august-31-2018.

8. David Ramsay Steele, *The Mystery of Fascism: David Ramsay Steele's Greatest Hits* (South Bend, IN, 2019), 104.

9. As intellectual historian David Gordon observed in a note to me after reading Steele's judgment: "Saying something is closer to something else doesn't mean it's the same as what it's presumably closer to" (personal communication, November 26, 1919).

10. Dennis Prager, " Tolerance, Health, and Fascism, "*National Review*, August 27, 2013, https://www.nationalreview.com/2013/08/tolerance-health-and-fascism-dennis -prager/.

11. Clement Atlee, BBC-History, http://www.bbc.co.uk/history/historic_figures/attlee _clement.shtml.

12. James Kirchick, "Why Putin's Defense of 'Traditional Values' Is Really a War on Freedom," *Foreign Policy*, January 3, 2014, https://foreignpolicy.com/2014/01/03/why-pu tins-defense-of-traditional-values-is-really-a-war-on-freedom.

13. James Kirchick, "Everybody Hates Nazis," *Tablet*, November 7, 2017, https://www .tabletmag.com/jewish-news-and-politics/248926/everybody-hates-nazis.

14. See John T. Flynn, *As We Go Marching* (Auburn, AL: Ludwig von Mises Institute, 2007) and Justin Raimondo, *Reclaiming the American Right: The Lost Legacy of the Conservative Movement*, 2nd ed. (Wilmington DE: Intercollegiate Studies Institute Books, 2008).

15. Albert J. Nock, *Myth of a Guilty Nation*, repr. (Charleston, SC: Nabu Press, 2010).

16. See Albert Jay Nock, *The State of the Union: Essays in Social Criticism,* edited by Charles H. Hamilton (Indianapolis: Liberty Press, 1991), 89–90.

17. Nock, *The State of the Union,* 91; 76–88 passim.

18. Stephen Engelberg, "Ex-Rival Accuses Buchanan of 'Flirting with Fascism,'" *New York Times,* July 10, 1995, https://www.nytimes.com/1995/07/10/us/ex-rival-accuses-bu chanan-of-flirting-with-fascism.html.

19. William D. Gairdner, "Getting Used to the F-Word," *New Criterion,* October 2011, https://newcriterion.com/issues/2011/10/getting-used-to-the-f-word.

20. A. C. Bowen, "David Horowitz Awareness Week, Islamofascism Comes to Columbia," Lewrockwell.com, October 30, 2007, https://www.lewrockwell.com/2007/10/ac -bowen/david-horowitz-awareness-week-islamo-fascism-comes-to-columbia/.

21. See George H. Nash, *The Conservative Intellectual Movement since 1945,* expanded ed. (Wilmington, DE: Intercollegiate Studies Institute, 1996).

22. Hannah Arendt, *The Origins of Totalitarianism* (New York: Harcourt Brace Jovanovich, 1973).

23. See Eric Voegelin, *The New Science of Politics* (Chicago: University of Chicago Press,1952) and *Science, Politics and Gnosticism,* trans. William J. Fitzpatrick (Chicago: University of Chicago Press, 1968).

24. Nash, *The Conservative Intellectual Movement in America since 1945,* and Patrick Allitt, *Catholic Intellectuals and Conservative Politics in America, 1950–1985* (Ithaca, NY: Cornell University Press, 1993).

25. David Marcus, "Conservative cowards are to Blame for the Falling Statues," The Federalist, June 20, 2020, https://thefederalist.com/2020/06/20/conservative-cowards-are -to-blame-for-falling-statues/.

26. See Gerald Casey, *Freedom's Progress? A History of Political Thought* (New York: Imprint Books, 2017) and the podcast with Tom Woods, "What Is Fascism?" (August 20, 2019), https://tomwoods.com/ep-1474-what-is-fascism/.

27. See Erik von Kuehnelt-Leddhin, *Leftism Revisited: From de Sade and Marx to Hitler and Pol Pot,* rev. ed. (Washington, DC: Regnery, 1991) and *The Left from de Sade and Marx to Hitler and Marcuse* (New Rochelle, NY: Arlington House, 1974).

28. See Hermann Broch, *Modernismus, Kulturkrise und Hitlerzeit* (London: Institute of German Studies, 1994); Alfred Döblin, *Judentum und Katholizismus* (Berlin: Duncker & Humblot, 2010); and Waldemar Gurian, *Totalitarianism as Political Religion* (New York: Grosset and Dunlap, 1964).

29. See Heimito von Doderer, *Die Dämonen* (Berlin: Deutscher Taschenbuchverlag, 1985), https://www.britannica.com/biography/Heimito-von-Doderer.

30. A collection of essays that discusses most of these Christian critics of Nazism and the problem of a despiritualized modernity from a sympathetic perspective is Eric Voegelin, *Hitler and the Germans* (Columbia: University of Missouri Press, 1999); see also Gregory Wolfe, "Discerning the Spirits: Gerhart Niemeyer as Culture Critic," *Imaginative Conservative,* March 4, 2020, https://theimaginativeconservative.org/2020/03/discern ing-spirits-gerhart-niemeyer-culture-critic-gregory-wolfe.html.

31. See, for example, Pierre-André Taguieff, "L'identité francaise et ses ennemis: le traitement de l'immigration dans le racisme francais contemporain," *L'homme et la société* 77–78 (December 1985); Michel Winock, "Les flambées du nationalisme francais,"

*L'Histoire* 73 (December 1984): 11–25; Jean-Paul Honoré, "Jean-Marie Le Pen et le Front National," *Les temps modernes* 41 (April 1985): 1843–47; and Nicolas Baverez, "La longue marche du Capitano," *Le Point*, January 25, 2020, https://www.lepoint.fr/editos-du-point /nicolas-baverez/nicolas-baverez-matteo-salvini-la-longue-marche-du-capitano-25-01 -2020-2359558_73.php.

32. https://www.open.online/2019/10/17/salvini-intervista-fiume-per-la-rivista-fran-cese-le-point-il-fascismo-e-unidea-morta/; Salvini famously added to this observation that "although dead and not likely to return, like Communism, fascism is worth studying" (*un fenomeno da studiare*).

33. See Marco Tarchhi, *Cinquant'anni di nostalgia: La destra italiana dopo il fascismo* (Milan: Rizzoli, 1995)

34. Élisabeth Lévy, *Les maîtres censeurs* (Paris: Jean Claude Lattes, 2002), 158.

35. Manohla Dargis, "Dunkirk is a 'Tour de Force,'" *New York Times*, July 20, 2017, https://www.nytimes.com/2017/07/20/movies/dunkirk-review-christopher-nolan .html.

36. See Arnaud Imatz, *Droite/gauche pour sortir de equivoque* (Paris: Perre-Guillaume de Roux, 2016), 120–73.

37. See Jean-Luc Coronel de Boissezon, "Le questionnement populiste de la démocra-tie," *Cahiers de L'Issep* 2 (Winter 2019–20): 13–24; and Christophe Boutin, Olivier Dard, and Frédéric Rouvillois, eds., *Dictionnaire des populisme* (Paris: Cerf, 2019).

38. See Hermann Rauschning, *The Revolution of Nihilism* (London: William Heine-mann, 1939) and, perhaps of less interest, by the same author *Masken und Metamorpho-sen des Nihilismus* (Frankfurt am Main: Humboldt Verlag, 1954).

## 7. The Antifascist State

1. Hans-Gerd Jaschke, "Streitbare Demokratie," published bu Bundeszentrale für Politische Bildung, September 9, 2006, https://www.bpb.de/politik/extremismus/recht sextremismus/41891/streitbare-demokratie; Hans Jürgen Papier and Wolfgang Durner, "Streitbare Demokratie," *Archiv des öffentlichen Rechts*, 128, no. 3 (2003): 340–71.

2. Aristotle, *Politica,* Oxford Classical Text (Oxford: Oxford University Press, 1957), 252b, 1–25.

3. See Michael Oakeshott, *Rationalism in Politics and Other Essays*, expanded ed. (In-dianapolis: Liberty Press, 1991), ed. Timothy Fuller, xvi and 6–42; see also Kenneth Mi-nogue, *Politics: A Short Introduction* (Oxford: Oxford University Press, 1995).

4. Karl Lowenstein, "Militant Democracy and Fundamental Right, I," *American Po-litical Science Review* 31.3 (June 1937), 417–32.

5. Charles Davis, "Trump Announced a 'Surge' of Federal Agents to Cities Led by Democrats," *Business Insider*, July 23, 2020, https://www.businessinsider.com/is-trump -fascist-jason-stanley-says-it-is-wrong-question-2020-7?op=1.

6. Emily Jashinsky, "What Ever Happened to the Anti-Corporate Left?," *Federalist*, October 29, 2018, https://thefederalist.com/2018/10/29/ever-happened-anti-corporate-left/.

7. Jason Stanley, *How Fascism Works: The Politics of Us and Them* (New York: Ran-dom House, 2018), 103.

8. See Michael Hardt and Antonio Negri, *Empire* (Cambridge, MA: Harvard University Press, 2001). See Daniel Bensaid's comments on this book on his website, Le Site Daniel Bensaid, "Negri, Hardt: Un empire sans dehors," March 2001.

9. Jens Renner, "Griff nach fünf Sternen, " Der Freitag Wochennzeitung, ed. 36, 2019, https://www.freitag.de/autoren/der-freitag/griff-nach-fuenf-sternen.

10. On the intended transformative effect of migration during Blair's tenure as British prime minister, see Will Somerville, "The Immigration Legacy of Tony Blair, *Migration Information Source*, https://www.migrationpolicy.org/article/immigration-legacy -tony-blair/.

11. See Ernst Cassirer, *Myth of the State* (New York: Anchor, 1946).

12. See Carl Schmitt, *Staat, Bewegung, Volk: Die Dreigliederung der politischen Einheit* (Hamburg: Hanseatische Verlagsanstalt, 1933).

13. Renzo De Felice, *Breve Storia del Fascismo* (Milan: Arnoldo Mondadori, 2000), 41–42.

14. De Felice, *Breve Storia del Fascismo,* 43–45.

15. Erwin von Beckerath, *Das Wesen und Werden des faschistischen Staates,* repr. (Darmstadt: ND Buchgesellschaft, 1979).

16. See *Encyclopedia of the Social Sciences,* ed. Edwin R. A. Seligman and Alvin Johnson, reprint (New York: Macmillan 1951), vol. 5: 134.

17. *Encyclopedia of the Social Sciences,* vol. 5: 137.

18. Renzo De Felice, *Mussolini il fascista: L'organizzasione dello Stato fascista 1925–1929* (Turin: Einaudi, 1968), 525–47m provides two different plans for a labor charter: a socialist-leaning one by Giuseppe Bottai and a less collectivist plan by S. E. Alfredo Rocco, which is the one that was later adopted.

19. Renzo De Felice, *Breve Storia del Fascismo* (Milan: Mondadori, 200), 41–52.

20. Although most English biographies depict the leader of the interwar New Zionists implausibly as an ethnically tolerant friend of the Arabs, the work by Hillel Halkin, *Jabotinsky: A Life* (New Haven: Yale University Press, 2014) is factually useful. See also Dan Jacobson, "A Memoir of Jabotinsky," *Commentary*, June 1961, www.commentary magazine.com/articles/a-memoir-of-jabotinsky/.

21. The best study of Polish history in the English language is Norman Davies, *God's Playground: A History of Poland*, 2nd ed. (Oxford: Oxford University Press, 2006), especially the second volume that deals with Polish history since 1795.

22. De Felice looks specifically at Italy's national past and the efforts to include the entire Italian people in a unitary concept of national identity through fascism in "Il Problema dell'Identità nazionale," 127–35. See Renzo De Felice, *Breve storia del fascismo con due saggi: il problema dell 'identità nazionale e dall'eredità die Adua all'intervento* (Turin: Il Giornale Mondadori, 2002).

23. In an illuminating essay on the self-described Colombian reactionary Nicolas Gomez Davila, German intellectual historian Till Kinzel observes that, for his subject, the essential polarity in politics was between "indiscriminate equality" and "the regulative principle of hierarchical distinctions." See *Gegen die Krise der Zeit: Konservative Denker im Portrait,* ed. Daniel Führing (Graz: Ares Verlag, 2013), 27. For other studies on the those traditional rightist movements that look nothing like the present American conservative movement, see Paul Robinson, *Russian Conservatism* (Ithaca, NY: Cornell Uni-

versity Press, 2019) and Grant Havers, "The Tory Right and the American Conservative Movement," in *The Vanishing Tradition* (Ithaca, NY: Cornell University Press, 2020), ed. Paul Gottfried, 32–62.

24. See Kevin H. O'Rourke and J. G. Williams, eds., *The Spread of Modern Industry to the Periphery since 1871* (Oxford: Oxford University Press, 2017), especially chapter 6; Piero Craveri, *La Repubblica dal 1958 al 1992* (Turin: UTET, 1995), 19–26; and Guido Crainz, *Storia del miracolo italiano: Culture, identità, trasformazioni fra anni cinquanta e sessanta* (Rome: Donzelli, 1996).

25. Here it is being assumed that one can speak about a "generic fascism," which is a concept that looms large in my work; see *Fascism: Career of a Concept* (Dekalb: Northern Illinois University Press, 2016), 36, 95, 123 136–38, and 151–53. For a more exhaustive treatment of this subject, see Stanley G. Payne, *A History of Fascism, 1914–1945* (Madison: University of Wisconsin Press, 1995), 462–86.

26. See Christopher Lasch, "The Obsolescence of Right and Left," *New Oxford Review* 56 (April 1989): 6–15; and on the New Class takeover of the American Right, see Paul Piccone, "The Crisis of American Conservatism," *Telos* 74 (Winter 1987–88): 3–29.

27. Typical of what will have to be done in the short and perhaps middle term to allow our true beings to emerge is the motion introduced in the French National Assembly by Paris deputy, Danièle Obono, an Afro-feminist and ecosocialist, to remove all mention of gender from public records. Apparently, such conventional designations are dangerous social constructs that work to repress our true but perpetually changeable identities. Boulevard Voltaire, "Danièle Obono est le honte des Noirs en France," Verlaine Djeri, July 5, 2020, https://www.bvoltaire.fr/daniele-obono-est-la-honte-des-noirs-de-france/

28. "La Réaction d'un trentenaire patriote à la mort du Président Chirac," Le Cercle Aristote, September 26, 2009, https://cerclearistote.com/2019/09/reaction-dun-trente naire-patriote-a-la-mort-du-president-chirac/.

29. Tony Woodlief, "The Fires Foretold by Willmoore Kendall and the Burning of America," *The American Conservative*, June 8, 2020, https://www.theamericanconserva tive.com/articles/the-fires-foretold-willmoore-kendall-and-the-burning-of-america/.

30. See Carl Schmitt, *Concept of the Political*, trans. and intro. by George Schwab (New Brunswick, NJ: Rutgers University Press, 1976); and Paul Edward Gottfried, *Carl Schmitt: Politics and Theory* (New York: Greenwood Press, 1990), 57–82.

31. Douglas Murray, *The Madness of Crowds: Gender, Race and Identity* (London: Bloomsbury Continuum, 2019), 16.

32. Ezra Klein, "The Problem with Twitter as Shown by the Sarah Jeong Fracas," *Vox*, August 3, 2018, https://www.vox.com/technology/2018/8/8/17661368/sarah-jeong -twitter-new-york-times-andrew-sullivan

33. Sarah Jeong, "I was equating Trump to Hitler before it was cool, tweet, December 7, 2015, https://twitter.com/sarahjeong/status/674008878514700289; "New York Times Defends Hiring Asian Reporter Who Mocked White People in Old Tweets Including 'White Men Are Bullsh*t" and "Cancel White People," *Daily Mail*, August 2, 2018, https://www.dailymail.co.uk/news/article-6021015/New-York-Times-defends-hiring -Asian-reporter-mocked-white-people-old-tweets.html.

34. Oswald Spengler, *Jahre der Entscheidung* (Munich: C. H. Beck, 1933), 134–35.

35. Spengler, *Jahre der Entscheidung*, 135.

36. "Supreme Court to Hear Case of Michigan Transgendered Woman Who Says She Was Fired After Transitioning, " WXYZ-TV-Detroit, October 18, 2019, https://www.wxyz.com/news/supreme-court-to-hear-case-of-michigan-transgender-woman-who-says-she-was-fired-after-transitioning.

37. Kevin Drum "A Very Brief Timeline of the Bathroom Wars," *Mother Jones*, May 14, 2016, https://www.motherjones.com/kevin-drum/2016/05/timeline-bathroom-wars/.

38. Goldman Sachs, "Bringing your Authentic Self to Work: Pronouns," company directive, November 19, 2019, https://www.goldmansachs.com/careers/blog/posts/bring-your-authentic-self-to-work-pronouns.html.

39. See this confusing use of the f-word to scold the gay lobby on the Republican Red State website, https://www.redstate.com/streiff/2015/04/28/fascism-homosexual-marriage-advocates/

40. "Hungary Prepares to End the Legal Recognition of Transpeople," *The Guardian*, April 26, 2020, https://www.theguardian.com/world/2020/apr/26/hungary-prepares-to-end-legal-recognition-of-trans-people.

41. Jason: *The Politics of Us and Them* (New York: Random House, 2018), 43.

42. Stanley, *How Fascism Works*, 102.

43. Stanley, *How Fascism Works*, 104.

44. Lida Käykö, " Feminist Movements Are Our Best Chance of Defeating the Far Right," The Feminist, Anti-Fascist Assembly, March 8, 2019, https://www.hopenothate.org.uk/2019/03/08/feminist-movements-best-chance-defeating-far-right/.

45. Rolf Wiggershaus, *Die Frankfurter Schule*, 6th ed. (Munich: Deutscher Tschenbuch Verlag, 2001), 172–78; and Ludwig von Friedeberg and Max Horkheimer, *Studien Über Autorität und Familie* (Paris: zu Klampen Verlag, 1936). The negative views of homosexual behavior in inter alia *The Dialectic of the Enlightenment*, written by Theodor Adorno and Max Horkheimer during World War II, would easily qualify among our current antifascists as extreme hate speech. https://books.google.com/books?id=lwVjsKcHW7cC&q=homosexuality#v=snippet&q=homosexuality&f=false.

## Excursus

1. Thomas Hobbes, *Leviathan*, ed. C.P. Macpherson (Penguin Books: London, 1968), 35.

2. Hobbes, *Leviathan*, 35.

3. Thomas Hobbes, *Elements of Law*, ed. J.C. H. Gaskin (Oxford: Oxford University Press, 1990) chap. 5, sec. 6.

4. Hobbes, *Leviathan*, 105.

5. Hobbes, *Leviathan*, 105.

6. There is a vast literature on Hobbes's epistemology and efforts to devise scientifically reliable "definitions." See for example F. S. McNeilly, *The Anatomy of Leviathan* (New York: St. Martin's Press, 1968), particularly 35–47 and 52–53; Michael Oakeshott,

"Introduction to Leviathan," in *Rationalism in Politics and Other Essays*, foreword by Timothy Fuller (Indianapolis: Liberty Press, 1991), 221–95; and Ferdinand Tönnies, *Thomas Hobbes: Leben und Lehre*, 3rd ed. (Stuttgart: Bad Canstatt, 1971). Tönnies, whose study of Hobbes originally appeared in 1896, helped create what is the established interpretation of his subject as an epistemological materialist and the father of liberal natural rights thought. Although other plausible readings of Hobbes's work are abundantly available, Tönnies buttresses his interpretation with a wealth of evidence.

7. Tönnies, *Thomas Hobbes*, 109–10.

### Afterthoughts

1. Paul Gottfried, *Fascism: The Career of a Concept* (DeKalb: Northern Illinois University Press, 2016).

2. Entirely typical of this contrition was Angela Merkel's emphasis on "German shame" in a recent speech given by her at Auschwitz, https://abcnews.go.com/International/wireStory/germanys-merkel-begins-visit-auschwitz-67539712.

3. A. James Gregor, *The Ideology of Fascism: The Rationale of Totalitarianism* (New York: Free Press, 1969) and *The Fascist Persuasion in Radical Politics* (Princeton, NJ: Princeton University Press, 1974).

4. Gregor, *The Ideology of Fascism*, 14–21, 365–74.

5. See Norman G. Finkelstein, *The Holocaust Industry: Reflections on the Exploitation of Jewish Suffering*, 2nd ed. (London: Verso Books, 2003).

6. See the detailed discussion of the selective appeal to historical memory in Paul Gottfried, *The Strange Death of Marxism* (Columbia: University of Missouri Press, 2005), 84–102.

7. Über Horst Selbiger, author profile page, https://www.horstselbiger.de/ueber-mich.

8. Über Horst Selbiger, author profile page; and Selbiger's self-published autobiography, *Verfemt, Verfolgt, Verraten: Abriss meines Lebens* (Berlin: self-published, 2018).

9. Victims of Communism Memorial Foundation: Teaching Truth, seeking justice, keeping memory, website, https://www.victimsofcommunism.org/memorial; see also Stéphane Courtois, ed., *The Black Book of Communism*, trans. Jonathan Murphy and Mark Kramer (Cambridge, MA: Harvard University Press, 1999). On the difficulties encountered by Lee Edwards who promoted the project in obtaining government funding from the Clinton administration, see Paul Weyrich, "A Memorial to the Victims of Communism and my Tribute to Lee Edwards" Paul Weyrich, "A Memorial to the Victims of Communism and My Tribute to Lee Edwards," *Townhall*, May 15, 2007, https://townhall.com/columnists/paulweyrich/2007/05/15/a-memorial-to-the-victims-of-communism-and-my-tribute-to-lee-edwards-n1335881.

10. See Peter Novick, *The Holocaust in American Life* (Boston: Houghton Mifflin, 1999).

11. This line of accusation reached perhaps its high point in Daniel Jonah Goldhagen's polemic, *A Moral Reckoning: The Role of the Catholic Church and Its Unfulfilled Duty of Repair* (New York: Vintage, 2003). Although this work received rave reviews in the national press, it was also picked apart in scholarly journals. See, for example, Ronald J.

Rychlak, "Goldhagen v. Pius XII," *First Things* (June 2002), https://www.firstthings.com/article/2002/06/goldhagen-v-pius-xii.

12. Ernst Nolte, " Die Vergangenheit, die nicht vergeht: Eine Rede, die geschrieben aber nicht gehalten werden konnte," Frankfurter Allgemeine Zeitung, June 6, 1986.

13. See Habermas's response in *Die Zeit* (July 11,1986); Stefan Kallitz, *Doe polititische Deutungskultur im Spiegel des "Historikerstreits"* (Wiesbaden: Westdeutscher Verlag, 2001); and Gottfried, *Fascism: Career of a Concept*, 59–86.

14. See Peter Hoeres, *Zeitung für Deutschland: Die Geschichte der FAZ* (Munich: Benevento Verlag, 2019), 323–26.

15. Frank Schirrmacher, "Aufklärung?" *Frankfurter Allgemeine Zeitung* 11, no. 7 (1986): 25.

16. Panajotis Kondylis, *Machtfragen: Ausgewählte Beiträge zur Politik und Gesellschaft* (Darmstadt: Wissenschaftliche Gesellschaft, 2006); Falk Horst, ed., *Panajotis Kondylis und die Metamorphosen der Gesellschaft* (Berlin: Duncker & Humblot, 2019); and Paul Gottfried, "Panajotis Kondylis: ein skeptischer Aufklärer," https://www.blauenarzisse.de/panajotis-kondylis-ein-skeptischer-aufklaerer/.

17. A devastating satire on the righteousness of the current Left is Jim Goad, *The New Church Ladies: The Extremely Uptight World of Social Justice* (Stone Mountain, GA: Obnoxious Books, 2017).

18. Philip Bethge, "Apartheid, Rassismus, AfD, Rassenlehre," *Spiegel*, September 14,2019, https://www.spiegel.de/wissenschaft/mensch/rasse-selektion-apartheid-rassismus-afd-rassenlehre-9-11-a-1286518.html.

19. Hannah Arendt, *The Origins of Totalitarianism* (New York: Harcourt Brace and Jovanovich, 1973), 220–30, 234–36, and 474–79. Arendt views this willful manipulation of facts as an exercise in power by totalitarian leaders.

20. Two iconoclastic commentaries on academic intolerance in the United States are by Robert Paquette, "The World We Have Lost," *The New Criterion* (May 2008), https://newcriterion.com/issues/2008/5/the-world-we-have-lost-a-parable-on-the-academy; and Heather MacDonald's feature commentary, "The Snowflakes Have a Chilling Effect even beyond the Campus," *Wall Street Journal*, April 17, 2017. Although MacDonald does not mention antifascism as a thematic focus for academic riots, she correctly observes that "ideological aggression" lies behind them.

21. See Paul Gottfried, *The Vanishing Tradition: Perspectives in American Conservatism* (Ithaca, NY: Cornell University, 2020),152–62.

22. A former Yale professor, William Deresiewicz, in a best-selling book *Excellent Sheep: The Miseducation of the American Elite* (New York: Simon & Schuster, 2014) expresses disgust at the zombie-like manner in which his students mechanically stated unreflective opinions: "Their minds were like a chemical bath of conventional attitudes that would instantly precipitate out of a solution and coat whatever object you introduced" (80). As an academic for forty years, I think Deresiewicz may be understating the rote-like conformity in today's college students. The availability to them of more sources of information than ever before seems to have had no effect in encouraging them to think independently.

23. "The Communist Persecution of Homosexuals: 9 Facts That Some Silence and Many Ignore," Counting Stars, July 8, 2019, http://www.outono.net/elentir/2019/07/08/the-communist-persecution-of-homosexuals-9-facts-that-some-silence-and-many-ignore/.

24. See Tillmann Lahme, *Golo Mann: Eine Biographie* (Frankfurt am Main: S. Fischer, 2014) and Peter Hoeres, *Zeitung fur Deutschland*, 331, www.faz.net/aktuell/feuil leton/buecher/autoren/zum-100-geburtstag-von-golo-mann-war-so-ein-mensch-als -kollege-wuenschbar-1926434.html. Although it cannot be confirmed, as Joachim Fest and others once thought, that Adorno or Horkheimer wrote accusatory letters to the responsible authorities, what can be confirmed, according to Lahme, was that Adorno went around telling lurid stories about Mann's homosexuality while his appointment was under consideration.

25. Illustrative of this attempt to treat fascism as a fixed concept with equally fixed practices from the 1920s through the presidency of Donald Trump is Carl Boggs, *Fascism: Old and New: American Politics at the Crossroads* (New York: Routledge, 2016).

26. For Weber's seminal essay on the nature and struggle of values, see *Gesammelte Aufsätze zur Wissenschaftslehre*, ed. Johannes Winckelmann, 7th ed. (Tübingen: Mohr-Siebeck, 1988), 489–540.

27. A work that treats the totalitarian aspect of modern democracy as the administered pursuit of equality is Bertrand de Jouvenel, *Sovereignty: An Inquiry into the Political Good*, repr. (Cambridge: Cambridge University Press, 2012).

28. Nicolas Sarkozy, "Egalité des chances et diversité," video, December 17, 2008, https://www.youtube.com/watchh?v=E8QsOz4u54M.

29. See Edouard Berth and George Sorel, *Les méfaits des intellectuels*, repr. (Auckland, New Zealand: Wentworth Press, 2018).

30. An excellent study of the confrontation between artistic modernism and Communism produced by a modernist champion is Hilton Kramer's *The Twilight of the Intellectuals: Culture and Politics in the Era of the Cold War* (New York: Ivan R. Dee, 2000)

31. Paul Gottfried, *The Strange Death of Marxism: The European Left in the New Millennium* (Columbia: University of Missouri Press, 22005) argues this thesis at considerable length.

32. "Democratic Rep. Deb Haaland Calls Antifa 'Peaceful Protesters,'" video, August 18, 2019, https://www.youtube.com/watch?v=HXYB-U0V3lU.

33. Peter Hasson, "Antifa Members Have Repeatedly Attacked Journalists Who Cover Them," *Daily Caller*, July 1, 2019, https://dailycaller.com/2019/07/01/andy-ngo-antifa -attack-journalists-list/

34. Andrew Buncombe, "Seattle's CHAZ: Inside the Occupied Vegan Paradise— and Trump's 'Ugly Anarchist' Hell," *The Independent*, June 12, 2020, https://www.inde pendent.co.uk/news/world/americas/us-politics/seattle-chaz-occupied-protest-trump -vegan-washington-a9562066.html

35. John Bowden, "Fox News Poll Shows Trump Losing to Biden, Warren, Sanders and Harris," *The Hill*, August 15, 2019, https://thehill.com/homenews/campaign/457645 -fox-news-poll-shows-trump-losing-to-biden-warren-sanders-and-harris

36. R.R. Reno, *Return of the Strong Gods: Nationalists, Populists, and the Future of the West* (Washington, D.C.: Regnery Gateway, 2019), 124–25.

37. Michael Brown, "The Cancel Culture Is Ruthless, *Townhall*, June 7, 2020, https:// townhall.com/columnists/michaelbrown/2020/06/07/the-cancel-culture-is-ruthless -n2570167.

38. Ernst Nolte, *Der Faschismus in seiner Epoche*, 10th edition (Munich: Piper,2000), 419–24, 485–514.

39. Samuel Earle, "The Terrifying Rehabilitation of Nazi Scholar Carl Schmitt," New Statesman, April 10, 2019, https://www.newstatesman.com/2019/04/terrifying-rehabili tation-nazi-scholar-carl-schmitt.

40. For an easily accessible English-language study of Schmitt that deal with the facts of his life, see Joseph Bendersky, *Carl Schmitt: Theorist for the Reich* (Princeton, NJ: Princeton University Press); and for works centered on Schmitt's *The Concept of the Political*, translation George Schwab (New Brunswick, NJ: Rutgers University Press, 1976), see George Schwab, *The Challenge of the Exception: An Introduction to the Ideas of Carl Schmitt between 1921 and 1936*, 2nd edition (Westport, Ct.: Greenwood Press, 1989); and my own *Carl Schmitt: Politics and Theory* (Westport, CT: Greenwood Press, 1990). A particularly informative collection of essays on Schmitt can be found in *Telos* 70 (Summer 1987).

# For Further Reading

All the books listed here influenced this study of antifascism. These sources and explanatory works were not all of equal value, but each in varying degrees helped shape my thinking about the subject of my work. Varieties of antifascism have changed dramatically since the 1920s. This development has occurred as antifascism's object of attack has been made to fit a changing concept or image of the enemy. Not all the authors cited would agree on what fascism is or where the problem should be located. Where possible, books written in English or English editions of non-English works are cited.

Adorno, Theodor W, Else Frenkel-Brunswik, Daniel J. Levinson, and R. Nevitt Sanford. *The Authoritarian Personality*. New York: Harper, 1950.

Arendt, Hannah. *The Origins of Totalitarianism*. New York: Harcourt Brace Jovanovich, 1973.

Bray, Mark. *Antifa: The Anti-Fascist Handbook*. Brooklyn: Melville House, 2017.

Brüning, Heinrich. *Memoiren, 1918–1945*. Stuttgart: Deutsche Verlag-sanstalt, 1970.

Buckley, William F. *Up from Liberalism*. New York: McDowell and Obolensky, 1959.

Caldwell, Christopher. *Reflections on the Revolution in Europe*. New York: Random House, 2009.

Casey, Gerald. *Freedom's Progress? A History of Political Thought*. New York: Imprint Books, 2017.

De Felice, Renzo. *Mussolini il Rivoluzionario, 1883–1920*. Milan: Einaudi, 1965.

De Felice, Renzo. *Breve Storia del Fascismo*. Milan: Mondadori, 2017.

DiAngelo, Robin. *White Fragility: Why It's So Hard for White People to Talk about Racism*. Boston: Beacon Press, 2018.

Diggins, John P. *Mussolini and Fascism: The View from America*. Princeton, NJ: Princeton University Press, 1972.

D'Souza, Dinesh. *The Big Lie: Exposing the Nazi Roots of the American Left*. Washington, DC: Regnery, 2017.

Eatwell, Roger and Matthew Goodwin. *National Populism and the Revolt against Liberal Democracy*. London: Penguin, 2018.

Eco, Umberto. *Il Fascismo Eterno*. Buenos Aires: La nave di Teseo, 2018.

Faderman, Lilian. *The Gay Revolution: The Story of the Struggle*. New York: Simon & Schuster, 2016.

Farrell, Nicholas. *Mussolini: A New Life*. Burlington, VT: Phoenix Books, 2005.

Fraenkel, Ernst. *The Dual State: A Contribution to the Theory of Dictatorship*. Clark, NJ: Lawbook Exchange Ltd., 2010.

Fromm, Eric. *Escape from Freedom*. New York: Holt, 1994.

Gentile, Emilio. *Chi è fascista*. Bari: Laterza, 2019.

Gentile, Giovanni. *Origins and Doctrine of Fascism*, trans. A. James Gregor, 2nd ed. New York: Routledge, 2004.

Goldberg, Jonah. *Liberal Fascism: The Secret History of the American Left, from Mussolini to the Politics of Meaning*. New York: Doubleday, 2007.

Goldhagen, Daniel J. *Hitler's Willing Executioners: Ordinary Germans and the Holocaust*. New York: Alfred J. Knopf, 1996.

Goldhagen, Daniel J. *A Moral Reckoning: The Role of the Church in the Holocaust and Its Unfulfilled Duty of Repair.* New York: Vintage, 2003.

Gottfried, Paul. *Fascism: The Career of a Concept.* DeKalb: NIU Press, 2016.

Gottfried, Paul. *The Strange Death of Marxism: The European Left in the New Millennium*, paperback edition. Columbia: University of Missouri Press, 2018.

Grabar, Mary. *Debunking Howard Zinn: Exposing the Fake History that Turned a Generation against America.* Washington, DC: Regnery History, 2019.

Gramsci, Antonio). *Prison Notebooks*, trans. Joseph A. Buttigieg, 3 vols. New York: Columbia University Press, 2011.

Gregor, A. James. *The Ideology of Fascism: The Rationale of Totalitarianism.* New York: Free Press, 1969.

Gurian, Waldemar. *Totalitarianism as Political Religion.* New York: Grosset and Dunlap, 1964.

Habermas, Jürgen. *Legitimation Crisis*, trans. Thomas McCarthy. Boston: Beacon Press, 1975.

Hobbes, Thomas. *Leviathan*, ed. C. P. Macpherson. London: Penguin Books, 1968.

Hocking, W. E. *Experiment in Education: What We Can Learn from Educating Germans*, paperback edition. Palala Books, 2018.

Hodgson, Keith. *Fighting Fascism: The British Left and the Rise of Fascism.* Manchester: Manchester University Press, 2010.

Holborn, Hajo. *Germany's Aims in the First World War.* New York: W. W. Norton, 1968.

Jardina, Ashley. *White Identity Politics.* New York: Cambridge University Press, 2019.

Jay, Martin. *The Dialectical Imagination: A History of the Frankfurt School and the Institute of Social Research, 1923–1950.* Berkeley: University of California Press, 1994.

Kendi, Ibram X. *On Being an Antiracist.* London: One World First Edition, 2019.

Kershaw, Ian. *The Defense and Destruction of Nazi Germany, 1944–1945.* New York: Viking, 2012.

Klemperer, Klemens von. *The German Resistance to Hitler: The Search for Allies Abroad.* Oxford: Clarendon Press, 1994.

Kolakowski, Leszek. *Main Currents of Marxism*, paperback edition. New York: Norton, 2008.

Kuehnelt-Leddhin, Eric von. *The Left from de Sade and Marx to Hitler and Marcuse.* New Rochelle, NY: Arlington House, 1974.

Kuehnelt-Leddhin, Eric von. *Leftism Revisited: From de Sade and Marx to Hitler and Pol Pot*, rev. ed. Washington, DC: Regnery, 1991.

Langer, Bernd. *Antifaschistische Aktion: Geschichte einer linksradikalen Bewegung.* Münster: Unrast, 2015.

Lasch, Christopher. *The True and Only Heaven: Progress and its Critics.* New York: Norton, 1991.

Lévy, Bernard-Henri. *L'idéologie Francaise.* Paris: Grasset, 1981.

Maccoby, Michael, and Ken Fuchsman, eds. *Psychoanalytic and Historical Perspectives on the Leadership of Donald Trump.* New York: Routledge, 2020.

Mack Smith, Denis. *Mussolini: A Biography.* New York: Knopf, 1982.

MacWilliams, Matthew C. *On Fascism: 12 Lessons from American History.* Netley, Australia: Griffin Press, 2020.

Marcuse, Herbert. *Hegel and the Rise of Social Theory.* Boston: Beacon Press, 1960.

Mises, Ludwig von. *Bureaucracy.* Dead Authors Society, 2017.

Mises, Ludwig von. *Omnipotent Government: The Rise of the Total State and Total War.* Indianapolis: Liberty Fund, 2011.

Mitscherlich, Alexander, and Margarete Mitscherlich. *Die Unfähigkeit zu trauern: Grundlage des kollektiven Verhaltens.* Munich: Piper Verlag, 2009.

Murray, Douglas. *The Madness of Crowds: Gender, Race and Identity.* London: Bloomsbury Continuum, 2019.

Murray, Douglas. *The Strange Death of Europe*, enlarged edition. New York: Bloomsbury Continuum, 2018.

Neiman, Susan. *Learning from the Germans: Race and the Meaning of Evil.* New York: Farrar, Straus, and Giroux, 2019.

Neumann, Franz. *Behemoth: The Structure and Practice of Fascism, 1933–1944.* New York: Oxford University Press, 1944.

Ngo, Andy. *Unmasked: Inside Antifa's Radical Plan to Destroy Democracy.* New York: Center Street, 2021.

Nolte, Ernst. *Der Europäische Bürgerkrieg: 1917–1945: Nationalismus und Bolschewismus*. Berlin: Propyläen, 1987.

Novick, Peter. *The Holocaust in American Life*. Boston: Houghton Mifflin, 1999.

Orwell, George. *Homage to Catalonia*, intro. Lionel Trilling. Orlando: Harcourt Books, 1952.

Payne, Stanley G. *Fascism: Comparison and Definition*. Madison: University of Wisconsin Press, 1980.

Payne, Stanley G. *A History of Fascism, 1914–1945*. Madison: University of Wisconsin Press, 1995.

Rauschning, Hermann. *The Revolution of Nihilism: Warning to the West*. Whitefish, MT: Kessering Press, 2005.

Reid-Ross, Alexander. *Against the Fascist Creep*. Oakland: AK Press, 2017.

Reno, R. R. *Return of the Strong Gods: Nationalists, Populists, and the Future of the West*. Washington, DC: Regnery Gateway, 2019.

Schmitt, Carl. *Concept of the Political*, trans. and intro by George Schwab. New Brunswick, NJ: Rutgers University Press, 1976.

Scholl, Inge. *The White Rose: Munich, 1942–1943*, 2nd ed. Middleton, CT: Wesleyan University Press, 1983.

Schöpner, Horst. *Antifa heißt Angriff*. Hamburg: Unrast, 2015.

Schrenck-Notzing, Caspar von. *Charakterwäsche: Die Politik der amerikanischen Umerziehung in Deutschland*. Munich: George Müller Verlag, 1981.

Snyder, Timothy D. *The Road to Unfreedom*. New York: Tim Duggan Books, 2019.

Snyder, Timothy D. *On Tyranny: Twenty Lessons from the Twentieth Century*. New York: Tim Duggan Books, 2019.

Stanley, Jason. *How Fascism Works: The Politics of Us and Them*. New York: Random House, 2018.

Stern, Fritz. *The Politics of Illiberalism: Essays on the Political Culture of Modern Germany*. New York: Columbia University Press, 1992.

Sternhell, Zeev. *Les anti-Lumières du XVIII siècle à la guerre froide*. Paris: Fayard, 2006.

Sturzo, Luigi. *Italia e Fascismo*. Rome: Edizione di Storia e Letteratura, 1926.

Testa, M. *A Hundred Years of Antifascism*. Chico, CA: AK Press, 2015.

Vergnon, Gilles. *L'antifascisme en France: De Mussolini à Le Pen*. Rennes: Presses Universitaires de Rennes, 2009.

Voegelin, Eric. *Hitler and the Germans*. Columbia: University of Missouri Press, 1999.

Voegelin, Eric. *Political Religions in Voegelin's Collected Works*, vol. 5, ed. Manfred Henningson. Columbia: University of Missouri Press, 1999.

Wiggershaus, Rolf, *Die Frankfurter Schule: Geschichte, Theoretische Entwicklung, Politische Bedeutung*. Munich: Deutscher Taschenbuchverlag, 2001.

Williams, T. Harry. *Huey Long*. New York: Viking Books, 1981.

Zeskin, Leonard. *The History of the White Nationalist Movement from the Margins to the Mainstream*. New York: Farrar, Straus, and Giroux, 2009.

# INDEX